Aviation
at the
EDGE

John Flexman

Aviation at the EDGE

MEMOIRS
Cirencester

Published by Memoirs

MEMOIRS
PUBLISHING

Memoirs Books

25 Market Place, Cirencester, Gloucestershire, GL7 2NX
info@memoirsbooks.co.uk www.memoirspublishing.com

Aviation
at the
EDGE

CONTENTS

INTRODUCTION

Re-telling my exploits to so many so often, I was frequently told
I should write a book. Good idea. Our life has been so full of drama
and excitement that I thought a book would not only be of interest
to family and aviation devotees but might inspire those other quiet
kids, now at school, to just "go for it".

To Mum for always being there, and to Janet
for sticking it out through thick and thin.

Three thousand feet above the Zambian bush, the
DHC2 Beaver had only ten minutes' fuel remaining.
Night was drawing in; ground features were indiscernible.
I could not raise anyone on the radio.

Would this be the end?

Chapter One

EARLY DAYS

1944

My earliest memory (I must have been around fifteen months old) is of sitting on my potty in the kitchen. Space at our house in London Road, Wokingham, was limited. There were bunk beds in both front rooms and the kitchen/diner was used for storage. The cramped conditions were a result of our living room being home to a family of Polish refugees. Although they were good people, we were forbidden any contact. They were not allowed to be part of the family, as Mum was for all intents and purposes a single mother. It was 1944, wartime, and Dad was serving in the Royal Navy.

As a gesture of appreciation, one of the ladies made me two teddy bears. The regular-sized bear was covered in grey herringbone tweed and the little one in black felt with green features. I called the tiny chap Bemu, my name for Dad's best friend Jack. On her weekly visit my grandmother (on Mum's side) asked me what their names were. Not having a name for the larger bear, on the spur of the moment, I said it was Freckenue. This confused all present, I now suspect it was my attempt at a half-remembered curse.

My father's homecoming was dramatic, and it upset my little world. Up to this moment Mum had given us all her loving attention. Suddenly this total stranger appeared. Mum burst into tears, put me in the playpen and disappeared with this chap for what seemed an eternity. Annoyingly the fellow stayed around for a number of days, but thank goodness he went away again, albeit temporarily. When he returned my irritation dissipated, as our dull and shabby paintwork was transformed with new colours. Mum was a different person, the distant stare replaced with a new sparkle. Our now-happy family bubbled with life. The Polish family were relocated, much to their relief and ours. The much-needed renovation of fittings and furniture gave our lives a real boost.

The property came with a large garden (it seemed vast to me). The undergrowth was cleared and I took any opportunity to escape and explore.

There was a small lawn, an air raid shelter and a play area next to the house. At the far end was a fenced-off, untended kitchen garden. My elder sister Elizabeth (Liz) could not open the gate, but had discovered she could crawl under it. One warm day of early spring she got jammed in the puddle under the gate and burst into tears (she was growing fast). Dad rescued her, but could not control his mirth.

I found this mystifying, and it continued to worry me for some time. When I started school I discovered how common it was to be amused by the misfortune of others.

The kitchen garden was out of bounds, and therefore of great interest. I learned how to open the gate, and discovered the magnificent world of insects. There were the obvious butterflies and many wasps and bees, as the garden contained a small orchard overgrown with tall grass and weeds. I secretly tried the fallen fruit, not only apples and pears but plums and greengages. I got stung by a wasp of course, but accepted this as retribution and keep quiet. I worried that the sting would get worse and swell up into some monstrous growth.

More interesting creatures were to be found hiding in the dilapidated shed and under the rotting woodpile; earwigs, woodlice, centipedes and some amazing spiders. My favourite flower was the dandelion and of the insects, the ladybird, with its patient acceptance of my interfering scrutiny. No scurrying away in panic for this apparently gentle creature.

The air raid bunker was forbidden territory, which sparked my curiosity. When I managed to crack open the door, the total darkness filled me with horror. I never tried again.

Elizabeth brought round the neighbours' children, a boy and girl about the same age as herself. Liz showed them the curious delights to be found in the garden and persuaded me to put on the wartime gas mask that was hanging in the garden shed. I assumed her intention was to amuse the guests. I was the only one who had ever donned this monstrosity and was unaware of its frightening appearance to the onlooker. I came out of the garden shed toward the two kids and was stunned when they both screamed in panic and fled. They never ever came back. I was severely scolded and left to ponder the injustice of it all.

Mum took me to the corner shop, where she spent her meagre supply of food coupons. For company and a chat she often popped into the store next door, which was an Aladdin's cave of electronic wonder where strange equipment blinked, glowed and hummed. Walking into the premises was not like entering a shop at all. Inside one was confronted by an overfilled workbench behind which racks of second-hand spare parts reached to the ceiling. On each side were stacked items awaiting repair or collection. Available floor space dictated a limit of three visitors. The proprietor, an ex-RAF radar technician, mostly did repairs to radio sets, but was willing to try his hand fixing anything powered by electricity. His latest project was to convert a Government-surplus radar set to receive TV signals. In those days broadcasts were limited to late afternoons and evenings, and Mum arranged one of our outings to coincide with one such programme. Although the screen showed only green on black, a discernible moving picture could be detected - it was magical. My boy's love of gadgets sparked into life.

Christmas I remember as an unreal assortment of events taking place at night in the semi-dark. Carol singers were a charming but boisterous lot who laughed at my attempts, spoken through the letterbox, to explain why Mummy could not come to the door right now. Father Christmas worried me. Despite his occasional "ho ho ho" he came across as a stern figure of authority rather than one of compassion. This might have been the result of my father's warning that I would get a present from Santa only if I had been good. For a year or two I failed to realise he was my father, but I was well aware it was someone in disguise. Why did he have to hand over the toys I had pestered my parents for? I would have preferred it if they had given them to me in person. My fathers' attempts to be jolly turned out scary, so I was glad when this buffoon went out of the door.

Our gardener, Mr Butler, was a friend of Dad's from the pub who occasionally helped out in the kitchen garden. Mr Butler would have made an excellent Santa. He had a large sand-coloured walrus moustache, twinkling eyes and a beautifully soft and broad Berkshire accent. I can never remember what he said, as I was totally entranced by the overall effect. He used to arrive in his grey and shabby three-piece suit before taking off his jacket and waistcoat to work. He tended the garden in a pin-striped white collarless shirt, braces and wellington boots. He kept his cap on while gardening, a shock of straw like hair sticking out from underneath. He had a beautiful onion-shaped fob watch which I found fascinating. It was a large device with a brass case, intricate hands and antique-style Roman numerals. Just before he retired he asked Mum if he could present me with it, but she of course refused. Mum shooed him away when I asked him to show me how he rolled his hand-made cigarettes. This operation he carried out with bewildering speed and dexterity.

I attended nursery class at a nearby Catholic girls' school where the staff were all nuns. We were escorted between lessons to one of many small shrines in the school gardens. There we were made to bow our heads while the sister said prayers for what seemed an inordinate amount of time. I was glad to leave when we relocated. I found it quite stressful not knowing if the class would be taken by a fierce nun or a gentle one.

My grandparents on my mothers' side lived on the other side of town and visited every week. They owned a car, an immaculate black Austin Ten. Dressed in what seemed to me very formal new clothes, they seemed a bit severe and were always asking me questions. I now realise that they just wanted reassurance that I was in good health and was being brought up properly. Occasionally when they had enough petrol coupons we might drive over to Finchampstead Ridges, an escarpment area with a grand view. The Ridges were a mix of heather, gorse and woodland, and I came to know this area intimately when I got my own bicycle.

Granddad owned a greengrocer's shop in the centre of town, a corner shop just opposite Wokingham town hall. "H. Spencer" was emblazoned in gold black-shadowed lettering on a bold green background above the shop front. On entering one was greeted by a rich smell of fresh fruit and the tangy earthen smell of root vegetables. Underfoot the bare floorboards indicated many years of continuous wear. Produce was displayed in carefully-arranged wooden fruit boxes lined with green tissue paper. The bill was hand written on forms from a perforated roll contained in a till made from oak trimmed with brass. Harry, as he was known to his customers, served his customers wearing a beige and brown herringbone striped three-piece suit. The business must have been fairly profitable as it enabled Harry to give Mum and Dad a loan to buy their first house.

Our new home, 20 Park Road, was conveniently located a

hundred yards from my grandparents. The road was private, unadopted, and unpaved. A layer of heavy gravel prevented it from becoming muddy and potholed. Our house was on the right-angle turn in the road where Park Road became Park Avenue, a more salubrious address. If cars turned this corner at speed they spat stones in our direction.

We move to 1947. At age five I was to attend Palmer School, the real thing. Initially Mum escorted me to and from it but I was quite keen to go by myself, because I could check out shop windows without being chivvied.

It was during my first year at school that I discovered my true self. I realised from observing the behaviour of the other kids that I was one of the few quiet, shy and introspective types. I was an obedient child, horrified at the behaviour shown by some of the other kids, yet I was jealous of the attention received by my more outgoing classmates.

Kids have a knack of finding others' weaknesses and a talent for inflicting mental pain. My retiring nature made me a prime target for the bullies. I had what were then called "buck teeth" and protruding ears, so I got called "Bugs Bunny" and "Dumbo". Even in primary school the extortionists were busy harassing the smaller pupils. One fortunate consequence of my parents not having the funds to issue me with pocket money was that these budding criminals gave up their attempts to extort any cash I might have.

I teamed up with another kid who the bullies had ostracised because of his mixed-race heritage. Brian Lord was another sci-fi fanatic and like me a fan of the Eagle comic and Dan Dare, Pilot of The Future. Brian was taller and of stronger build than average, so between us we managed to keep the morons at bay.

Mum became aware of the taunts I suffered and arranged for orthodontic work to be carried out. This turned out to be a protracted business as both my upper and lower jaws were too narrow. The machinery fabricated for correction of this condition was extraordinary and consisted of upper and lower plates. Each of these plates was made of two halves joined by screw jacks. These jacks had to be given a half turn every week, forcing my jaws to broaden laterally. With all this machinery in my mouth my speech gained a lisp, more fodder for my tormentors. It took eight years, but the treatment was successful.

Our house in Park Road was close to Wokingham Railway Station, and like all small boys at that time I became obsessed with the mighty steam engines. Seeming almost alive, these behemoths constructed of large and heavy moving parts demonstrated their immense power by effortlessly hauling their trains out of the station. It wasn't far to walk and I spent long periods on the footbridge over the tracks, often enveloped in steam and smoke. Although Mum made me bath and change when I got home she never complained about the coating of soot and grime. One day when a TV program on steam engines was being aired Mum rode her bicycle to the school to collect me, and I rode home on the basket carrier.

Dad was a sportsman. He played hockey for Ranelagh Old Boys, and cricket and football for the Wokingham Town teams. Until my bicycle years I had to accompany Mum as a spectator to his fixtures. Dad was greatly disappointed that I did not share his enthusiasm, but I was dragged along to attend his sporting events anyway. Dad was normally a caring father, so I was deeply hurt when he casually described me to Mum as pathetic. I tried and occasionally played for the Palmer School football team, but when my bike arrived I lost interest.

Encouraged by me, Brian Lord persuaded his parents to get him a bike. We were mobile, and it was a life-changing moment. Our first outings were to Finchampstead Ridges and we rode the footpaths down the escarpment. This was scary, exhilarating, and addictive. We named the rides and rated them by number, favouring the longest, which though less severe still allowed maximum speed. Occasional walkers had to leap into the adjacent foliage when we came screaming down. The gently-descending trails were less damaging when we lost control, as they were bordered by deep bracken. Patches of gorse alongside some sections added to the frisson. Number Ten was a fearsome gulley lined with trees. It was very steep, no pedalling required and the only ride that required the constant use of brakes. Mum was concerned at the ever-increasing number of scratches, cuts and bruises I sustained, but most of her attention was now focused on my younger brothers Robert and Roger.

I discovered that the thrill of being close to danger gave me a welcome release from my pervasive state of anxiety and introspection. That revelation dictated the course my life would follow.

Dad's family were from Sonning Common and Peppard near Henley. We had visited his mother by car on several occasions and I had noticed that Sonning Common had some really good slopes. With bikes, we could go there unsupervised. The only problem was the distance, fifteen miles from Wokingham via Twyford and Wargrave. It was hard work, my little bike had no gears and tiny nineteen-inch wheels. No fizzy pop (soda) was carried. We relied on standpipe water for refreshment; sometimes on hot summer days we drank from the streams, which in those days were relatively unpolluted. It was worth the journey. The rides were fast but safe, being down broad expanses of open grass.

In those days of little traffic the freedom of the road was a hugely liberating experience, for we had no adult supervision – well, almost none. When we were observed by my uncle Ernest as we careered down the hill into Henley High Street, he regaled Dad with an exaggerated version of our downhill sprint. Dad was unaware how far we cycled for a day's fun, thinking we just went to the local park or maybe even the Ridges (three miles). I was grounded, but Dad relented after pressure from Mum, who didn't like me moping around the house.

Elizabeth and I were made to go to church on Sunday dressed up in embarrassing fashion. That's a whole morning from breakfast to the Sunday roast. Twenty five percent of our precious weekend wasted and no chance to go riding! I got pressured by Mum Dad and the vicar to join the choir, groan. Now twice on Sunday and practice on Thursday after school. I did get a shilling per week for my services though.

The choirmaster, a Mr Gould, was a stern fellow who had no patience with us little tykes. He was a balding gnome with NHS spectacles who could stop any smirk, murmur or loss of attention with a look as terrifying as the business end of a double-barrelled shotgun. During choir practice he played a harmonium, a curious mobile reed organ operated by foot pumps.

Once when I was late for practice and feared Mr Gould's wrath, I rode my bike at speed into the churchyard toward the bike rack. Braking too late, I slammed into the rack and my head went forward and down on to the pennant I had attached to the handlebars. The metal spike pierced my lower lip and entered my mouth, extracting itself as I reared back. I sat there dazed and bleeding from my torn lip. Concerned as to what I should do next, I lurched into the church trailing blood to confront Mr Gould.

I was quite shocked by his look of compassion, which was completely unexpected. There being no telephone at the church or at home, he gave me his starched linen handkerchief to staunch the flow and sent me home. I still have a crescent-shaped scar under my lower lip. I resumed choral activity when my lip healed, because I needed the pocket money.

I read the adventures of Biggles and science fiction magazines. The Eagle I read again and again, becoming immersed in space travel and the world of the future. Brian and I built a space-ship cockpit in the under-stair cupboard, our imagination running wild.

Wokingham was close to RAE Farnborough, and I got a real kick from the sound of sonic booms when the prototype Hawker Hunter was put through its paces, I saw the movie Sound Barrier and one day as I was coming back from the railway station an Air Force flypast went overhead on the way to the air show. I was hooked.

My Dad's ex-navy friend was an air show exhibitor. "Jack" (real names Francis Valentine Parker) was in business with his brother Cecil making exhibition hardware. These machines were amazing for their time. Jet engines, undercarriages and other aircraft systems were cut up, painted, motorised and internally illuminated to allow viewing of their vital actions. Jack had VIP tickets for the weekday (industry only) shows, there were no crowds and one could sit and watch at leisure. It was fantastic! I attended the Farnborough Air Show from 1947 to 1959.

This was an exciting time for aviation and displays were given by weird and wonderful aircraft like the Avro Ashton, the SR53, the Fairy Delta and the giant Saunders Roe Princess. Unfortunately weekday entrance passes were limited to immediate family, so my mate Brian attended on public days.

Unfortunately Brian was at the show on September 6 1952 for the appalling accident when a De Havilland 110, later named the Sea Vixen, broke up in mid air. One of the engines arced over into the densely-packed public enclosure, and 29 people were killed as well as the pilot and observer. Brian was close to the impact site and was splattered with blood. This traumatic experience destroyed his desire for a future in aviation.

Chapter Two

BOARDING SCHOOL

1952-1959

Mum and Dad enrolled me at The Royal Hospital School at Holbrook, near Ipswich, hoping to toughen me up and make me less of a dreamer. The plan was partially successful. It was a comprehensive boys' only boarding school for the sons of seamen, and in those days no school fees were charged. The school moved to its present site from Greenwich in 1932. It was constructed in impressive Queen Anne style and has a great history.

I vividly remember leaving Mum on the platform at Liverpool Street Station. I am not sure who was the more distressed, but we contained ourselves in true British fashion.

Life away from home was an alien experience. I and all the other new boys silently went through the joining routine, trying to take it all on board. New intakes arrived several days before the other pupils in order to become familiar with the surroundings and receive briefings on procedure. Before going to our respective houses (named after famous admirals) we stayed together in one, Cornwallis. Each house was in the shape of a large H, the senior and junior wings separated by the Housemaster's apartment downstairs and the ablutions upstairs.

I was struck by the grand scale of the establishment and the Spartan appearance of the accommodation. The quality of build was impressive.

Gleaming teak floors and cabinets graced the day rooms and dormitory. In the toilets and showers brass and copper fittings dazzled.

We rattled around in this huge new world. There were stifled sobs from under the covers after lights out, for this new institutional environment was intimidating. Mr Burbage, the stern housemaster of Cornwallis, made it very clear that school rules and routine would be followed. With a total of 660 boys I can now see why. Instructions were given to us by Burbage and an experienced prefect. A fair amount of the daytime was taken up with lessons on how to march in step and change direction as a troop.

We gaggled off to the quartermaster's stores and were equipped with uniform and sports gear. We were then split up and sent to our respective houses to await the remaining pupils. St Vincent, with housemaster Mr Tate, was to be my home for the next six years. Tate was a firm but fair Yorkshireman. Typical of most men from that county, he was blunt in manner and mad about cricket. The deputy, Mr Wright, was an ex-army officer of perfect manners who was kind but careful not to give the impression he favoured any above another.

Holbrook, as a military boarding school, was not as extreme as you might imagine in regard to initiations for new boys. We were of course assessed to see who would be where in the pecking order. Mr Wright was well aware of the potential for bullying and patrolled constantly, making us jump by appearing like a wraith anywhere and at any time. Corporal punishment was used sparingly but to good effect. The separation by age worked well, preventing the older boys from antagonising or otherwise taking advantage of the younger ones.

The dormitories were open, like old-style hospital wards, with thirty beds each. We slept with the windows open, the heating only switched on during the coldest nights. The day started at 7.00 with a call of "Out of your beds!", after which we trooped naked to the communal showers. No talking was allowed. When we were in place, lined up under the shower heads, three feet apart, Mr Wright would turn on the water at the appropriate temperature. If we had generally been of good behaviour, this would be warm. After 30 seconds the water went off and we had ten seconds to soap down, then the water came back on warm for 30 seconds while we rinsed off. Then we were "woken up" with a three second drench of icy cold. After towelling dry it was back to the dorm, where we dressed, stripped the bed, flipped the mattress and dressed the navy issue beds in standard envelope style, no creases. Sheets had to be precisely folded back in line with all the other beds. This had to be achieved in two minutes or practice in free time would ensue.

House cleaning followed; still no talking. A list was posted with our particular roles for the week, which could be sweeping, dusting or cleaning the brass, copper and chrome fittings. The chores took about twenty minutes. On completion we cleaned up and went to the dayroom (no loitering) where we could talk for the first time that day. In the dayroom we each had a small under-counter locker made of teak. There we stored our personal effects and "tuck". The dorm was then out of bounds until bedtime.

In no time we were called to the house square to "fall in" and form ranks. We marched everywhere under the control of prefects. First to the dining hall for breakfast, then to the impressive school chapel. After a short service during which we practised singing for special occasions, all 600 boys were to sing, and sing clearly. Our full-throated efforts were impressive, and often brought tears to the eyes of visitors. They were unaware that our vocal "enthusiasm" was due more to the threat of extra practice than religious fervour.

I became an atheist and remained so for many years. This decision was the result of discussions with the school chaplain. I needed explanations concerning our existence, insisting on an answer that could withstand the light of reason, which of course was not possible.

The chaplain was aware that his answers had failed to impress me and I sensed a certain wavering of his own conviction.

It seemed to me that the Christian religion had become an outdated and ramshackle edifice desperately in need of an overhaul. I did not reveal my conclusions to anyone, thinking that "they" might attempt to brainwash me. In retrospect I realise that half the staff were of similar disposition. There was no consensus on how to deal with unbelievers, but chapel was compulsory.

The curriculum was arranged to enable sport on a daily basis. This could be cross-country running, team games on the sports field (fifty acres) or use of the swimming pool. Organised use of the gym was a regular class period. After supper we returned to the classrooms for an hour or two of prep, after which we returned to the house for supervised hobbies before bedtime. No time for mischief. During my early years I was occasionally the target of a bully called Attridge, but I solved the problem when I snapped and whacked the offender with a football boot.

Although the school had its own well-equipped infirmary, each house had a resident Matron for minor ailments. Much to the chagrin of us St Vincent boys our matron was spectacularly ugly. At Drake house the housemaster, Mr Bartlett, was a divorcee and the matron a stunner. They got on noticeably well. The inevitable rumour factory generated so much speculation and smutty jokes that the governors gave them an ultimatum. They got married. The staff were happy with this outcome but the Drake boys were furious, now deprived of their beautiful nurse's ministrations.

One of my favourite activities was small-arms instruction. At the far end of the parade ground was an underground firing range where we were taught basic target shooting with .22 rifles. The range was situated in "The Ship", a bunker-like construction at the bottom end of the parade ground. It was so called because it had the bowsprit and figurehead of Training Ship Fame III on the end overlooking the playing fields.

I made it on to the school shooting team, which meant away matches. Leaving the school to experience life on the outside was a major source of excitement, for we got to see real live girls. The only other school team I played for was the rugby fifteen. I was too small really, but played fullback and successfully brought down potential try scorers. Competing against teams from co-educational schools meant seeing more girls, close up. We showed off like mad and strutted about in our navy uniforms. What we would have done if a girl had responded I hate to think. Girls seemed like angels to us, but with so little experience we would have messed up any encounter for sure.

As far as the fair sex was concerned older brothers and outside sources were totally unreliable, thanks to hopelessly ill-informed bragging and the influence of cheap pornography. The school did at least give new entrants a lecture on the birds and bees. They hoped it might prevent masturbation, but it only gave our fantasies a boost.

The only practical instruction on how to manage the opposite sex came from the drill instructor, a Mr Bates. Always smartly turned out as a gunnery instructor, Bates also ran the rifle range. Being isolated from the rest of the school enabled him to pass on his secrets undisturbed. It couldn't last and Bates was eventually shopped and dismissed, but his talks were of great value, especially in regard to prevention of pregnancy and STDs. We were very grateful.

I tried to approach the very cute daughter of one of the gym instructors by writing her a love letter - big mistake. The contents were made public knowledge and it took quite a while for the ribbing to subside. The staff were even worse than my fellow pupils. I also lost the attention of the art master's daughter because of this revelation. I had made definite eye contact on several occasions and had even received a hint of a smile. She very much resembled a young Angelina Jolie in looks and attitude... really.

Our testosterone raged. There were one or two seriously queer fellows who tried to cajole others to join them in more intense activities, but these chaps were well known and avoided. One's macho reputation would be shot to hell if seen fraternising with them. One of the most predatory of these lads announced his intention to enter the church on leaving the school. We were stunned but said nothing, for we were wary of any inquisition that might follow a denunciation.

Chemistry, a favourite subject, enabled me to make my own explosions. I did not necessarily wish to blow anything up, enjoying the effect as an art form more than a means of destruction. At home I had been secretly hiding fireworks when on school holidays, and had modified rockets etc in order to understand their capabilities. I replaced the starburst payload of one example with another small rocket as a second stage, and the result was interesting. The pyrotechnic hybrid whooshed into the sky. I had hoped to achieve a record altitude but the second stage only ignited when the booster, fuel exhausted, had arced over. The mini missile separated and rocketed down straight for our neighbour's rooftop, luckily ricocheting into his garden. My Wokingham mate Richard Talbot related the incident to his parents, who declared me out of bounds.

I then learned how to make serious bombs. After a couple of near disasters with metal canisters I settled for the very effective rolled-up magazine bound with string. My initial and very dangerous attempts included a pipe bomb, whose shrapnel narrowly missed my younger brother, and a tin-can variety whose Jetex fuse ignited when under construction. I had to leap over the kitchen table, open the door and lob my "grenade" into the garden. Mum sensibly banned any further production, threatening to inform my father.

Proud of my handiwork, I smuggled a remaining device back to school. We let it off one Sunday well away from the premises, as in those days penalties for serious misbehaviour were severe (caning or expulsion). Present day Holbrook is a very different place. It is co-ed now and has adopted a democratic and modern approach, moulding its pupils into well-balanced easy-going youngsters.

No opportunities to kick start any love life occurred while at Holbrook. The school did hold sixth-form dancing classes with a nearby girls' school but these classes were closely supervised and proved too intimidating for self-conscious teenagers.

Robert Outred, David West and myself hung out together and occasionally went for Sunday afternoon "leave out", hoping in vain to chat up the local girls. No chance, they regarded RHS boys as an alien species. Pupils were allowed two or three exeats during term time if we had not received any minus points like extra prep or detention. Detention was imposed for misbehaviour in class and meant exclusion from the Saturday night movie in the assembly hall. I only suffered this indignity once, for failing to provide a History essay. I did not think this was bad behaviour, but our dry-as-dust history teacher (who resembled Sam the Eagle on the Muppet Show) did not accept my explanation that I found the topic in question irrelevant. I had tried in vain to conjure up something interesting to put on paper but could only provide a summary of two lines. History was the only subject I failed at the GCE "O" level examinations.

In the sixth form I was prompted by the careers master (same old dry history chap) to consider my future. He suggested a career as a geologist, and this seemed the most likely. However my instincts led me in a completely different direction.

Pelham Ship, a classmate and the son of the school band instructor, was a like-minded aviation freak. We were concerned that British combat aircraft always looked so plebeian and competed to design the ideal jet fighter. We had been inspired by the recent low flypast of an American McDonnell Voodoo. The F101 Voodoo, along with the F105 Starfighter, were revolutionary in appearance as a result of new USAAF criteria demanding supersonic performance. Our concerns evaporated when the Supermarine N113 arrived on the scene. This mean machine cheered us up with regular fast and low overflights. The school with its 200-foot clock tower was used as a turning point on a low-level training route.

I was sixteen and a half when I saw the same aircraft in a recruitment ad for Royal Navy pilots. I promptly completed and posted the form. The response was immediate; I should proceed to HMS Ganges for an initial medical. I was classed as "small and wiry but fit" and was given dates to present myself, first at RAF Hornchurch for flying aptitude, then HMS Sultan in Gosport for interviews and a general assessment.

At Hornchurch they used a primitive video game to test co-ordination. The idea was to keep a wandering dot in a centre circle by use of control column and rudder pedals, tricky when they upped the speed. At Sultan candidates took an IQ test and were assessed for team member skills by being challenged to devise a method using gym equipment to cross a "ravine". Our team failed due to an argument between two of our members.

At the end of the course we were asked to critically assess the other applicants. As the other chaps on the course were twenty-something adults I felt uncomfortable assessing what I considered grown ups.

About 75% of us were accepted for initial training, I was written up as "intelligent but immature and overly sensitive" - fair enough. The board then asked if I wanted to join the Navy immediately or complete my second year sixth and A levels. I couldn't wait and signed on the dotted line. I was to have a short service commission, eight years on the Supplementary List (S.L.).

My Mum and Dad gave my brother Rob and me all the encouragement we could possibly need in regard to our flying careers. This support was extraordinary considering my Mum's brother Eric had died when his Hawker Hart was involved in a mid-air collision. The accident occurred while Eric was serving with the RAF in Aden in 1936.

Chapter Three

THE ROYAL NAVY AND FLIGHT TRAINING

1959-1961

It was now October 1959. As I was an ex-Holbrook boy, the Navy had made me an exception, so barely seventeen years old and four months short of the stipulated age of entry, I found myself on the Cornish Riviera Express en route to Plymouth. My destination was *HMS Thunderer*, the Royal Navy's Engineering School at Manadon. In those days SL aircrew received their basic naval instruction at Manadon, not Dartmouth.

I joined 89(P) Course. We learned parade drill, regulations, and the responsibilities and administrative tasks required from a junior officer. We also learned how to pack a cabin trunk and keep a journal.

At weekends we were allowed shore leave as long as we wore the approved clothing, ie sports jacket and cavalry twill trousers or blazer and grey flannels. A hat was required when "walking out", which made us feel a touch incongruous in downtown Plymouth. Course mates Les Ingham, Bob Roffe, Neville Featherstone and Ed Twinberrow were keen to demonstrate how to enjoy fine dining and fancy clubs; I had only read about such things.

At the end of the course I was assessed as young for my age. Being 20 percent younger than the rest of my course mates I imagined this must mean they thought me childish.

There followed survival and emergency training at Seafield Park, Stubbington, near Portsmouth. This included a fully-clothed and very painful dip in the Solent, in March when the sea was very, very, cold. Ejector seat training included live firing up a ramp, which was later abandoned as it caused back problems. The parachute instruction and anoxia/hypoxia experience (in a hypobaric chamber) was fun. When sitting in the chamber we were given pen and note pads. Air was evacuated, simulating atmospheric conditions at high altitude. When at 30,000 feet we were instructed to take off our oxygen masks and write down the words spoken over the headphones. At first the writing appeared normal, but after a while it became large and childish. When it became illegible we burst out laughing and were told to put our masks back on. One or two had to be assisted, as at this stage mental deterioration was pretty rapid. This experience was valuable and years later proved very useful.

The excitement increased, our next step being attendance at the No. 1 Flying Training School, RAF Linton-on-Ouse. The training was managed by the Royal Air Force for Royal Navy students. There were however a small contingent of RN flight instructors more or less kept under control by Commander Cedric Coxon. We were to fly the Piston Provost T1, progressing on to the Vampire T11 jet.

The general list (GL) career officers joined 89(P) Course for pilot training; they were Jonathan Todd, Jeremy Nichols, Chris Allen, Jeremy Devitt, and Peter Murison. These Dartmouth-trained chaps were a surprisingly genial bunch who were generally tolerant of our sometimes uncouth S.L. behaviour.

The Provost T1 looked good. It had a powerful radial engine and was tailwheel configured. These attributes demanded a considerable amount of physical and mental co-ordination from the trainee pilot. As a basic trainer it served its purpose well, weeding out the weaker candidates at an early stage. The Jet Provost, its replacement, proved to be an expensive mistake. Underpowered and easy to fly, it allowed marginal candidates to escape detection until they commenced operational training.

After a week of ground school we were issued with flying clothing and prepared for our first flight. It was April 21 1960, I was $17^1/_2$, and the familiarisation flight was my first time off the ground, ever. I had been determined that my first flight would be from the cockpit.

As we lifted off I felt a surge of excitement, feeling "at home". After that first familiarisation the hard work began. All flights were preceded by an extensive briefing, and much had to be assimilated, for our futures were at stake.

My first instructor, a Flt Lt Butler, was RAF, young, and newly qualified, and I was his first pupil. In trying to ensure a correct and complete delivery his briefings were stilted and boring. I tried to take it in, but this by-numbers instruction left me numb. After ten flying hours I had failed to reach the standard required for going solo. There came a change of instructor. This was ominous, as it was a first step towards being "chopped" or sent home. I felt the beginnings of despair.

The new instructor, Lieutenant Robin Doe, Royal Navy, was outrageously flamboyant. When we were introduced he took one look at my anxious face, slapped me on the back and jovially said "cheer up, this is going to be fun", and it was. Instead of flying round and round in the circuit doing touch and goes he took me over to the low flying area. As we entered the zone he rolled the Provost over and dived for the "deck". He pulled out about twenty feet above the hedgerows taking my breath away. Swooping around electricity pylons and farmhouses, the adrenalin rush was staggering. Back in the circuit at Rufforth, the satellite airfield, he flew an unbelievably tight and steep circuit, proving that the normal circuit was "easy peasy". I got the idea.

If I made any errors Doe would cuff my flying helmet and exclaim "not that way you clown, like this" and then demonstrate the correct technique in exaggerated fashion. He encouraged me to fly boldly and without hesitation. A week later we parked in front of the control tower at Rufforth, engine running, and he opened the canopy and climbed out, saying "OK, one circuit and landing, then come back for me". It was a strange and wonderful feeling taxiing out with an empty seat alongside. It was easy after all. Not long after, when we were into precision aerobatics, my previous instructor found it hard to believe Robin Doe's report on my progress and asked to check me out. He found the experience hard to swallow and the debriefing was short and sweet, "very good" he said with a tight smile.

Only two of our twelve-strong course had been "chopped", whereas only two remained on the course behind. Two candidates had to be re-assigned to 90 Course. Being the two youngest, Mike Todd and I were back-coursed, which was disappointing but understandable.

My flying career nearly ended prematurely on two occasions, for totally different reasons. The first was a disciplinary matter, when I was reprimanded for unauthorised low flying, an offence which normally resulted in automatic termination. The second occasion could have been the end; it was when I experienced "G-LOC".

In a tight turn or when pulling out of a dive G forces cause progressive loss of vision, eventually leading to loss of consciousness. These forces can be countered by tensing tummy and leg muscles, which prevents blood draining from the brain to the lower body.

I planned to carry out a loop using 6G rather than the authorised 4. Shortly after entering the manoeuvre I blacked out.

I regained consciousness as if waking from a very deep sleep, it seemed to take forever. I could see a gleaming orb directly in front of my eyes... it didn't make sense. The sound of the engine gradually filtered through. Who am I? where am I? I wondered, struggling to collect my thoughts. Suddenly I recognised the bright disc as my parachute release button. My head was slumped on my chest. The realisation that this was not a dream slowly took hold. The Provost was in a shallow dive and passing 3000 feet. I levelled out and groggily took stock of the situation.

I was shaken and returned to base, saying I had the runs. Fortunately I had started the aerobatics at 7000 feet.

I did not mention the incident for fear of being grounded for investigation. Despite the use of G-suits, G-LOC has claimed many lives, including those of experienced test pilots.

I did not enjoy instrument training. To block any external reference amber Perspex screens were placed against the windscreen and side panel and the students wore blue-tinted goggles. The combined effect was that of total darkness outside (similar to opposing Polaroid filters). We practised instrument take-offs and recovery from unusual attitudes, the latter including spins and aerobatic manoeuvres. Military flying is freeform and presents many opportunities for pilot disorientation. When experiencing G forces in low visibility the inner ear balance mechanism will misinterpret the situation. It can tell you that you are turning in one direction when the opposite may be true. It is extremely difficult to follow the instruments in these circumstances, and many have died following their instincts rather than their instruments.

When Peter Murison got married we all attended the wedding near Manchester, on a perfect sunny day. My course mates thought it an appropriate time for my champagne initiation. I loved the stuff, upgraded to cognac and became ridiculously drunk. Thinking it a good idea to also initiate me into the joys of smoking, someone stuffed a cigar in my mouth. That was the end - I threw up and passed out. They put me to bed in the hotel. When I awoke my head felt like a red hot beach ball and I thought I was going to die.

Chris Allen gave me a lift to London in his self-maintained MG

TC. We drove with the top down to disperse engine fumes, so a fine spray of oil covered us both. Chris had goggles, but I had to keep my eyes closed. Badly dressed and stupefied, I staggered black-faced across London. On the tube I sat like a zombie, attracting curious stares. When I got home Mum burst into tears.

At the end of basic training those deemed to have slower reactions (they might dispute that) departed for training on Helicopters or the "Airborne Early Warning" Gannets. The remainder continued at Linton for jet training on the Vampire T11.

During that summer break, Commander Coxon thought it would be a good idea for me to spend some time afloat. He and two others with sailing experience, Dartmouth general list chaps, were to proceed to Hamble and begin a sailing trip across the channel.

The boat was an ex-Luftwaffe Windfall yacht commandeered at the end of the war. It carried about 100 square metres of sail and was ten metres in length. On arrival at Hamble we stocked the boat with supplies and ordered the duty-free. With preparations complete there was time to spare; it was three in the afternoon and time for a beer.

We reeled out of the pub at about ten that night. How we all got into the dinghy I'll never know. After rowing around for about ten minutes in the dark we eventually found the Windfall. Now we were told by Cdr. Coxon that we had to leave harbour straight away as bad weather was imminent! We motored out into the channel and set sail with the wind increasing. My bunk was a pipe cot in the foresail locker. It got very rough, a force nine in fact. I had to strap myself in to stop getting thrown about. My orders were to remain below and let the "real sailors" do their thing.

They had left it too late to reef in the sail and the bow was tucking in. We butted across the channel semi-submersed, The "head" (toilet) was under my bunk, I was seasick, we all had hangovers and were soaked through. Sleep was out of the question. Carrying too much sail and unable to tack, we were blown up the English Channel. Cherbourg would have to wait. As we rounded the lee side of the peninsula the wind dropped and we anchored off Barfleur. I thought we might get some sleep, but no, we were to go ashore. It was late afternoon, and we had spent the whole night and the following day coping with the weather and baling out.

The fishing fleet was secured inside the harbour sheltering from the storm, so our arrival aroused considerable interest. What fools were these, going for a cruise in gale force 9? We piled into our little dinghy (pram) and with only inches of freeboard rowed into the harbour. "Les Foux Anglais" were invited into the nearest bar and given hot toddy. As the current focus of interest we were plied with drinks and engaged in a lively conversation in fractured Franglais.

At nightfall we were informed by the harbourmaster that we would not be allowed back on board until the following day, a commendable decision. We continued socialising until the ability to form words failed. We slept on the tiled floor and awoke in a state resembling rigor mortis. Strong coffee and calvados enabled us to revive enough to murmur our thanks and re-embark, and we sailed on to Cherbourg.

After loading up with more duty-free we continued round Cap de la Hague to Jersey, where they speak English. We slept. I did not think I would be capable of a night on the town but the stamina of youth prevailed and we had yet another interesting evening, managing to invite a couple of girls back to the boat. Our hopes of sensual delight were shattered when the Commander returned, alone and singing sea shanties, his raucous presence destroying any enthusiasm the girls might have felt. They left.

The following day we stocked up yet more duty-free and set sail for Hamble. Glorious weather, thank god. Downwind with spinnaker set and sails goose winged, we raced across the channel. There was very little to do, so I sunbathed and slept. The others consumed our excess duty-free. I could see another boozy saga unfolding, so on reaching Hamble I made my apologies and left for home.

The transition to the Vampire T11 was exhilarating. Welcome to the world of speed and high altitude flight!

In an effort to enhance my social life I bought a 1947 Vauxhall 14 from my course mate John Middleton for £25. It resembled one of the old gangster autos. Not having a licence, I drove around with L plates, accompanied by those friends with sufficient nerve. The Vauxhall had two lethal faults - dodgy steering and an accelerator pedal that stuck unpredictably.

During a lesson with John one day I drove around the officers' mess. Turning into the garage parking area I applied a touch of accelerator pedal and the throttle jammed. In front of us were four or five scattered vehicles being washed or maintained (normal on Saturday morning). I leaned on the horn and we tensed, expecting impact. Amazement and disbelief showed on the faces of those leaping to safety. Braking was out of the question, but by wrenching the wheel from one side to the other we managed to exit the other side unscathed.

Not being able to afford the many repairs required, it was probably good fortune that on one very cold night lack of de-icing fluid resulted in a split engine block. The Vauxhall was scrapped and I felt inadequate, for a set of wheels provided considerable flexibility for social activity. I would receive my wings years before I passed an MOT driving test.

Alan Hickling, being a real motorhead, had a collection of classics, including a 1927 Rolls Royce Ghost. His Railton "Straight Eight" was not roadworthy, but it got a good workout round the perimeter track at weekends. This vintage machine finally met its end when with fuel boosted by "nitro" it reached about 150 mph down the main runway and blew its engine. The brakes failed to stop the mighty beast, which demolished part of the boundary fence and came to rest a smoking wreck in a field of wheat. Luckily no fire ensued.

Our social life was probably what you would expect. Much time was spent in the officers' mess bar and there was silly behaviour on "dining in nights" and weekends in London. Those weekends started on Friday at five with the race down the newly-opened M1. An eclectic collection left the air station, a Ford Prefect, two MGs, a new Issigonis Mini, the Rolls Royce, and a Daimler SP 250. The racers soon separated as drivers tried to beat individual journey times. The motorway had no speed limit at that time, and the Daimler always arrived first, closely followed by the Mini.

The Daimler owner had a girlfriend who owned a basement flat in Harley Street. The parties started there. Saturday morning was messy, only one bathroom. Hair of the dog was imbibed at the Shepherds in Mayfair. There were plenty of girls, but my youth and inexperience were very apparent. The girls enjoyed chatting to me but then partied with the older guys, sigh. Sometimes I continued home to Wokingham, only thirty minutes by train. There I met a sweet young thing at the youth club, a more suitable choice. Alison was just as green as myself. We were good friends for some time.

Back at Linton I occasionally escorted Commander Coxon's daughter to functions, but she was a wild child. I couldn't keep up and it didn't last.

I was awarded my wings on the 14th July 1961. The jet graduates' future role depended on the grade they achieved. The options at this stage were - Night fighter Interceptor (Sea Vixens) and Day fighter, Ground attack (Supermarine Scimitar). I was hoping for, and got, fighter/ground attack. After summer leave, advanced tactical training would commence at RNAS (Royal Naval Air Station) Lossiemouth.

Chapter Four

ADVANCED FLYING TRAINING, LOSSIEMOUTH

August 1961

The Fighter and Ground Attack school was located at RNAS Lossiemouth on the Moray Firth in the north of Scotland. This air station was ideal for training due to its persistent good visibility and freedom from low cloud.

Basic fighter training was carried out by 738 Squadron with the Hawker Seahawk FGA6, which though small was a beauty. This was the first single seater we had been let loose on and the cockpit felt very personal, even intimate. For the first time I felt at one with the machine. Flying in formation was exhilarating, as it enabled a close-up view of this purposeful-looking aircraft in workmanlike camouflage, not training day-glo.

After tactical formation training came an eagerly-anticipated new experience, armament practice. For air-to-air gunnery we used much stylised intercept profiles (curve of pursuits), and the trigger operated a gunsight camera not the 20mm cannons.

Specialised WRNS developed and assessed the cine film when we returned. In those days it was OK for girls to make the coffee (no vending machines), so long as they were not busy. We drank lots of coffee, which was free and gave us the opportunity for a little flirting.

They were a good bunch. The girl in charge, Sally, effectively ensured we complied with the no-fraternising rule. She had an excellent line in putdowns. Fortunately the rules only applied during working hours and we often let our hair down during rave-ups ashore (off base). They were good company but a canny bunch, they knew full well that the chances of a permanent relationship were pretty slim.

The only scandal at Lossiemouth had nothing to do with the Air Wing. The Chaplain and the first lieutenant's wife were caught canoodling on the golf course, by, of all people, the Captain (of HMS *Fulmar*). He was out walking his dog, it was dark, but the runway approach lights straddling the course were unexpectedly switched on. The skipper might under normal circumstances have chosen to ignore the couple, but there were other witnesses in nearby bushes. The golf course was a convenient dual use facility. I believe the "sinners" were transferred.

There were three bombing ranges in the Moray Firth, Rosehearty, Banff, and Tain, and these we pounded regularly with three-inch rockets and twenty-five-pound practice bombs. My schooldays experience with small arms proved good value, as a similar gentle touch was required for aiming the aircraft. My ground attack scores were satisfyingly high.

Low-level navigation was exhilarating. In the Seahawk it was carried out at 360 knots and 200 feet. The specified routes wove their way through the Scottish Highlands across spectacular terrain. The opportunity to experience these rarely-seen unpopulated vistas was a privilege much appreciated.

The Seahawk had suffered problems during its introduction to the front line and remedies included an improved fire warning system and an addition to the primitive fuel control system, the latter an isolation switch for the barometric fuel control unit. The BFCU had proved unreliable on occasion, reducing fuel at inappropriate times. To avoid problems it was isolated for take-off and reinstated during checks at 200 feet. If the engine failed while at slow speed and close to the ground a safe ejection was unlikely, as early ejection seats were primitive.

A faulty BFCU got me at 200 feet when I reselected it and the engine quit. I re-activated the isolation switch, closed the throttle and pressed the relight button, hoping to get re-ignition. Meanwhile I lowered the nose to maintain flying speed, my eyes glued to the exhaust gas temperature gauge, which would tell me if the relight drill had been successful. It was. Pulling up at around tree top height I shakily returned for landing.

Back at the crewroom the Senior Pilot (second in command of a squadron) Mike Kennet entered, smiled and asked me what I was waiting for, as another aircraft was now ready. I asked him if I could finish my coffee. He paused, gave me a sideways glance and nodded.

More fuel problems. While carrying out circuit and bumps at the adjacent Milltown airfield the fuel gauge got stuck. Not paying enough attention to the time, I was surprised when ATC called and said I should return to base, time out. I was stunned when I realised I had exceeded my one hour sortie time by twenty minutes. Expecting the engine to cut at any moment I asked for a straight-in approach and coasted back on minimum power. I made it back to the ramp and was told that there was just a few seconds' worth of fuel remaining. More jelly legs.

Instructors also had their moments; one who shall be nameless led us through a "tail chase". This was a preliminary exercise prior to air to air combat training, where two or three students attempt to follow the leader through a series of extreme manoeuvres. In this instance we were led into a stall turn. This involves a vertical climb until the speed runs out, when the aircraft is coaxed to wheel over to one side before diving back to flying speed. At the top there is little or no control. So there we were, three students in a vertical climb facing the leader now falling back down toward us. I was number two.

Avoidance is hazardous at these low speeds, as overt control movements can result in a spin. I could only grit my teeth and hope for the best. The lead aircraft passed by... my turn. Wheeling over the top I was confronted by the next two on the way up, we were powerless. The first near miss was too quick to notice, but passing the second I saw the pilot's helmet fixed in my direction. His visor was down, but I bet his eyes were so wide open it hurt. The formation was scattered in disarray. I guessed the instructor was appalled at how close to disaster we had been, but he managed to reassemble the formation for a return to base. The debriefing was a subdued "well done". We didn't tell on him. but the guy lost his credibility with us three.

The Seahawk Instrument flying practice had been carried out in the good old Vampire (two seats with a QFI, qualified flying instructor). At this stage I was just OK, but I had to work hard at it. On completion of the initial training we carried out the swept wing conversion course on the Hawker Hunter T8. Now equipped with macho-looking G-suits we felt more like the fighter jocks we aspired to be. The flying became exciting, more speed, better acceleration. An altitude of 35,000 feet was now reached in twelve minutes rather than half an hour. Intensive instrument flying on the Hunter gave us the skills to handle recovery from unusual attitudes under high G forces.

Then the ultimate thrill, advanced flying training on the Scimitars of 736 Squadron. The last of the Supermarine dynasty, the Scimitar was a twin-engined single seater, a fifteen ton beauty, eighteen feet high at the tail fin and 57 feet long. All through ground school one felt its awesome presence.

Final ground instruction was in the flight simulator. This machine was vital, there being no two-seat variant of the Scimitar. We practised the many emergency situations again and again. The simulator instructor, Lieutenant Maurice Hynett, was an amiable character but he could be merciless. If Maurice thought students over-confident he would increase emergencies until the inevitable crash, which always hurt even though you knew it to be inevitable.

Unfortunately the simulator was only a systems trainer. It had a navigation plotter for the controller but the pilot could only fly on instruments as there were no visual display screens.

In the days and hours approaching the first Scimitar flight the tension and excitement mounted. After the briefing, I signed the paperwork and walked out to the aircraft. I was very conscious of the onlookers, it was always a big event. They were grinning broadly in an encouraging manner but were also alert for signs of nervousness. I was small, skinny and only nineteen years old. I was nervous, but not of flying the aircraft, only of making a silly mistake. The ground crew were easy-going and considerate and treated me like a kid. We had practised many inspections and cockpit checks in the previous few days but not in full flying kit. This was the real thing.

Strapped and plugged in, the ejection seat safety pins were removed and the teardrop Perspex canopy motored forward. After meticulously reading the checks off the knee pad I gave the thumbs up and the Rolls Royce Avons wound up with a rumble. The Palouste external air starter was towed away. The aircraft gave the impression it was straining at the leash. After a few checks I waved the chocks away. From the pilots position, out on the nose, no part of the aircraft was visible. The aircraft's size was obvious because of the lofty view. Taxiing out I felt the enormous reserve of power ready under my left hand.

Once given take-off clearance I tentatively advanced the throttles and the engines wound up to a muted roar. There was a small but intense vibration. As I released the brakes, the acceleration was unbelievable. Lift off was one third the way down the runway at 175 knots (325 kph). The landing gear and flaps had to be raised quickly as the gear limiting speed of 300 knots was reached as I passed the end of the runway. OK you modern fighter types, that's no big deal, but in 1961 it was awesome. When 500 knots was attained the nose was raised sharply and 35,000 feet could be reached in four minutes. If there was no cloud the airfield could be seen in the rear view mirror until level off.

During the first flight we carried out basic manoeuvres, just a few steep turns and configuration changes, before returning to Milltown for "touch and go" approach and landing practice. On the short return for a final landing at Lossie I was exhilarated, and it took quite a while for the adrenaline to subside.

The Scimitar approach was very different from previous aircraft. Precise speed control was required. Once configured for landing (wheels and flaps etc) the angle of attack and a speed of 132 knots had to be retained until touchdown. Speed was controlled by raising or lowering the nose and height by adjusting power.

The Scimitar, in common with other steeply swept-wing aircraft, had a tendency to pitch up if speed decayed too far (see the F100 Super Sabre Crash on You Tube). If the nose started to rear up, forward pressure on the controls alone would not help, only full power and a missed approach would resolve the situation. Several Scimitars were lost by slow reaction to "pitch up".

Other than being careful with the approach, the Scimitar was easy to fly and very responsive. If you know your sports cars, then it could be compared with the Dodge Viper rather than a British thoroughbred.

Armament training was carried out with the same practice bombs, but the rockets were the two-inch variety carried in pods. The Scimitar had four 30 millimetre cannons but during target practice we only fired one at a time. Releasing that barrage of steel was strangely satisfying. During a shipboard demo for the press I saw and heard the effect of all four guns being fired. Very scary, and this was from about a mile away. The rate of fire for each gun was 1200 rounds per minute. Each shell had three reports, one as it left the barrel, another from its supersonic shockwave, and the final impact explosion. All three were of a different timbre, like different notes played on a vast organ. Even when firing blanks, (during the Indonesian confrontation) it scared the poo out of their troops.

I struggled with low-level navigation, getting off track (one is never 'lost') on the tougher exercises. I sometimes lost the plot in lowland farming areas. It was not easy in those days. Flown at 420 knots and with no auto-pilot, computer or GPS, it was done with a plastic map, a grease pencil and "dead reckoning". I subsequently discovered that other members on the course had flown considerably higher than the 200 feet specified without really giving a s..t, but I was still a kid and followed instructions to the letter. I took criticism of any poor performance to heart and suffered a few sleepless nights. Sensitivity can be a curse.

I only had one incident on the course, a fire warning. The alarm sounded when we were rolling into a dive at Tain range. It was a bit awkward, as we had about 120° bank in a section of four. I had to ease out without endangering the following two (out of sight underneath). Once clear I carried out the much-practised fire drill and informed Pete De Souza, the instructor. Pete conscientiously ran through the fire drill instructions, taking up valuable airtime. I had to change frequency to alert Lossie of my return on one engine. It turned out the warning was spurious, but it was good practice.

Last on the agenda, dummy deck landing practice. No wires but a painted deck on the runway paired with a mirror deck landing sight. An instructor would be out by the mirror to record accuracy. It was important to touch down without any flare or round out, i.e. not to reduce the rate of descent (750 feet/min) but to drive the aircraft on to the touchdown point. The Scimitar's industrial-strength landing gear could take it, no problem. Touch down speed was about 132 knots. This figure was well below the clean stalling speed, but we had augmented lift (blown flaps). A constant speed approach was flown with airbrakes out and a high power setting, so if there was a problem, eg missing the arrestor wire, the engine pickup was immediate. With an airbrakes "in" selection, climb away was assured.

Toward the end of the course on the 19th March, we flew down to RAE Bedford for catapult launch experience. I was lucky and flew the Scimitar, which took 35 minutes. The others travelled the day before as passengers in the Sea Prince, flight time four hours.

I was to get first shot (I suspect the others had hangovers) and taxied round the airfield and up on to the ramp for launch. In front of the ramp was a ten-foot drop and about 400 yards of runway. A nylon net was stretched across the end to capture any aircraft that failed. Not to worry, we were told that we would safely get airborne straight off the ramp. This land-based catapult required a minimum of ten knots of natural wind for a successful launch. The Met Office had forecast at least this much, but it was wavering up and down.

I was the first to go, and the launch officer was unsure whether the wind indicator was reliable. The wind dropped and we waited for a few minutes. When it suddenly picked up I got his "go" signal and set full power, arm straight, elbow locked, gave the thumbs up and the launch button was pressed. There was a slight delay as steam pressure built up to the required amount. The wind dropped to zero! Now beyond the point of no return, the launch officer maxed the steam pressure. The acceleration would now be over the limit (3.7G). The Scimitar launched with an almighty kick.

I was not impressed when the aircraft dropped on to the tarmac. I saw that one throttle lever had closed. I could not bring myself to abort and take the barrier so I "firewalled" both throttles and stomped hard on the left brake, jerking the nose of the aircraft to the left. The aircraft lurched off the tarmac and headed off across the grass. With 220 psi tyre pressure the Scimitar sunk into the grass.

I raised the nose and a temporary lift-off ensued. Progress toward the perimeter fence continued in a series of kangaroo leaps. ATC assumed the worst and hit the crash alarm. The Scimitar finally staggered into the air across the airfield boundary fence and nearby village rooftops.

I assumed I had screwed up and suffered grave thoughts concerning my career while circling to land. Taxiing back to the ramp, the aircraft was closely followed by the fire engines and crash crew. After shutdown the launch officer ascended the ladder. "I'm so sorry lad" he stammered. I would like to have replied "no problem" but I was lost for words. It was a minute or two before my legs would enable me to descend the cockpit ladder safely. The remaining launches were cancelled, launch candidates and the RAE naval contingent retired to the bar.

I was debriefed and found the others already into their second pint. Despite peer pressure I resisted Bedford's best bitter as I had accepted the Sea Prince pilot's request for a volunteer co-pilot (there was no serviceable autopilot). I was to fly the aeroplane while he managed the navigation and radio.

On the flight back to Lossie our hooligans down the back became rowdy on extra beer brought along for the ride. Resuscitating an old air force prank, they secretly worked their way forward up the cabin. The change in centre of gravity required application of nose up trim which was instinctively applied. On reaching the cockpit door, shouts of "gotcha" were followed by a rapid retreat to the rear and much raucous laughter. This sudden rearwards change of trim could not be countered and the nose reared up, sending the Sea Prince into a vertical climb which was followed by a hammerhead stall. Now plummeting earthward, our passengers fell from the rear of the cabin to the cockpit bulkhead, followed by half the contents of the chemical toilet. It was both dramatic and alarming. As we recovered back to level flight the passengers, bruised, bright blue and pungently aromatic, returned silently to their seats.

Back at Lossie I sank a few double brandies and went to bed. I slept well; a double shot of adrenaline will do that. The Sea Prince was grounded for decontamination. "Severe turbulence" seemed enough to satisfy the inquisitors.

On graduation day we were handed our qualifying certificates by the HMS Fulmar captain. At the presentation in the hanger, only the 736 Squadron members were present. We were advised of our posting, which could be 800 Squadron, HMS *Ark Royal*, or 803 Squadron, HMS *Hermes*.

Chapter Five

803 SQUADRON, HMS HERMES, THE MEDITERRANEAN

1962

In the event I was posted to 803 Squadron, Commanding Officer Tommy Leece, Senior Pilot Brian Wilson. I was to replace Lt Paddy Waring.

I joined 803 on the 1st April 1962. The squadron was based at Lossiemouth across the other side of the airfield. They had just disembarked from HMS *Victorious* and were to re-embark on the refurbished HMS *Hermes*.

I was still a midshipman, and there were smirks and raised eyebrows as I appeared in the hangar. I don't think any 'midi' had joined a squadron for decades. My squadron colleagues seemed a likeable bunch. I was to be Fred de la Billière's wingman. Fred's proper name was Arthur Michel De La Coeur de la Billière; he was the brother of Sir Peter de la Billière, CiC British Forces during the Gulf War. Fred was the 803 squadron Air Warfare Instructor, my section leader, and would monitor my operational progress.

During the short work up period before embarkation I suffered two hydraulic failures. Thank you Maurice for the intensive simulator training. I started to worry about the standard of maintenance, but was told that the odd hiccup was only to be expected, as the aircraft concerned had recently undergone a complete overhaul and upgrade at RNAY Fleetlands, Gosport.

The work up consisted of ACT (Army Co-operation Training), weaponry at Tain range and Sidewinder interception practice. I was given early promotion to Sub-Lieutenant to avoid any embarrassment. On board ship midshipmen were tolerated but generally ignored, ratings referring to them as "snotties".

I was to escort the ratings on the train to Portsmouth. The squadron was shipping a large stock of stores and a sizeable complement of ratings, British Rail having provided a train for our sole use. This setup ensured control over bar supplies and alcohol consumption, essential when the military is on the move. This was a twelve-hour journey and believe me, sailors with time on their hands can be a whole load of trouble. This trip could have been a nightmare, but luckily for me the squadron Chief Regulator was a wise and experienced old timer. His foresight enabled him to nip trouble in the bud saving me the hassle of dealing with defaulters.

There is always one, however. This particular hooligan was expected to misbehave and liked to deliver. He had of course smuggled supplies of his own. He got rowdy and threw a few punches. The regulating staff were waiting for just this moment and piled in. After a brief scuffle the offender ended up handcuffed in the baggage car "for his own safety". Having acted true to form and lived up to expectations, he was content to spend the remainder of the journey in situ.

Arriving in Portsmouth the next day, we transferred to buses for the short journey to the dockyard. Our stores and freight were later shunted all the way to the wharf and hoisted aboard by crane.

This was my first time on board a Royal Navy warship and *Hermes* looked mighty impressive. I was struck by the constant muted roar of ventilation and other machinery. How on earth did anyone sleep? A steward led me to my cabin. Officer territory on board HM ships is traditionally at the stern and on *Hermes* the aviation section was allocated a section of its own. Each squadron enjoying neighbourly sub-sections. Our accommodation was compact and neat (caravan/trailer owners will know what I mean). As a newbie and a youngster I enjoyed the privacy of a single cabin. After unpacking and stowing my flying kit I suddenly realised that my brain had cancelled out the background noise.

I was tasked with issuing our technicians their flight deck clothing. This I did in the hangar on some hastily-improvised trestle tables. Being as green as they come and not now having the support of the regulating staff, things soon got out of hand. Organised crowding and jostling enabled the less honest to obtain extra supplies. I was saved the embarrassment of responsibility for these inconsistencies, as the hangar fuel main burst drenching our location with aviation fuel. Everyone bolted for the exits. The emergency evacuation provided the ideal excuse for attribution of losses.

The next day *Hermes* sailed out of harbour for the "work up" area in Lyme Bay. Ships' systems were tested, guns fired and various states of alert were simulated. I used the opportunity to try and find my way to the wardroom, the briefing room and various other sites important for my survival. It would be a few days before I was able to get directly to my intended destination.

The ship went to flying stations to receive the squadron aircraft. I located the viewing area or "goofers" on the roof of the ships bridge in order to watch our bunch landing on. I was shocked by how small the landing area was and how large the Scimitar seemed.

Landings were swift and dramatic. Immediately aircraft hit the deck they would decelerate with a scream as the steel wire rope was torn out of the "sheaves". Brakes were not applied, allowing wire tension to drag the aircraft rearward. A thumbs up from the marshaller indicated that the wire had dropped to the deck. Power was used to stop the rollback, as the instinctive application of brake would tip the aircraft on to its tail bumper. It was just a short taxi with wings folding into Fly 1 deck park. The next to land hit the deck twenty seconds later.

After all aircraft had been recovered, mini tractors repositioned the aircraft to be parked herringbone style down the deck edge for refuelling and re-arming. Unserviceable aircraft were sent wings folded down to the hangar. *Hermes* had two lifts, one in the centre of the landing area and another forward at end of the angled deck.

Expecting my first sortie to consist of circuits with practice touch and goes, I was surprised to see myself programmed for high-level interception exercises. I would be allowed one touch and go before my first deck landing.

In cooler climates we wore immersion suits, which proved a bit warm during the briefing, so it was a relief to finally climb up on deck, where a stiff breeze was blowing. As I walked to the aircraft I had that funny feeling at the nape of the neck, knowing that I was again being closely observed. After carrying out the external check I got back in the groove and focused on the pre-flight details, start up, and taxi out to the catapult.

Easing into position on the catapult, the Scimitar gently hit the chock and was grabbed by the centring rollers. The strop was attached and as the shuttle pulled forward the nosewheel lifted into the air. The Scimitar was now propped up with about 12° nose-up attitude. As it rested on the tail skid the blast deflector was raised and the power up signal given. I applied full throttle, gave a thumbs up to the launch officer and locked my left arm behind the throttle. The launch was exhilarating. With *Hermes* at 28 knots and the prevailing wind, the Scimitar soared into the air.

The section leader, Simon Creasy, constantly fed me instructions regarding formation keeping and instructions for speed and positioning. He was keeping me busy, and I had no time to worry about the landing. On return to the ship we broke formation into the circuit wheeling into line downwind. I was last in sequence, and after the others had landed on I was to carry out my touch and go with the tailhook up before making another approach for final landing. Commander Air, the CO Tommy Leece and the Senior Pilot, Brian Wilson, were all in Fly-Co to observe. If I couldn't handle it I would be instructed to divert to Yeovilton.

Being a curved approach, it was only when on short finals and looking for the centre-line that I got the full landing picture. Jesus! The deck seemed impossibly small. I peed myself (just a bit). Focus, line up, check the mirror, speed 132 knots... impact, full power, airbrakes in, climb away to circuit height. This time round include "hook down" in the checks. I would only apply full power on touchdown if there was no instant retardation. I was feeling good, an adrenaline high. Concentrating all the way round the circuit it was over too quickly, I was down and hooked. The landing felt great. It took one second to stop the aircraft.

All the others knew, but no one had told me, that *Hermes* was really too small to operate aircraft the size of the Scimitar and Sea Vixen. It had been designed for single engine types of half the size and weight.

As I taxied into "Fly One" I could see flight deck crews and squadron maintenance men moving into position. It felt good to be part of this impressive setup. As I climbed down from the cockpit, a very loud raucous northern accent proclaimed "F... me, he'd look better with a bucket and spade".

The ship was a village. By dinner time I was referred to as the Milky Bar Kid (from the TV advert).

Aircrew cabins were below the flight deck, mine immediately so. The impact noise when tailhooks hit the steel above could waken the dead. I calculated my bunk was about six feet below the touch-down point. When Vixens were night flying I normally stayed in the bar until completion of their programme. If I was on early start the next day this could prove a problem; I along with many others drank brandy and soda at a duty-free 4 pence each.

The more seasoned members of our outfit, Paddy Anderson and Simon Creasy had larger double cabins across the passageway along with Phil Cardew and Bob Ponter. Adjacent cabins accommodated the younger members, John Middleton, Ben Bosworth, Mike Harwood and Chris Wilson. The CO and Senior Pilot were on the next deck below, more suited to their rank of Lieutenant Commander. Residents there supposedly led a more sedate existence.

HMS *Hermes* set course for the Mediterranean for a six month work-up. Having come out of refit and with a new crew, this six months would be used to iron out technical bugs and turn the ship's company into a "well-oiled fighting machine".

After each session of operational training for the air group and the ship's company, *Hermes* docked for shore leave. The first port of call was Lisbon. Relations with the Portuguese were a bit strained due to Salazar's authoritarian policies, and those taking shore leave were warned that the secret police would be watching. Lisbon's impressive architecture and strangely quiet night spots were checked out with an unusual display of restraint.

At Gibraltar RN dockyard, *Hermes* took on stores and underwent troubleshooting maintenance. Time for a bit of fun. The wardroom hosted the usual cocktail party. These occasions generated fevered anticipation as daughters of local notables always accompanied their parents. The availability of many eligible bachelors was too great an attraction to resist, and I can only imagine the pleading and moral blackmail used to effect their attendance. The dads were more worried than the mums, making frequent furtive glances at their girls surrounded by attentive young officers vying for attention. Punishment for taking girls below was severe, but secret assignations ashore were sometimes arranged.

Trips across the border to La Linea and the city of Malaga afforded entertainment of very different kinds. A bunch of us took a taxi to attend a bullfight in Malaga. We watched the young El Cordobes in action. Bulls have a rough deal, so it seemed apt when one of the bulls jumped the barrier and gored a press photographer.

In Barcelona we were overwhelmed by the hospitality of the Spanish Navy. They entertained us in style with much sherry and visits to exclusive gentlemen's clubs (and a high class brothel). I purchased a Toledo sword. I still have it. It was to prove an effective weapon many years later.

As Hermes cruised the length of the Mediterranean the air group hurled assorted ironmongery into the sea (via our towed "splash" target) and occasionally into the designated real estate of Spain, France, Italy and Greece. Flying periods were interspersed with periods of "action stations". The anti-aircraft guns would be fired and many of the watertight doors would be secured. This made progress around the ship annoyingly pedantic and the air became oppressive. The ship's ventilation system was switched to recirculate as protection from possible atomic, biological, or chemical attack. When the ship was in transit and the air group stood down, squadron COs arranged various distractions to occupy our worryingly imaginative aircrew.

The traditional formal dinner held every Thursday usually ended up with typically moronic hi-jinks. Military standard after dinner games consisted of mess rugby, "High Cockalorum" and "Are You There Moriarty?" There was in addition one that seemed peculiar to the RN, where beer-filled condoms were attached to the ceiling fans. Participants formed a circle underneath while the fan spun at ever increasing speeds. You had to stand rooted to the spot and were allowed only to lean outwards. Those who fell or staggered incurred penalty drinks. The condoms would extend to incredible lengths before bursting.

At Malta, 803 and 849 disembarked to Hal-Far while the ship tied up alongside Parlatorio Wharf in Valetta Harbour for scheduled self maintenance. In Beirut *Hermes* again anchored alongside - there are advantages to being a small carrier. Simon, Paddy, Bob and myself attended a cocktail party at the British Embassy hosted by the naval attaché. After an hour of fuelling up on cocktails we were raring to go and persuaded Sally, one of the embassy secretaries, to join us for some fun downtown. The four of us, with Sally driving, set off in her trusty Hillman Minx. Speeding over a hill we were confronted by a road block, the pole was up. Spurred on by our shouts of "Go! Go!" Sally put her foot down and slalomed between the barrels. The guards came out shooting. We grovelled on the floor and Sally took a corner to avoid the bullets. Fortunately only one hit registered, on the rear fender. Sally was shaken and dropped us off at the nearest night club, no longer in the mood for our raucous cheering and laughter.

The club was a crappy little joint with no action and a steep cover charge, so we left for The Casino de Leban in a taxi. The main attraction featured dancing girls from the Moulin Rouge and it was first class. After that first evening and with purchase of the obligatory mementos the following day, most of our cash was gone. We spent the remaining two days sipping Bacardi cocktails and eating iced watermelon by the pool at the Phoenicia Hotel. The bikini-clad beauties were stunning but aloof. They fed our fantasies for the time being.

Back at sea *Hermes* positioned off Crete for more exercises. Mike Tristram suffered a birdstrike, not just clipping a seagull, we'd all done that, but a head on with a Sea Eagle. The mangled bird smashed through the armour-plated front windscreen and Mike was temporarily blinded. Fortunately the sloping windscreen deflected most of the hard bits but some flesh and gore got under his visor, now broken. He reduced speed and removed bird parts from his face. Now able to see, Mike returned to the ship under the direction of his wingman, Ben Bosworth.

Although authorised to eject, Mike elected to try for a landing. Most of the air group assembled on the goofers platform to observe his arrival. Mike first carried out a practice approach to check feasibility. It was a little erratic, but good enough to hope for a successful outcome. Mike commenced another approach. The landing was askew but his alignment was straightened out by the arrestor wire. The aircraft ended close to the edge but safe and sound. Mike was told to shut down the engines and stay in the cockpit.

The aircraft was towed into a more accessible position. All eyes were focused on the canopy, the interior of which was coated with blood. A mechanic attached the cockpit access ladder and climbed up to insert the ejection seat safety pin. Mike turned to see the confirmation thumbs-up. He took one look at Mike's blood-covered face and fell back in shock, landing on the guy who was about to insert the wheel chocks.

A stretcher had been placed on the deck and Mike, under protest (he insisted he was OK), was ordered to lie down. He stayed there, as only one sick berth attendant had arrived. I could see all this from the goofers.

In the hustle and bustle of the flight deck no one noticed Mike still lying on the stretcher, and he was not going to wait. Convinced he could make his own way off the deck, he stood up. Unfortunately the aircraft now hitched to the tractor moved forward and the leading edge of the wing caught Mike on the back of the head. Stunned, he fell and was replaced on the stretcher. The other stretcher bearer then arrived and Mike was carted off for attention. My cine camera was never available when I needed it. Mike was awarded the Queen's Commendation for his achievement.

Using El Adam bombing range in Libya. we carried out army co-operation training using live 1000lb bombs. Under direction from an FAC we flew in to deliver time-delayed ordnance. It's not easy in the desert as there few obvious reference features. Pilots are normally guided on to the target by the FAC's reference to land marks. In the desert a mortar fired a smoke round to act as a reference point. Time delay bombing is more accurate as the release height is lower; you just hope the timer works.

The exercise proved successful, but the FAC chap later told us that itinerant scrap metal collectors had appeared from behind the dunes to collect what they thought was unexploded bounty. The delay used was ten seconds. After many shouted warnings they dropped to the sand and the bomb exploded. It must have made their ears ring.

Back at sea, at the other end of the Med I witnessed the most extraordinary weather phenomenon. Descending out of cloud I levelled off to see five enormous waterspouts descending from a cloud base of about 3000 feet down to the surface of the sea. With the columns on either side it seemed I was flying down the aisle of some gigantic cathedral - it was breathtaking. Back on board I recounted the experience to the others, but their only response was raised eyebrows.

USS *Forrestal* was off Cannes and the squadron (now ashore in Malta) used the opportunity to fly over and train on their Bullpup (a primitive air to surface missile) simulator. When our American hosts learned that it was my 20th birthday, they arranged for a party at their admin. Block, ie local apartments. I was carted off to a downtown night club and plied with much champagne. The floorshow was an Egyptian belly dancer, who was persuaded to accompany us to the admin block to party on. The girl performed again, this time without her kit on, wow!

We returned to Malta and re-embarked. Having completed night operations the Sea Vixens were being recovered and I was dozing in my bunk waiting for the noise to subside. After an ear-splitting crash I found myself airborne six inches above the bed. I could see my cabin as if in broad daylight and watched as ceiling and light fittings fell in slow motion and dust filled the cabin. I seemed to sink slowly back on to the bunk. Energised by a sudden realisation of catastrophe I leapt out of bed, donned my overalls and lifejacket and made tracks for the nearest abandon ship station, the port rear gun platform. On opening the watertight door I was confronted by a wall of fire. I slammed the door shut, clamped the latches and crossed over to the starboard sponson. On the way I bumped into the admiral on his way to the bridge. "Steady lad, it's a crash on deck, wait for the broadcast" he said. I returned to my cabin, and sure enough there followed the alarm with instructions to essential personnel.

A Sea Vixen had hit the "round-down", the back edge of the flight deck, and burning fuel from ruptured tanks had cascaded over the side. The wreckage, under its own momentum, had continued into the sea off the angled flight deck. There was much speculation as to the cause of the accident, which in the end was put down to pilot error.

Prior to returning to the UK we disembarked for a short spell of operating out of North Front Gibraltar. Weapons training continued as always, this time at a designated firing range at sea just out of sight of the Moroccan Coast, north of Ceuta. The squadron flew sorties, firing two-inch rockets at a splash target towed behind an RAF rescue launch. Pilots took it in turns to act as on board Range Safety Officer.

During my spell on duty the prevailing conditions were dangerous. It was hazy with no visible horizon, no wind, the sea smooth as glass. One of our new guys left his recovery too late and bottomed out about twenty feet above the sea. The vortex whipped up spray and left a wake several hundred yards long. I cancelled for the day. In another time and another place this same problem claimed a Scimitar and a pilot, Andrew Mcphee from 800 squadron.

Our CO, Tommy Leece, was replaced by NJP Mills, nicknamed "Freddy" after the boxer - nobody ever called him Nelson. Mills wore a permanent expression that suggested he had just eaten green oranges. He only enjoyed the company of his general list contingent, treating his supplementary members with suspicion. All pilots had secondary duties, and S.L. members got the menial tasks, the serious stuff being handled by the G.L. crowd. To be fair our limited experience made most of us S.L. types pretty average administrators. I was nominated Divisional Officer responsible for the welfare of our small complement of cooks and stewards. I thought this unfair as they were a bunch of troublemakers and I was the squadron junior.

Hermes was preparing for the upcoming ORI, or Operational Readiness Inspection. During high altitude exercises news came that the after lift had jammed down. Our flight of four, including the CO and Senior Pilot, diverted to RAF North Front in Gibraltar. We were advised that the problem was severe and *Hermes* would be heading for Gibraltar dockyard for repairs; we should expect to be in "Gib" for several days.

It was early Sunday lunchtime, which in any officers' mess is a social occasion, guests being invited to join the residents for drinks. The PMC (President of the Mess Committee) made an exception and allowed us to enter the bar in our flying kit. Initially the atmosphere felt awkward. Members had brought their families and had their own social scene. After a Red Barrel or two things loosened up and one or two of the air force guys joined us at the bar. I was drinking a half pint and was told this would ruin our reputation. Resistance was futile, so I switched to pints.

An hour or so quickly passed. At about three o'clock the duty officer arrived and handed Freddy a signal from *Hermes* which said the lift was now in working order and we should return ASAP. The ship was now heading to Beirut, as the Lebanon was suffering yet another internal crisis. The CO and the Senior Pilot, Brian Wilson, were gung ho types, no problem, send for transport. Freddy then received a call from the station commander, who point blank refused permission for our departure. Mills called the Hermes captain and informed him of this order. "Are you fit to fly?" the captain asked. "Absolutely" said Mills. The captain then radioed Whitehall, who signalled the North Front Station Commander, who promptly washed his hands of the affair. The station duty officer confirmed we had fire cover and we manned the aircraft.

I felt tipsy, but thought I would be able to manage. I completed the checks from memory twice, feeling that something somewhere was amiss. This was pushed from my mind when the CO announced that we would take off in a box four formation! No one said a word after that.

As we accelerated down the runway we were all obviously thinking the same thing, and on lift off we opened out to allow some elbow room. The unintended result was a starburst on take-off... impressive. I heard that the Station Commander almost burst a blood vessel. We eased out into battle formation, much wider apart, and continued back to Hermes.

My nagging doubt resurfaced, but I was concentrating on carrying out the arrival and landing in proper fashion. Touchdown was good, but the source of my concern became apparent. I shot forward to be stopped by the control column between my legs and the gunsight in my face. "Clear the deck, clear the deck" was bellowed in my ears. I snapped out of my stunned inertia and taxied into the deck park, blood streaming down my face.

I had not strapped myself in. When the lad came up the ladder to insert the ejector seat safety pins he was surprised to say the least. I said "You should see the other guy". I climbed slowly down the ladder and made unsteady progress to the briefing room, I needed a strong coffee. The others seemed quiet, but none of our landings could be classed as dangerous. The Lebanon situation cooled off and *Hermes* resumed its preparations for the inspection.

The ORI went badly and failed to satisfy Admiralty observers. Further scrutiny was required, which took place during exercise "Riptide", in the Atlantic. This time *Hermes* just qualified, to great relief all round.

During our last exercise before returning to Portsmouth we were in the Western Approaches when our radar picked up a bogey orbiting at the edge of our radar coverage. It had all the hallmarks of a Soviet intelligence-gathering flight. The contact was suspected to be a Soviet four-engined "Bear", and I was despatched to intercept and identify it. When vectored in behind the bogey I recognised it as one of the Boeing 707/720 series. Because of its flight pattern I assumed it to be a USAF tanker and thought I might give them a buzz. Piling on the power I zoomed under the right wing and did a couple of snap rolls. As I passed I recognised the green stripe and shamrock of Air Lingus. Oops, I hoped they enjoyed the show.

On my return I was told to report to Commander Air in Flyco. "Spiv Leahy" (who had also been a bit of a lad in his time) asked me in his sternest voice if I had followed the international procedure for identifying. I looked blankly at him. "Two kilometres" he prompted. I said I might have been a bit closer than that. He tightened his lips and tried to look disapproving, and all in attendance turned away to hide their smiles. I was shown the signal from Whitehall, which recounted the Irish captain's alarm at being buzzed by a "large military twinjet". I thought the captain's recognition ability pretty poor so I mailed Aer Lingus Operations some photos including a grimacing Phil Cardew captioned "large military pilot". Childish, but I hope it was taken in the spirit intended.

Shortly after I was diverted from exercises for another identification, I recognised the type to be a ten-engined version of the obsolete B36. I flew alongside and was beckoned closer by the crew. I could see quite a crowd behind the large observation windows, they were taking photographs. I thought they deserved something extra and rolled inverted while extending the landing gear (I would like a copy of any picture, if there is one). This manoeuvre would have come as a surprise, but at that altitude the indicated air speed was below the Scimitar's landing gear operating speed of 300 knots.

During the exercise I was taken to one side and briefed to simulate an attack on *Hermes* by a "Kennel" anti-ship missile; it was to be a surprise to test the ship's alertness. I was tasked to descend toward the ship at high subsonic speed and break off at the last moment. I did this, and descending from starboard I crossed the deck in front of the bridge. I had to pull up smartly to level out just above the sea, below deck level. Out of view, hidden behind the island, the SAR helicopter (a Wessex) was on station off the port quarter. He got caught in my vortex. The pilot managed the turbulence with great skill but was quite annoyed.

Deciding to finish with a flourish, I wrapped the aircraft around the ship at about fifty feet and ninety degrees of bank, seriously frightening myself in the process. It wasn't as easy as I had thought to maintain height during this manoeuvre. Reporting to Commander Air again I received two weeks' stoppage of leave, but fortunately we were due to disembark in fourteen days.

Back at Lossiemouth we brushed up our instrument flying in the Hunter T8s. Mills flew with the junior pilots in the Hunter in order to make his own assessment. I got the feeling that he didn't trust the reports already on file, either that or he had still had a thing about Supplementary List. While at Lossie I sponsored a move to get the tail logo changed as it was bloody boring, just a plain white H for *Hermes*. Knowing that Freddie would turn down any of my ideas I channelled the new design through the AWI, Simon Creasy. The scheme proved successful and the black and yellow checkerboard was soon on all the tailfins, great. You've got to have style.

Chapter Six

FAR EAST TOUR

November 1962 - October 1963

Before flying back on board we were warned that the weather was bad, with the ship pitching close to limits. When we descended through the murk the conditions were atrocious, the light was poor and the sea wild and stormy. *Hermes* was rolling in corkscrew fashion, presenting an unnerving scene on the approach. It was vital to focus on the centreline and mirror. The first few aircraft, including myself, landed on without incident. The weather deteriorated further, but the following flight led by the Senior Pilot chose to continue.

I was on my way down to Wardroom Two (the annexe where aircrew could eat their meals dressed in flying kit) when I heard a crash and was showered by ceiling panels, light fittings, dust and other debris. The annexe was directly under the round down, the impact point. I opened the door and was presented with a frozen tableau of ten or so diners covered in dust and soup. The soup bowls had been flipped by falling fluorescent light fittings. It would have been funny, but we were dreading the possible loss one of one of our squadron. Expressions had set in a grim blank-eyed stare.

Brian Wilson had hit the round down and his hook and tail section had caught the back end of the deck as it pitched into the approach path. They needn't have worried. The Scimitar was a tough beast and despite damage the hook managed to snatch No.1 wire.

Later Brian brushed off his near catastrophe with some flippant aside, but he was pretty quiet for the rest of the day. The remaining aircraft diverted to Yeovilton, coming on board the following day.

Hermes steamed through the Med with only limited time at "Flying Stations". At the other end of the Mediterranean I woke up to an unusual stillness. Investigating, I climbed up on deck and was stunned by the view. We were anchored, waiting for the pilot who would monitor our passage through the Suez Canal. The ethereal panorama of early morning Alexandria was spread out in a thin line of low sand-coloured buildings along the horizon. The city was just a thin strip between the calm blue sea and the cloudless sky. Mesmerised, I slowly took it all in before finally going down for breakfast. I'm told that I was lucky, as visibility was not always that good.

The slow transit of the Suez Canal was equally hypnotic, the magic broken by a low flying Mig 15 probably flown by one of the Soviet "advisors" and collecting photographic intelligence. This brought everyone back to earth with a bump, reminding us that the Cold War was real.

Clearing the canal at Port Suez, the air was dry with a hint of aromatic shrubbery. The harsh rock and sandy terrain was sandwiched between the gunmetal sea and the grey-blue sky.

Hermes sped through the Red Sea and anchored in Aden harbour. Keen to go sightseeing and get my first real experience of the East, I was told to calm down and wait for the cool of the evening. I accompanied my colleagues to the Aden Club, a surviving remnant of the Empire. We focused on having a decent cold beer, as Watneys Red Barrel was on tap in the club bar. The club's quiet elegance impressed me after the taxi ride (no aircon) through the hot and noisy streets. At six o'clock things changed as the bar received an influx of determined drinkers. They were pleased to see new faces and get news of the UK. When tired of the questions and well-meaning advice we retired to the dining room.

The food was basic in the extreme, but under the circumstances forgivable. I guessed the menu had not undergone any changes during the last half century. We went back to the bar and sank a few more beers before the taxi back to the jetty was ordered. Most of my squadron mates had been here before on Victorious, but I was desperate to check out the bazaars and side streets. Foreign ports had the potential to satisfy my craving for excitement. My colleagues sought out the best pint in town and perhaps latched on to a wealthy expatriate (a practice known as "baron strangling"). I thought this routine limited the whole overseas thing.

Alone the following day, I searched the stalls and back streets noted for their bargain duty-free prices. I was soundly fleeced, and hoped my naivety would eventually be replaced by a cool worldly know-how.

803 flew one or two close air support exercises in the desert before *Hermes* set course for the Far East, steaming across the Indian Ocean. No flying took place out of range of land diversion airfields. I compiled entries for the squadron line book (a pictorial diary) but got bored and joined the others out on the gun sponson to watch the ships wake and the flying fish. Passing RAF Gan in the Maldives, *Hermes* took the opportunity to go to flying stations. We dive-bombed the splash target, being very careful to monitor the altimeter. The sea of glass gave no indication of height or distance, and the accompanying destroyer marking our fall of shot looked like a toy.

Passage to the Far East can be tedious for the air department due to the many non-flying days. The CO arranged early morning PT on deck and the junior pilots were made to assist the ground crew with aircraft cleaning. Senior members were mentally exercised with practice strike planning, or at least that's what they claimed. The message the CO was trying to convey is that we would suffer if late nights in the bar become too frequent. Adapting to the situation, I spent much time in the ship's photo department (as assistant to the squadron photo-recce officer) "swotting".

Entering the Straights of Malacca, we were challenged to defend ourselves against a strike by F86 Sabres of RAAF Butterworth. They laid down the parameters for the exercise, which weighted the odds very much in their favour. We were trounced and humiliated, the Aussies added insult to injury by sending some annoyingly smug signals to all and sundry.

Hermes went alongside in Singapore for maintenance and a spot of shore leave. As part of my training I had to carry out the duties of Second Officer of the Watch. In harbour this meant manning the forward gangway with regulating staff to monitor the dress of ratings going ashore. We also assessed their condition on return. Being drunk on board is hazardous and the offenders are (if quiet and orderly) escorted below and put in the charge of the Leading Hand. If any aggressive behaviour was attempted the offenders were put in cells to be charged in the morning. This happened frequently.

Sometimes "Jack" returned injured, normally a result of drunken brawls, but occasionally it was more serious. One sailor returned to be assisted up the gangway by his mates. His white bell bottoms were covered in blood. The sick bay attendants were called, and when I asked what had happened, he opened his hand without a word and there in the palm was his penis. His mates would not comment. Subsequent investigation indicated that he had molested a local girl and received instant "justice".

We were now the Far East flagship with Vice Admiral Donald Gibson on board. Gibson was a staunch Fleet Air Arm supporter and a hero in his own right, as he had flown with 803 squadron on several daring raids during the war. At the welcoming cocktail party he invited his friend Noel Coward on board, who true to form requested he be introduced to the youngest serving officer - me. Noel was in his element. He was immaculately attired in white linen and smoked a black cigarette in a 12-inch white holder. *Hermes* had spruced up the quarterdeck with fancy awnings, much polished brass and tropical flowers. With the dockside background of palm trees, the scene could have been a setting from one of his plays.

Gibson introduced me and Coward asked if I was enjoying life on *Hermes*. My stammered "Yes sir" proved my obvious lack of sophistication. Thankfully he immediately lost interest. Gibson, with a just detectable wink of the eye, said I could go.

The CO organised our first few nights ashore with visits to restaurants and clubs. He was well aware of the temptations on offer and hoped to keep tabs on our behaviour. Singapore was great. Loads of shopping and plenty of atmosphere. There not being much traffic in those days, rickshaws were a pleasant experience.

The newly-married members bought Noritake dinner sets, and Paddy Anderson proudly showed his wife (one of several who had come out to Singapore) the 92-piece set he had purchased for the bargain price of £18. She turned up her nose at it, saying she didn't like the pattern. I heard the crash of breaking crockery from my cabin. On enquiring if they were OK, I was asked if I wanted to buy the set. I glanced at the shards on his cabin floor. "Sixteen pounds" said Paddy sheepishly. I liked the pattern, Wild Ivy, and said OK. We still have it, minus one or two pieces.

Hermes went back to sea, dockyard maintenance complete, and the air group disembarked to Singapore air stations to continue training. 803 Scimitars disembarked to RAF Tengah, the Vixens to Changi and the Gannets and choppers to Seletar. *Hermes* carried out a purely naval workup for the ship's company. This included gunnery and damage control exercises. The Commander said these exercises would inhibit air operations, which was true, but we suspected it might be more to do with not allowing the air group to observe their "Fish-head" cock-ups.

It was Christmas 1962. At the Officers' Mess Christmas lunch I sat with an RAF chap who seemed to have Parkinson's disease. His hands were shaking so much he had to drink his wine from a baby's cup with a lid. He explained the origins of his predicament. He was the station electrical officer and before each routine check of the sub-station he had the habit of tapping the terminals to ensure power was switched off. Murphy's Law rules, and one day he received a near lethal bolt of 11,000 volts and was blown clear out the door of the sub-station. I felt for him. His face, hands, and presumably other areas were covered with purple bruises.

To avoid the heat, tropical routine was observed, ie duty commenced at 0700 and was complete by 1300. We flew low-level navigation sorties using the newly-installed plotter. This device was nothing more than a rolling map set to the speed required, 420 knots in our case. Freddie gave me the task of preparing these maps for our low-level sorties by cutting navigation charts into four-inch strips and pasting them together.

Meanwhile inter-service relations at the Tengah Officers' Mess suffered as a result of unwise moves by some of our number. Tengah's resident Squadron of Hawker Hunters was detached to Thailand for an exercise and to release accommodation for our use. Some of the young wives had remained at Tengah. These temporarily unattached ladies and girls attended the Sunday curry lunch. It was inevitable that during pre-lunch drinks these two groups would be drawn together. The sound of their laughter and excited conversation did not go unnoticed. Concerned on behalf of their colleagues in Thailand, one of their number was nominated as spokesman and despatched to forestall any untoward developments. He was ignored.

Rumours, whether based on truth or not, spread like wildfire and reached the ears of those on detachment. With the morale of these chaps now threatened, the powers that be instructed Freddie to divert our guys with other pursuits. Arrangements were made. We attended sporting fixtures and cocktail parties arranged at local country clubs etc. One of the best functions was lunch with one of the rubber planters near Johor Bahru. In a fine old colonial mansion we were entertained in style with enormous gin and tonics and stories Somerset Maugham would have been proud of. After a curry lunch we slept in wicker armchairs.

When the monthly allocation of flying hours was used up, time was spent on various ground training drills. Those of us who had no previous jungle survival training were sent to the specialist school at Ulu Tiram. After basic instruction in the classroom there followed three days and two nights in the rainforest in the care of the Gurkhas. Pretending we had been shot down, we trekked off into the jungle in flying kit with survival rations and a parachute.

We were shown how to recognise edible plants, trap insects and animals and locate sources of water. We were also warned about poisonous species and other dangers.

Chris Bynoe, one of the 892 Vixen pilots, was in cavalier mode, having smuggled several cans of lager in his backpack. He excitedly exclaimed "football" and hoofed a ground level hornet's nest. There was general panic. A few ran for cover pursued by the infuriated swarm. "Freeze!" shouted a Ghurkha. We froze, and the threat dwindled. Well covered for protection against mosquitoes, Bynoe was only stung three times, but it must have been painful.

Wearing flying overalls, bush hats and neck scarves, our faces were smothered with insect repellent. Effective stuff, it could melt plastic and had to be kept away from mouth and eyes. When I once used it on the beach as protection from sandflies, an accidental smear on my goolies had me leaping around in agony.

We were shown how to build a temporary shelter with sticks and the parachute, a "basha". This task completed, we sat around the camp fire to eat. The Gurkha officer had thoughtfully provided canned beer. Chris, determined to prove he could outdo us all, was building an impressive structure. As a temporary shelter it was serious overkill. Well into the campfire rugby songs we could hear his parang still chopping away. We retired to our bashas, the lumberjack soundtrack continued. Sometime later an ominous creaking was heard, shortly followed by the scream "TIMBER!". Some of us leapt out of our bashas, staring into the dark for the falling tree. It came down straight across the campsite and the smouldering embers of the campfire and sparks and hot charcoal flew everywhere. A branch struck the end of another basha and the occupant was catapulted into the branches of the falling tree; luckily he suffered only bruising and scratches. His basha destroyed, he slung his hammock from the lower branches of the fallen tree and threw the parachute across the top. It rained heavily that night and we all got soaked apart from the guy in the impromptu tree setup.

The remaining time in the jungle seemed pretty tame after that, making snares and traps and eating snakes, frogs etc. we drew the line at monkeys but made a mental note of how to catch and cook them, just in case. Even Chris Bynoe was given a pass. I don't think they wanted him back for a rerun.

Early in January the squadrons re-embarked. *Hermes* sailed across the South China Sea to the Philippines to join exercise "Dovetail" with the American Fleet. It was stimulating. We checked out *USS Ranger* and were impressed by the size of its vast deck. A few of their experienced pilots came over to *Hermes* for touch and goes. Their aircraft were bigger than ours, and it was all a bit hairy. They thought our accident rate pretty low considering the size of the deck.

The Americans were envious of the *Hermes* 984 three-dimensional radar. The innovative aerial enabled the radar to determine height as well as position information. The extra information on incoming threats more or less guaranteed interception. The success rate of our combat air patrols ensured *Hermes* received a high score when the results of the exercise were analysed.

As always the Americans had greater size and numbers and operated by the book, while British equipment was limited but effective. Lacking resources, we were experienced at improvising when having to make do.

A classic case occurred during Dovetail. *USS Ranger* launched four Vigilante aircraft to find their nominated photo-reconnaissance target. Our sole photo-recce Scimitar was unserviceable in the hangar, our lads working furiously to rectify the problem. The Ranger's aircraft returned and we were about to accept defeat when they launched another four. We rushed our Scimitar airborne and it found the target. On return, the photo was developed and our skipper, Captain O'Brien, had a presentation copy made framed in oak with an engraved silver plaque. A helicopter flew it over to the Ranger, where it was presented, one hour after it was taken, to the US admiral.

On completion of exercise Dovetail we entered Subic Bay in the Philippines. It was to be a ceremonial arrival at the American Navy dockyard. O'Brien demonstrated his seamanship by pulling off an impressive white-knuckle arrival. He was a showman, and handled the carrier with the dash and verve he had learned in command of destroyers.

Hermes was arrayed for "Procedure Alpha". This entailed lining up freshly polished aircraft on deck with the ship's complement lining the sides dressed in best whites. I and other junior officers were in ranks across the forward edge of the flight deck.

We headed for the designated berth, a jetty at right angles to the shoreline. *Hermes* was to continue straight in, slowing to a halt with the jetty on the starboard side. O'Brien refused the offer of tugs. The

American reception party waited on the main dockside ahead, their marine band playing. *Hermes* came across Subic Bay at full speed, displaying an impressive bow wave. All of us on the front end were now concerned that O'Brien may this time have got it wrong. One way or the other it was going to be a spectacular arrival.

Entering the harbour "full astern" was ordered, and *Hermes* shook with vibration, lending an added sense of danger. Had O'Brien screwed up? Our posture changed subtly as we attempted to gain a more secure footing. If we hit we might be thrown over the rail on to the dockside. The welcoming band faltered and bum notes gave way to silence. Some even laid their instruments down and backed off. The ship finally stopped with the flight deck overhanging the dockside. There was silence, apart from heavy breathing. Captain O'Brien could not see the events below, but had radio contact with those who could. I am told he was grinning from ear to ear.

At the ships cocktail party I got chatting to the cute but very young daughter of the British Air Attaché in Manila. We sneaked off downtown Manila for some fun. We checked out the night clubs, and I was amazed by the security arrangements. Most establishments sported a gun check-in desk at the entrance. Often the entrance itself was half height and one had to duck down to get in. It's my bet the fire doors were locked. Rapid departures were out of the question.

After a few hours of clubbing the alcohol finally went to our heads, and feeling unsteady I suggested a coffee. My date said she just wanted to lie down somewhere, and suggested a motel. I thought this an excellent idea. In the room she lay on the bed and passed out, but I couldn't sleep. When the hour was up it took a few minutes to rouse the now dishevelled young thing and get her into the cab. I returned her safely home, untouched.... at four in the morning. I delayed leaving until the door was answered, avoiding the wrath of her parents by hiding in the bushes. I sneaked away when the door slammed shut to cut off the sound of raised voices.

Our CO had refused the junior officers permission to investigate the red-light district of Olongapo, the sprawling entertainment facility erected adjacent to the American base. Crime was rampant and the place was fenced off and guarded by MPs. Entry requirement for military personnel was a minimum group of six, enforced by the Military Police. Inside the entertainment was of the raw and rowdy kind; porn freaks would be in heaven.

On the base, the story going the rounds was of a bunch of guys who had booked Olongapo girls for a "picnic" on one of the islands. The girls brought extra booze, but it was spiked. The revellers woke the next morning to find their boat and all their possessions gone. When they finally got help from a passing fisherman they were naked, sunburned and badly dehydrated.

From the Philippines *Hermes* set sail for Hong Kong. To the delight of her crew she would tie up alongside at HMS *Tamar*. Those on shore leave would not have the irksome task of relying on the ship's boat to and from the anchorage. Most carriers were too large and moored out in the harbour.

Captain O'Brien's arrival alongside HMS *Tamar* was another event to be remembered. Again refusing the assistance of tugs (too ignominious) the captain came in from the east, reducing speed for the final approach. *Hermes* carried out a 180° turn, presenting its starboard side to the jetty. The ship was brought to a halt with the bow in position and the stern continued to swing in under its own momentum. It seemed to us on deck that there would be an almighty crash when 30,000 tons of steel met the dockside. Trust O'Brien. As he knew it would, the ship's side pushed up a wall of water, effectively cushioning the arrival. *Hermes* became stationary just feet from the jetty. A minor miscalculation meant that an inch or so of water swept across the jetty and into the inner basin, so the welcoming party performed a merry dance trying to keep their feet dry. The marine band played on without faltering.

R&R in Hong Kong was an eye opener for first timers. The city was at the height of its post-war revival. Brightly lit and teeming with life, its countless eating places, night spots and cheap shopping produced a celebration of life unequalled at the time. *Hermes* arrived for Chinese New Year 1963. Crossing the road in Wanchai proved hazardous as firecrackers cascaded down upon the unsuspecting. I could not resist the temptation, so I bought a bunch and smuggled them back on board. I also had some shoes made and bought a cine projector.

After Hong Kong we bypassed Singapore and sailed up the Straits of Malacca for Exercise Jet 63.

Chapter Seven

RAAF BUTTERWORTH, TYPHOON "POLLY" & ACCIDENTS

1963-1964

Jet 63 was held in the Andaman Sea south of the Nicobar Islands. It was a second audit to assess our operational ability. Hopefully we had improved since our poor showing at the ORI (Operational Readiness Inspection). We came out OK, thanks in part to John Middleton and myself hitting the target at Batti Malv. We dropped live 1000-pounders, totally demolishing the markers.

During the exercise, 814 Squadron's anti-submarine Wessex helicopters detected a submarine which refused to be identified. The captain, realising it to be our (HMS Hermes) Russian "tail", decided to prove our readiness by dropping a grenade or two. During exercises grenades were sometimes dropped nearby to prove a hit and effect a little realism. This time however they were dropped virtually on top of the sub concerned. If they complained the captain would say he thought the sub was one of our own.

Hermes was due a maintenance period in Singapore dockyard. The squadron was to disembark to RAAF Butterworth near Penang, but unforeseen delays meant we had to disembark to Tengah for two weeks. The RAF were not too happy to see us so soon.

We practised low level penetration extensively. The favourite route was up the east coast beaches of Malaya, all palm trees and white sand. It was hot and the air-conditioning struggled, in fact mine quit completely near Kuantan. Not only did it fail to deliver cool air, it suddenly started feeding compressed air at 450°C straight into the cockpit. I pulled up into an almost vertical climb and at 18,000 feet I rolled over and levelled off, slow enough to motor the canopy open. The relief was instantaneous, but a number of plastic and rubber fittings had melted. My flying suit saved me from severe burns, and only my exposed cheeks, throat and wrists had blistered. The visor had protected my eyes and the oxygen mask my lower face.

I coasted back to Tengah in an extended glide, having told them of the problem. I don't know what the tower passed on to our senior pilot, but from the casual cynicism displayed by the ground crew I realised they thought it to be a case of "no cool air", not a cooked cockpit. When the ladder was attached to the side I warned the rating installing the safety pins that he should be careful. He yelled when he touched them. Gloves were sent for and the seat made safe. This time my squadron mates said "wow" as opposed to raising their eyebrows. The CO said "Well done, don't forget the compass swings this afternoon".

Being the junior pilot was a pain, as I got all the tedious tasks. Calibrating the compass involved taxiing the Scimitar over to the compass base, a remote part of the airfield free from electrical or magnetic interference. The aircraft was twice aligned with the cardinal points. One of the lads would check with the Watts Datum Compass. After cockpit readings were taken corrections could be made, a check "swing" confirmed accuracy. This time-consuming business took place in the hot afternoon sun while my mates were off downtown sinking a few beers. I resented all this extra duty, but the

CO was intent on preserving my moral integrity.

The officers' mess accommodation at RAF Tengah was overstretched. Junior members were transferred to an army annexe in the boondocks. It turned out to be a bonus this time, as we were the only residents. The staff were splendid and we lived the high life. The old colonial style building provided some laughs. Open windows, high ceilings and fans meant we shared the mess with the wildlife, so we enjoyed a nightly invasion of moths, mosquitoes and small insects. One night the big lazy fan over the dining table batted a rhinoceros beetle the size of a golf ball into my beer.

HMS *Ark Royal* had arrived, and some of their pilots joined us. Ian Frenz, a pilot from 800 Squadron, had a close call. Returning from a night on the town he decided to raid the refrigerator in the kitchen. Encountering a snake that reared up to strike, he kicked out, breaking its neck. Early the next morning we were awoken by shouting from the kitchen. Staff had found the defunct snake. It was a banded krait - one bite would have been fatal.

We were transferred to RAAF Butterworth. I am not sure what the Australians were told, but we got the feeling that they considered us a challenge they could easily meet.

The ground crew and support equipment were flown up in a C130 and the Scimitars followed. The CO led the formation and asked the tower if we could do a formation low pass before the usual fan break into the circuit. The request was firmly refused, with the added instruction that the break into the circuit must be flown at 150 knots and at standard circuit height. This was too much for Freddie, who tersely reminded the tower that it was too late to reduce speed. Descending to 200 feet, we accelerated to 500 knots.

After the fan break, the landing clearance was followed by instructions for all pilots to stand at attention by their aircraft and await the arrival of the Station Commander. We waited under the watchful eye of the duty officer for fifteen minutes. It was a hot afternoon, so we cooked. On arrival the Group Captain gave our CO a public dressing down. Freddy was not amused, but took it with a stiff upper lip.

No reception had been arranged, which was unusual to say the least. The CO instructed us to meet in the bar at 1800, when he would sponsor a happy hour. Only a few Aussies showed up, which we thought unsociable and most un-Australian. Unknown to us, the RAAF were imposing greater flight discipline following a recent serious accident. The clampdown had dampened the spirits of the normally-exuberant Aussie pilots. No wonder our disregard of instructions had annoyed their boss.

Those who did attend included girls of the teaching and medical staff. The few Aussie guys who were there apparently had the task of protecting the girls. It seemed as if Butterworth had been briefed regarding the predatory tendencies of RN pilots.

The men cornered us and talked shop. I found the discussion about fighter tactics repetitive and wandered off to read the notice board. The girls, keen to socialise with the newcomers, realised that they were being sidelined and resented it. One of them asked me over. I joined their animated discussion of the latest pop music but was interrupted by some drunk, who pulled me away with a few slurred insults. Simon and Paddy jumped to my defence; the situation looked like it might get physical. Luckily the PMC (President of the Mess Committee) chose that moment to arrive. Recognising a tinderbox situation he had a quiet word with the inebriate and restored calm. Gossip exaggerated the incident, so a decidedly frigid atmosphere developed whenever we entered the bar. The fact that the girls emphatically supported our version of events infuriated the Aussies even more. We chose to spend our off-duty periods in Georgetown, on nearby Penang Island.

This was more like it. We explored this historic "Straights Settlement". Our forays ashore started in the piano bar of The Eastern & Oriental Hotel, where the manager asked us if we could do a flyby. This request so contrasted with our reception at Butterworth that the CO agreed. Two days later our four Scimitars roared down the sea front. We added some simple formation aerobatics, including the 803 "twinkle roll". This delighted the crowd, and we were later awarded drinks on the house... all evening. Our air show was visible from the RAAF base. It was said that the station commander had gone apoplectic.

Butterworth was glad to see the back of us. We were keen to go, looking forward to the "runs ashore" in Japan. Back on board we set course stopping en route in Hong Kong.

I didn't think it a wise plan to have USS Ticonderoga in town at the same time as *Hermes*. "Jack" could not resist baiting American sailors and the inevitable fights broke out, one almost demolishing the China Fleet Club. What concerned the respective admirals however was the tension caused by damaged pride. After one riotous but amicable joint forces encounter, there followed the ritual tattooing of each others' flags to commemorate the occasion. Jack had to go one better, and our lot plied one Texan braggart with copious amounts of Southern Comfort. When the Confederate was comatose he was carted into the tattoo salon and received the Union Jack across his back, shoulder to shoulder. Our chaps kept a very low profile thereafter.

The ship's company took the opportunity of shore leave to obtain cameras, hi-fi sets, hand made shoes, and tailored suits. The family back home might receive some beautiful antiques, but more often they received weird stuff, thanks to Jack's warped sense of humour. At night, the destination switched from the shopping centres to the hotspots of Wanchai and the red light districts of Kowloon.

On one of our squadron "runs ashore" we were at a well-known bar ordering drinks when I got called to one side by an American, who said he was from the Ticonderoga. He bought the beer and we talked a lot about flying, but only in general. We had all been warned of Hong Kong's reputation as a hotbed of spies. I was to hear from him again about ten years later.

The excitement was building as *Hermes* departed north from Hong Kong and the courtesy visit to Osaka loomed. Some of the crew had actually signed on for years in order not to miss the rare opportunity of visiting Japan.

We tried out our Bullpup missiles at a US firing range near Okinawa. This primitive guided bomb was controlled from the cockpit by commands sent down a wire connected to the aircraft, and this unreeled as the missile sped toward its target. My attempt failed hopelessly. I claimed the pesky thing stopped responding to my commands. My mates took the mickey. I felt deflated.

During night exercises we lost a Sea Vixen and Chris Bynoe. According to the current record, he failed to recover from a rapid descent from 40,000 feet. I recall being told that the aircraft had flown into the sea during night dive bombing. During these attacks the target would be illuminated by Glow-worm flares launched from a lead aircraft. The whole enterprise was fraught with danger, as more than one Sea Vixen had been lost this way.

Continuing towards Japan, *Hermes* encountered Typhoon Polly. All aircraft on deck had to be repositioned into wind with extra lashings. For the benefit of my experience I was nominated to monitor the deck handlers carrying out this task. It was night, the deck was wet and the ship was beginning to pitch and roll in alarming fashion. The tractors cautiously manoeuvred the aircraft about the deck while handlers "walked" the lashings, ie some were released while others were fastened. At least four were attached to the deck at any one time. I followed, large rubber wheel chocks in hand. Under the impact of a freak wave the ship suddenly rolled over about 15° and the lashings on our aircraft parted with a crack. I was between the aircraft and the deck edge and it looked as if we were going to lose this one, and its tractor, over the side.

I hurled a chock at the starboard wheel, ten pin bowling style. It slotted neatly behind the wheel, lurching the aircraft to a halt. Before I had a chance to accept any applause the 10kg rubber chock squeezed like an orange pip, shot past my left leg and on out to sea. I retired to the wardroom and told my story - more raised eyebrows. There were suggestions I join the ships bowling team. That night the "Jumbo" mobile crane broke loose and crashed into a Vixen.

After the typhoon, the captain announced that flying operations were suspended due to severe corrosion of the steam catapults. We were close enough to Japan for the Gannet COD (Carrier On board Delivery) to collect the awaiting mail from Fukuoka before we hightailed it back to Singapore for dockyard repairs. Much chagrin was shown by those who had signed on for an extra tour.

Off the coast of Sarawak, the ship was steaming at speed. Lying in my bunk I heard a muffled bang from the bows. This was followed by an ominous rumbling. The volume increased and it became apparent that the ship was passing over a submerged obstruction. The rumbling passed underneath, ending with a bang, followed by vibration and a sharp reduction in engine speed. Whatever it was had hit the ship's propeller.

The prop would be replaced during the maintenance period. The next day the ship's divers reported the propeller damage. The foreign object turned out to have been a giant hardwood log that had broken loose from its raft. *Hermes* headed back to Singapore on one engine.

Unable to launch, we imagined several months of paid holiday. Not so. Approaching Singapore a passing storm provided enough wind over the deck for the Gannets of 849 Squadron to carry out free take offs. In the dockyard the jets were ignominiously lifted off by crane and towed to their respective airfields. With their wings folded this was feasible but tricky. With unforeseen obstructions along the way it took two days instead of overnight. 803 operated from Tengah again, the 892 (Vixens) Changi, and the Gannets and Wessex Seletar.

At RAF Tengah the inhabitants of the officers' mess could relax, as the admiralty had arranged for local country clubs to accept our guys as temporary members. It was a great solution and many friendships were made.

The Indonesian Confrontation was in its infancy and *Hermes'* presence was required off the coast of Sarawak. With the ship stationed offshore we demonstrated our presence to the Indonesian Army. Vectored on to their units by a Forward Air Control unit, we flew low overhead, firing our guns, only blanks, but they retreated in haste. After our little contribution to peacekeeping we cruised up and down the coast with the occasional session of armament practice.

After returning from a photo-recce sortie on the border, the control tower at RAF Labuan requested a low fly by. At that time the RAF had nothing to match the Scimitar for power and speed and they were keen to see our "mean machine". To give the viewers a chance I cruised past low and slow. This elicited the request for a fast pass. It's not very often that pilots are unleashed with a blank cheque. I powered up into an almost vertical climb, then wheeled over, accelerating in a descending curve back across the airfield. I aimed directly for the control tower at 650 knots and 15 feet, raising a minor dust storm. Approaching the tower I pulled up sharply and headed back to the ship. I now had a much lower fuel state than I could really afford. Scimitars only had about forty minutes fuel for low level sorties and the little demo for Labuan had cost me dear.

I had not heard any response from Labuan tower. The ship asked me to hold for landing Vixens. Now worried, I shut down one engine to preserve fuel, but told no one. If it came to the crunch I would request a priority landing. I did not want to have to explain my unauthorised (by the CO) activities. On one engine not catching a wire would mean a dip in the sea, which focused the mind somewhat. I landed with five minutes' fuel remaining, not extraordinary, but not routine.

Later that day when the CO was returning over Labuan the tower thanked him for the earlier display, apologising for not thanking the pilot concerned at the time. They explained that the reason for their silence was that my pull-up vortex had ripped some radio aerials off the roof of the tower, the noise being misinterpreted as a hit by my aircraft. After landing the CO called me up on deck and made me do a close inspection of the underside of 150, the aircraft in question. There was no damage of course, but this "cavalier" escapade was entered in my file.

Brian Wilson was a likeable Chief Pilot, but could be a little patronising, treating me as squadron mascot. I got my own back and regained some credibility during air to air combat training. During an intense "circle of joy", where both aircraft circle as tight as possible to get on each other's tail, I managed to tuck in behind him. I claimed a kill, Brian strenuously denied I was anywhere near, let alone in a firing position. All 803 pilots attended the debrief, eyes glued to the cine screen. OK, the clip showed I would probably not have scored a hit but there he was, in the frame only a whisker away from theoretical annihilation. Hah!

On Friday June 28 1963, Dave Phillips (pilot) and Mike Cooper (Observer) had arrived to replace the crew of the Vixen lost in the Sea of Japan, and at the end of their first flight they were carrying out deck landing practice. I had just landed and was walking back from Fly One, the deck park on the starboard bow. I saw the Vixen do a practice touch and go and then, for no apparent reason, rear up into an unsustainable vertical climb. The ship steamed on under the

Vixen, now stalled overhead. Directly below, I tilted my head back and stared up the jet exhaust, trying to figure out which way to run.

The adrenalin rush slowed the scene to a snail's pace. After what seemed an eternity the doomed aircraft slowly toppled over to starboard and dived into the sea only yards from the deck edge. The observer's hatch popped off a split second before impact, but there was no ejection. I looked around; no one else had noticed. The flight deck personnel were going about their business unconcerned. I raced down the deck into the Flight Deck Officer's position and yelled "crash alarm". I got a blank stare from the FDO while I described the accident. He looked doubtful and waited a few moments before hitting the alarm. That delay caused the marker buoy to be released late. At the enquiry this was said to be the reason the aircraft was never found.

I later went to the photo section to see the 16mm cine record of the event. The Vixen's elevator had never returned to neutral after the initial nose-up command. In my opinion, it had jammed. Why would any pilot in this position maintain nose up to the point of stall?

I recalled an incident that occurred at RAF Tengah. One of the Vixen pilots, Nick Dunsford, rejected a take-off, reporting that he had suffered an elevator control restriction. Both 803 and 892 squadrons shared the crewroom and everyone overheard the 892 Senior Pilot berating Nick for being "chicken". A brief inspection was carried out but nothing was found. The SP obviously thought Nick's report bullshit, claiming that he had aborted take-off because of doubts about sufficient runway length. I thought that this might very well have been the same aircraft that had crashed, and recounted the incident to Brian Wilson.

He told me to wait in my cabin. A few minutes later he returned and firmly instructed me "Do not repeat this information to anyone". My trust in authority was finished. Time to grow up I suppose.

Hermes returned to the Andaman Sea to play its part in Ark Royal's ORI. After the exercise we joined fellow Scimitar pilots from 800 Squadron at a "Banyan" (beach barbecue) in Langkawi. The consumption of beer never compensated for the lack of female company.

Hermes' Far East Tour now complete, the ship set sail across the Indian Ocean for R&R at Mombasa. The Air Department had fared well and with two or three days of no flying we congregated at the open air bar on the quarter deck to celebrate (any excuse).

Our behaviour became boyishly raucous. The ship's officers, led by Commander XO, stomped off down to the wardroom to watch a movie. A bunch of us decided to wind up these party poopers. We went down to the wardroom, and in front of the screen we performed our own song and dance. The grim-faced audience sat motionless until we finished, and I could tell from the glint in the Commander's eye that the Air Group would pay dearly for these antics.

The next morning saw aircrew out on the gun sponsons hoping the fresh air might assist hangover recovery. We stared at the wake and watched the flying fish skipping across the oily sea.

Passing merchant ships never seemed aware of our existence. O'Brien knew full well that their lookout was poor, and he could not restrain himself. One night an approaching supertanker seemed unaware of our approach, and our captain maintained course; it would be close. Passing abeam he sounded the ship's horn and switched on the floodlights. We roared past, port sides only 50 yards apart. We hoped it got their attention.

Each continent has its own distinctive aroma which can be detected far out to sea. Africa's heady mix of spicy perfume and corruption charged the senses. It would be an experience with just a hint of danger, I found this to be especially exciting. As *Hermes* slowly approached Mombasa the silence and decaying harbour fortifications lent the scene an eerily foreboding atmosphere.

Kenya, still a colony, was to become independent in just a few months time, so the atmosphere in town was highly charged. All the functions we attended were hosted by gloomy expatriates forecasting disaster. The few Kenyans we were introduced to were understandably enthusiastic, having no doubts about what their future held. The man on the street however held similar views to the expat old timers, and tribal rumblings were causing unease.

Our R&R included camping on the beach in Melindi and a motorised safari in Tsavo Game Park. The bus trip to Melindi was an adventure by itself.

Flight refuelling exercises off the Seychelles followed our visit to Mombasa. These, a test of pilots' skill and judgement, could be either very satisfying or a disaster. A smooth, steady approach and positive contact would result in a successful connection; fumble or bash the drogue and you might not get your fuel, or even worse you could damage the cockpit canopy.

After my refuel and having time to spare, I took the opportunity to re-route over Victoria. I was so entranced by the beauty of the islands that I was late returning to the ship, and *Hermes* had to remain steaming into wind (off course) for an extra ten minutes. I got another bollocking, this time from the captain.

In the Gulf of Suez *Hermes* handed over the baton to HMS *Victorious* and entered the Canal to commence the journey back to UK.

Back in the Med and probably in response to taunts from our Sea Vixen rivals, our CO, Freddy, decided that 803 squadron would become night qualified. This had been tried before by other squadrons, but after a few hair-raising incidents, abandoned. The Scimitar approach with its high angle of attack became even more of a problem at night. Having no visible horizon was considered the last straw.

Freddy volunteered to show us how and he was launched at dusk. The goofers' platform was full. His touch-and-gos were a bit on the high and fast side, decreasing the chance of hooking a wire. I don't know what Flyco was telling the CO, but it became apparent to us goofers that his chances of making a successful deck landing were diminishing at each attempt. It was still not quite dark when he put his hook down for a final landing.

In he came, high and fast. If he had let the aircraft continue to touchdown he would have missed the wire and carried out a "bolter". Realising that this attempt was a botched job, he commenced a go-around. Applying full power, he sharply raised the nose to initiate climb away. Raising the nose lowered the tail, the hook scooped the last wire... interesting. The wire screamed out of the sheaves and hauled the Scimitar out of the air. Whump. The Scimitar took the wire out to full travel, still rolling. The wire wrenched itself off the outboard drum. The broken end came up out of the deck, white hot and blazing like a firebrand. It swung out over the sea in a huge arc, leaving a stream of sparks. We were mesmerised. It would cut a swath across the forward deck and hit the parked Vixens in Fly One.

Freddy jammed on the brakes, his only hope. The Scimitar stopped, its front wheel right on the edge. The deck handlers were transfixed, watching the progress of the incoming wire. Some took refuge behind parked aircraft, while those out in the open attempted to skip the rope. The wire swept the deck and smacked into the parked aircraft. Two or three handlers now lay on the deck. One of them had his bum sliced off, another had the soles of his boots removed - no fatalities. Some parked Vixens were damaged. No more night flying for 803.

The Vixens of 892 had their interesting moments. After a 1000lb bombing sortie one of them returned with a hang-up (it had failed to release). This is awkward, as there is no way of knowing if the bomb is secure. Several attempts were made to shake it off, but to no avail. The book does not allow landings back on board in this condition;

the pilot should divert. If there is no diversion (there wasn't) he should eject.

With an arrested landing there is a strong possibility that the bomb will detach. There is also a remote possibility that it will be armed. The captain declared no objection and the pilot chose to land the aircraft back on. The ship went to action stations with the closing of watertight doors etc and the flight deck and goofers were cleared of all personnel. Non-active crew were positioned close to abandon ship stations.

The broadcast announced landing in ten seconds, and we heard the clang of the hook followed by the howl of the arrestor wires and another impact followed by a short screech. The bomb had released... we held our breath, staring each other in the eye, waiting. Those few seconds seemed an eternity.

Finally - "Stand down". We breathed again.

I went on deck to check out the scene. The nose of the bomb had cut a groove into the armour plate of the deck, extending from just forward of the touchdown point all the way to the end of the angle deck. Intrigued, I made a visit to the photo section to get a sneak preview of the 16mm cine. The film showed the Vixen being brought to a stop, the bomb dropped on to the deck and stood up on its nose. It somehow remained upright until it finally dived off the angled deck. That groove was thirty yards long and just under an inch deep, shiny and blued with heat.

We took part in several NATO exercises on the way back to UK. During one of these Brian Wilson suffered fuel starvation and engine flameout and he ejected after gliding over HMS Scarborough, one of our escort destroyers. Unfortunately, while being recovered by the ship's boat, he got bashed about a bit. Scarborough patched him up before our chopper returned him to *Hermes*. I suspect there was a problem with the automatic fuel balancing system. This was a known issue and a nightmare to manage manually. I only got the hang of it once, and that was after repeated attempts in the simulator.

Back in UK waters *Hermes* took part in Exercise Unison, a PR stunt really with the media on board to view the proceedings. I was wingman to Fred De La Billière, who had rejoined the squadron as our AWI. Tasked to attack the splash target towed behind a destroyer, I had a hard time following his tight and steep attack profiles. Slightly steep was more accurate but risky. I saw footage of our 2.75 inch rocket attacks, very impressive, each aircraft launched a salvo of 38.

After Unison, *Hermes* entered Portsmouth dockyard to undergo remedial work and we were detached to Yeovilton, where I was to do more compass correction work out on the airfield compass base. One aircraft, Reg. XD213, proved to be a real problem. It took up a lot of my time and kept me off the flying programme. It took eighteen attempts and the whole week before we finally got readings within acceptable limits.

John Middleton took the aircraft on its first flight and suffered a major hydraulic failure. Unable to transfer fuel from its drop tanks and only able to lower one wheel, John was told to fly the aircraft out over the channel and eject. The SAR helicopter was on the way. The Scimitar had on previous occasions shown it could fly a long way without a pilot, so the approved procedure to avoid collateral damage was to proceed to a clear area, wind the trim control hard over, then eject. The aircraft and pilot should then land in roughly the same vicinity. Several things might have crossed Johns mind:

1. The sea was very cold and we were wearing lightweight flying suits.
2. Would the automatic beacon in his life jacket operate efficiently, as claimed?
3. What if the SAR chopper winch was unserviceable?

John made the decision we all would have made. Just short of the coast, straight and level at 10,000 feet, he aimed the aircraft out to sea and ejected. John descended gently toward the Dorset countryside, near Chaldon Herring.

XD 231 headed out over Lyme Bay but then commenced a gentle turn. John watched the aircraft head back toward him. The Scimitar hit the ground in a shallow dive and disintegrated. The engines ricocheted into the air, describing a parabola over a nearby pub. John landed in a herd of cows and was picked up by the helicopter. Later that evening he drove to the pub, the Sailor's Return, where drinks were on the house.

RNAS Yeovilton was the chosen venue for the Fleet Air Arm Jubilee review. All Fleet Air Arm squadrons (bar those embarked overseas) were represented. Socially the event was a resounding success. The surrounding pubs were full of aircrew relating "there I was" stories. Beer sales reached record levels, and I bet there are a number of retired publicans who will never forget.

Alan Hickling was there with his ancient Rolls-Royce, providing much needed pub crawl transport. We managed to jam twelve passengers inside, but this had unfortunate results. Returning from a particularly drunken bash an occupant on the rear bench seat, bottom layer, announced "stop, I need to puke". the Rolls screeched to a halt in a quiet village high street. The doors were flung open, but before anyone could decant, the individual concerned, feeling the bile rising, clamped a hand over his mouth. This effectively ensured that a "five finger spray" soaked all the evacuees. They rolled out into the street, where they lay around screeching with mirth. Lights came on in the adjacent houses.

For the grand flypast it was decided, due to time constraints, that a mass formation take-off would be the most efficient way to get this large number of aircraft airborne. Lining up for take-off four at a time, there were many rows of aircraft on the runway. What had not been considered was the cumulative effect of jet efflux. I was close to last. In order to stop the engines overheating while ingesting the exhaust from in front, each row had to up the power a notch.

Apart from the higher fuel consumption those at the rear suffered serious overheating. I could see my Perspex cockpit canopy distorting. Just when it seemed that the air-conditioning was about to give up, off we went. My wheels failed to retract - I had suffered a hydraulic failure. Peeling off from the formation I went to the designated holding point and remained there for the whole event. I shut down one engine and flew at minimum drag speed to save fuel, but it would be a close run thing. My requests to return to land were refused. I was considering Bournemouth as a diversion when the flypast finished and was given permission to land. I returned with less than safe minimum fuel -again.

The Duke of Edinburgh as guest of honour thoroughly enjoyed the event; as a naval officer himself it must have brought back the "good old days". Junior officers were banned from the wardroom that evening. We weren't trusted not to repeat his sometimes outrageous remarks.

When the guys heard it was my 21st birthday they took me out to a pub for lunchtime drinks. I was taken off the afternoon's flying programme by Freddie the CO, who appeared disgusted, but I was not in any trouble.

Returning to Lossiemouth, the squadron practised air-to-air refuelling, I was the tanker. The drogue fuel valve stuck open after refuelling the first recipient, and there being no manual shut-off the fuel continued to escape. The only solution was to jettison the complete refuelling kit contained in an under-wing pod, expensive but no choice. The remains will be somewhere around Ben Nevis.

It was great to be back at Lossie. Notable occasions in the old wardroom included visits by the actor James Robertson Justice. Famous for his roles in the Carry On movies. JRJ was an enormous Scot with a red beard who wore the kilt and all the other stuff. Invited by the captain, he often overindulged and became extremely loud.

He was finally banned from the mess for emptying his beer over the head of his host.

The Scimitar would soon be replaced by the Buccaneer. The first squadron was doing its "work-up" at Lossiemouth. As the end of the Scimitar's operational role was in sight, restrictions on flying hours were lifted.

A period of intensive training followed. I was Fred's wingman again and life got exciting, with live 1000lb bombing at Garvey Island. I followed Fred in low-level battle formation, supposedly flying at 200 feet. I still wonder how close to the ground I came while focusing on formation keeping. Approaching the target I realised that this would be another of Fred's specials. We passed the agreed pull up point by a good few seconds, and I tensed up. Pulling up hard, I hung on behind. We seemed to be in an almost vertical climb. Fred wheeled over and on down toward the target. I delayed my turn to achieve a bit of separation, but I was alarmed at how steep the dive had become. With one eye on the altimeter I released, and pulled hard for the recovery. There was a loud bang as I was struck by a fragment from Fred's bomb.

There is a good reason why attacks should be carried out at the specified dive angle. Change one parameter, and you change them all. The steeper the angle, the higher must be the release height, something Fred had ignored.

Everything seemed to be OK. The controls functioned and Fred, now alongside, reported no signs of obvious damage. On the way back I carried out a slow speed check with gear and flaps down. Only a bit of wind noise and some vibration, so I felt somewhat reassured. Back at base a safe landing was made.

The post-flight inspection revealed a hole six inches across, punched right through the starboard wing. The shrapnel had passed through the wing at the only location where it would not compromise the safety of the aircraft. The space was occupied by an electrical junction box and covered above and below by access panels. Only a few inches in each direction lay: the fuselage and starboard engine, the main spar, the main fuel tank and the main fuel gallery (pipe). The repair simply consisted of replacing the junction box, two panels and a bracket.

I was not privy to the outcome of the enquiry, but Fred's enthusiastic style was in no way diminished. Early one winter morning he announced a "scramble". It was just the two of us and we raced out to the aircraft and fired up. Fred was much faster off the blocks than I, and he was half way round the airfield before I moved. I sped after him but he was rolling for take-off as I coasted downhill to the U-turn on to runway 05. I braked, but the wheels locked on the icy surface and I went straight off the end of the taxiway into the grass and mud. It was a bit of a swamp, and the aircraft settled down on to its drop tanks. I felt very silly.

The new CO, Pete Newman, said I must stay by the aircraft until it was recovered. It proved impossible to tow out by tractor and the crash crane was sent for. The crane only succeeded in winching itself down into the mud. By this time I was developing hypothermia as it was bloody cold, so I sneaked back to the hangar. The aircraft was successfully recovered the following day after all the fuel was drained out, a perforated steel track was laid down, and the addition of a second crane.

Never mind the mishaps - Fred was fun and good company, In retrospect I realise he was trying to imbue me with the "can do" spirit he thought necessary for a potential Air Warfare Instructor.

Air-to-air combat training began in earnest. This was the most thrilling, challenging but exhausting flying that I have experienced. Due to its high wing loading the Scimitar's turning circle at altitude was not good. There were however a number of tricks that could be used at lower altitudes when the power to weight ratio became more favourable. The Scimitar's high G barrel roll was particularly effective, and tight manoeuvring in the vertical plane could also produce good results. I'm not sure what purpose it would serve, but at low level the Scimitar could easily manage (if the pilot could take it) a 360 degree turn at a continuous 8G. The young and fit managed this manoeuvre with alacrity and took great pleasure in ribbing the older guys.

With hours unrestricted, the extra flying allowed us to explore the full performance envelope, sometimes reaching uncharted territory. Tempted by stories of previous legendary exploits, I tried to beat the unofficial record for the high-level loop. I failed and stalled the aircraft upside down at 33,000 feet, falling into an inverted spin. Spin recovery was not practised in the Scimitar, as it was considered unlikely to be successful. Instinct said full power... the nose of the aircraft pitched earthward. I pulled through (a "split S") and lost 25,000 feet in the process. All this occurred in just a few seconds. I was out of breath but exhilarated.

HMS *Fulmar* Air Day, open to the public and held in August, was always fun. The event was not only intended to impress the taxpayer but to assist recruiting. Apart from the flying displays there were various exhibits set up. One of these displayed opportunities for members of the WRNS to enjoy the outdoor pursuits of camping and orienteering. The display was being promoted by a rather attractive young Wren named Sandy Jones, and we got talking and became friends.

My replacement, Alasdair Gamley, joined the squadron. I had served on 803 for six months longer than normal, so a second-line appointment was overdue. Of the options available I chose 750 Squadron, based at RNAS Hal-Far in Malta, tasked with Observer (Navigator) training. Malta had a good reputation for outdoor activities and much sunshine.

750 was equipped with the Sea Prince, a navalised version of the Percival Pembroke and the DH Sea Venom similar in shape to the Vampire. It had a more powerful engine and improved aerodynamics.

Before departing for Malta I attended a course to learn multi-engine asymmetric flying and civil aviation airways procedures. This training was carried out at RNAS Lee-on-Solent by Mike Dench using a De Havilland Dove. The Dove might also have been used as an "Admiral's Barge", but even so his posting was a sinecure.

In the days before autofeather, an engine failure on take-off needed quick reactions and clear thinking. This was especially important when flying single crew, as control of the aircraft while securing the engine could be quite a handful. Woe betide you if you shut down the wrong one.

It was high summer and Cowes week, and having mastered the essentials we spent the remainder of the allocated time buzzing the yachts and trying to slalom the Needles (not possible).

Chapter Eight

750 SQUADRON, MALTA

September 1964 - July 1965

I flew out to Malta in an RAF Bristol Britannia, landing at RAF Luqa in the evening, it was very hot. I remember the aroma, a strange combination of hot stone, aromatic herbs and last night's Marsovin (the local wine).

The Mess at RNAS Hal-Far was quite homely and the accommodation brand new; it felt good. The 750 Squadron CO was Ken Sinclair and the Senior Pilot Pete Fish. Both were amiable souls and easy to like. Some old friends were there; The QFI, Pete De Souza, I knew from my time on 736 Squadron. Mike Tod and Pete McManus were there but it was Colin Morris (later to be one of the first Concorde captains) who took me under his wing and introduced me to the Valetta hotspots and various expat girls.

Local girls were not a practical proposition. It was impossible to have any sort of relationship when the obligatory chaperone loomed in the background. It would also mean church attendance with the family. Sunday being hangover day, this was out of the question. But then there were the QARNNS (Queen Alexandra's Royal Navy Nursing Service) nurses at Bighi Hospital. You could post party invitations with attendance lists on their notice board, but the girls had to be collected and returned by midnight. One of the benefits of having my own transport was being able to collect the partygoers, I could chat them up on the way.

Colin had rented a flat in Sliema at 7A M'Rabat Lane and he offered me a share, recently vacated. Sleeping ashore (off base) was forbidden, but recuperating after an all-night party was a grey area.

Two months after I arrived, the C in C Med Command decided to hold a mess dinner at naval HQ in Valetta to celebrate the victory of the Battle of Taranto. Taranto Night dinners were the occasion for the Fleet Air Arm to celebrate its greatest victory. On this occasion Chiefs of Staff and the top brass of the US 6th Fleet were invited.

Footnote: *On the occasion of this historic attack Fairey Swordfish biplanes (affectionately known as "stringbags") were launched at night from HMS Illustrious. Equipped with torpedoes and bombs, they attacked and sank or disabled most of the Italian fleet anchored in Taranto harbour.*

The Taranto Night dinner, wherever held, was a duty call for navy pilots, but as the junior officer I was nominated Hal-Far Duty Officer.

Luckily for me, oysters were on the menu and all who consumed them went down with typhoid. As one of the few serviceable pilots I did a lot of the flying during the next few days. Oh yes, we had sent a Sea Prince to collect the oysters from, guess where... Taranto.

On the social side and out of the blue I got a phone call from Sandy, who, surprise surprise, was now in Malta. I popped in to the Wrens' quarters and we had a chat. Sandy had impeccable manners and was far too nice. I had to explain that I was not yet ready to go steady. When I left she said she understood, but I felt really mean. The truth of the matter was that my taste veered to the exotic, even slightly dangerous, end of the female spectrum. Sandy became radio host on the local forces radio and eventually made it to the BBC.

Hal-Far had the normal complement of WRNS, but too many men were competing for their attention. As a result these girls were spoiled rotten and could be quite demanding. I teamed up with two inseparable WREN mechanics who proved to be very good company for nights on the town. Forget any love interest, these two had each other. Both the captain and the Commander of Hal-Far had daughters of suitable age, who were great fun at official functions and private parties if they could sneak away.

The Sea Prince was a good old bus, but it did have a design fault. Pilots had to taxi slowly and avoid centreline lights. Hitting a bump might cause the nosewheel bogey and tail assembly to oscillate at the natural frequency. Only an immediate stop would avoid a fractured rear fuselage and consequent separation of the tail assembly.

Malta is a tilted slab of sandstone, the west coast being an 800 foot cliff, the east sliding gently into the Mediterranean. Hal-Far airfield was situated in the southwest corner of the island. Luqa, Malta's only airport and the RAF base, was in the centre of the island. This set-up gave Hal-Far pilots a blank cheque for low flying.

All our training exercises started from the Island of Gozo, north of Malta. When the "Levanter" or East wind was blowing, turbulence in the form of a rotary vortex would form in the lee of the western cliffs. This was very uncomfortable and sometimes dangerous. In order to get to Gozo safely (or back to Hal-Far), our clearance would be "Clear to Gozo via the east coast not above 200 feet" (that's under the Luqa control zone). Needless to say most of the east coast transits were done at 20 feet. The sea was often like glass, making it very difficult to judge height. Any pilot with brains flew close to the beach for reference. Prior to my arrival a Sea Prince had skimmed the surface and torn off its fuel vent pipe. Following another aircraft in these conditions was classic Hollywood, the prop-wash racing like a shadow under the aircraft. Bighi Hospital, perched on a promontory at the mouth of Valetta harbour, was an ideal viewing point, and 750 squadron pilots showed off to the nurses on their way to work.

When the wind was in the opposite direction we returned to Hal-Far down the west coast, below cliff-top level. If we delayed the climb to circuit height we could turn on to final approach using a "wingover". Pushing your luck with a stall turn would result in an ATC report and a bollocking from the CO, Ken Sinclair. Ken was an amiable soul but he did his duty if misdemeanours were reported . We could get away with murder in those days.

After one practice divert to Luqa I held the Sea Prince down low, then pulled up into a wingover to Hal-Far. That got me an invitation to visit the RAF Luqa Station Commander on Saturday afternoon, prime beer-drinking time. I was advised that I had alarmed passengers at the civilian terminal and that the RAF had received complaints. The CO made me feel small. As far as I know 750 suffered no accidents in Malta.

The Sea Venom was a refreshing change from the Prince. It was a hot little ship, and 500 Kts on the deck (low level) could be achieved with ease. Venom flights were done early in the morning. When temperatures rose, take-off with full tip tanks was not possible.

Murphy's law struck again one day when I was returning to the mess and heard a WHUMP. A Venom had hit the stone wall off the end of the runway. The aircraft was from the Hal-Far Station Flight, not from 750. The results of the investigation were kept secret; there were suggestions that the tip tanks had been full but this had not recorded in the tech. log. The pilot did not survive his ejection due to lack of height. Most of us used runway "speed and distance" markers to assess take-off progress. If parameters were not met we could stop before the end of the runway.

I had one of my closest calls in the Venom. Being cleared for a low pass across the airfield, I went down to about twenty feet at 500 knots. Flying over the grass I failed to see a flock of seagulls which took flight directly in front of the Venom. If I pulled up we would collide. I nudged the stick forward and dipped under them. No bird strike, but my heart was racing. Sometimes I wonder.

The student's final navigation exercise was combined with a "land away" night-stop. These were a lot of fun. If Palma, Majorca, was the destination, we stocked up on Fundador brandy. We preferred the four-litre flagons, which came in a wicker basket and were easy to carry. The brandy would be left in the care of the residents of 7a M'Rabat for party purposes. Not being full strength, it was usually served 50/50 with ginger ale in half pint mugs. There was a party most weekends. These functions varied in size from small get-togethers to out-of-control, all-welcome madhouses.

Len Townsend joined the squadron, and he and his wife moved into a rented house. For the housewarming party I collected the nurses from Bighi. The nursing sister reminded me to drive carefully and return the girls on time. A serious little brown-skinned girl sitting in the back suddenly smiled. It was like the sunrise. For the first time in my life my heart skipped a beat. I mumbled a welcome, wondering if this little charmer would accept or reject my advances. The girls I had met previously were friendly, but there had been no chemistry.

Her name was Janet and she was from Trinidad. As I watched her from across the room, she appeared a little unsure, but then the rock and roll started. I had learned to jive and boogie at the youth club, but had rarely met a girl who could do the same. Half expecting a refusal, I asked Janet. I cannot remember a word we said, but boy did we move. Dropping the girls back at their quarters, I was too shy to attempt a kiss, but I did ask for a date and she said yes. I didn't sleep that night.

From that moment on we stayed together. Technically Janet, as a junior nurse, was categorised as a junior rating. The regulations forbade "fraternisation" between officers and ratings, but this was generally ignored if one was discreet. I crossed the line and sneaked Janet into the back row of the Sunday evening cinema in the wardroom - mistake. The Hal-Far nurse, Sister O'Leary, created a lot of fuss - she was a real dragon. Ken Sinclair advised me not to try it again. O'Leary, not satisfied, tried to put an end to our relationship by reporting our friendship to Bighi's Senior Medical Officer, but he just said "Don't worry".

O'Leary managed to get herself a seat on one of our navigation exercises to Rome, claiming she had an appointment to see the Pope. On arrival she said the meeting had been postponed due to unforeseen circumstances, then insisted on accompanying us chaps when we hit the town. We warmed up on pre-dinner sambucca cocktails and had dinner near the Trevi Fountain. We were wondering how to dump our hanger-on when Ken suggested we throw in some coins. We stared at him, and he winked. We tossed in the odd coin, and as O'Leary was rummaging in her purse Ken grabbed her round the waist and hoisted her into the pool. The crowd cheered, Ken said "run!" and we legged it.

When HMS Ark Royal anchored in Valetta Harbour, Colin and I invited a few friends for a party at 7A, but virtually the whole wardroom showed up. Upstairs, downstairs and the roof were full, and the flat, about 1000 sq ft, contained around 175. Things got hairy when the neighbours complained and the police were summoned. When they arrived at the front door someone chose that moment to knock a crate of minerals off the rooftop parapet and it landed dangerously close to the patrolmen. Those who were aware of what had happened sobered up, expecting serious trouble. As luck would have it the Times War Correspondent was right by the door. Seizing the opportunity he gave the two officers a glass of wine, welcomed them as old comrades and showered them and all Maltese with praise concerning their courage and determination during the war years. This went down well, and they left half an hour later with much laughter and backslapping.

Recovering quietly the next morning with breakfast on the roof, I was intrigued by a fast-moving pall of smoke racing along the eastern shore. Suddenly an RAF Vulcan pulled up hard over Sliema, presumably intending to join the circuit at Luqa. The big delta roared across the rooftops at 45° of bank. He was pushing his luck thinking he could emulate 750 squadron. The problem was that he was unaware that the procedure stipulated crossing the coast at circuit height. There was litigation. Claims were put in for an overturned fishing boat, two premature babies and a donkey with a broken leg. I believe the captain was court martialled. Colin Morris, sleep disturbed, awoke and consumed the beer ready on his bedside table. Colin would down two bottles before opening his eyes.

Some 7a parties were planned, while some were spontaneous. At weekends we often stopped off for a sundowner after a day at the beach. One memorable day the "few drinks" turned into a major session. We left the flat at 3 am the next morning, the streets deserted. Turning out of the bumpy and narrow M'Rabat Lane, our four cars accelerated down Sliema Hill. A wandering drunk chose that moment to cross the road. All four cars slammed on the brakes, but there was dew on the road and our wheels locked as we careered down the hill. The lead car slid to a halt, the drunk stationary in the middle of the road gazing at the oncoming vehicles. One by one the succeeding vehicles slammed into each other. Headlights, fenders, doors and windscreens showered into the road. Stunned and in total silence we checked ourselves for injury. Amazingly, no one was hurt. We clambered out of the wreckage, surveying the display of shattered vehicles.

In the surrounding buildings lights came on and doors opened. In the distance sounded the wail of police sirens. In an instant we were back in our vehicles, starter motors whirring. All of us managed to fire up and the cavalcade of battered vehicles lurched away, bonnet and boot lids flapping. Some had lost a door, and most were without windscreens. The convoy split up and disappeared down side streets, perspex and chrome fittings littering the road. I managed to make it back to Hal-far just as the engine of the Hillman Minx began to overheat. The hire car rep took it all in his stride, reminding me with a flicker of a smile that I only had third party insurance.

I changed my hire car for a battered Ford Prefect. The garage said that if I had any more accidents they would return it to a roadworthy condition but do no restoration. This arrangement would be easier on my wallet. Repairing the Hillman had cost me a bomb. The only problem was that there was no floor, so the dropping of sunglasses, wallet etc was to be avoided.

Janet and I got on OK and became an item. Ian Frenz, an ex 800 Scimitar pilot whose career paralleled my own, had joined the Squadron. He occasionally joined us for nights on the town. Most of the bars had juke boxes; our favourite music for jiving was *Woolly Bully* by Sam the Sham and the Pharaohs.

The Ford's clutch kept slipping. The garage would do a temporary fix but the problem always returned. One evening as I was taking Janet back to the hospital and climbing the hill to Bighi nurses' quarters, I lost my cool and floored the pedal, burning out the clutch. I got Janet back safely, but the clutch was totalled. Luckily it was all down hill to Birzebbugia. I coasted into the garage, telling the guys the clutch was playing up again.

As I was returning from a trip in the Sea Venom and flying down the east coast, I spotted the unmistakeable shape of a Russian Sverdlov cruiser. I had never seen one close up; now was my chance. Staying low, I flew in close before turning back toward Hal-Far. As I flew down the ship's port side I could see every single one of their many guns tracking my progress - impressive.

After Maltese independence, the writing was on the wall. 750 squadron was transferred to Lossiemouth, groan. We had to fly the aircraft back to UK, VFR (visual flight rules) as the Sea Prince had only basic instrumentation and no pressurisation. Aircraft spares and stores were properly secured in the back, but a last-minute decision to allow our personal effects meant these were only tied down with cordage. This might have been OK except that I had loaded my steel cabin trunk full of books and manuals.

After refuelling at Bastia in Corsica we had to set course across a range of mountains, not having enough fuel to fly the long way round. We calculated our climb would just clear us over with visual clearance, but we were not expecting the severe turbulence in the lee of the peaks (the rotor effect). My cabin trunk broke loose and slammed into the back of my seat.

We continued to Chateauroux French Air Base. The Red Arrows formation aerobatic team had performed there that afternoon, and in the mess that evening some of the French guys asked us if we were with the "British team". Ken said yes, and we were given dinner free of charge. Our hosts' command of English was as bad as our French, so the dinner passed off with everyone none the wiser. The Red Arrows were long gone.

When we landed at Yeovilton for HM Customs clearance, they tore us apart. I got charged 100 percent duty on some items that were several years old and much the worse for wear. I still wonder what put a bee in their bonnet.

Chapter Nine

LOSSIEMOUTH AND RNAS BRAWDY

1965 - 1967

It was July and quite warm, we didn't think to change from lightweight flying overalls. As we progressed northward to Lossiemouth it became apparent that we had underestimated the effect of increasing latitude. By the time we landed at Lossie we were numb with cold, the warm Mediterranean just a memory.

I had passed the Maltese driving test but needed a British driving licence. I took a few lessons, then applied for the test. The examiner was a dour middle-aged Scot who had little regard for irreverent and rowdy Sassenachs. The guy was not biased though, and I passed the test.

Flying out over the cold, grey and windy Moray Firth was an experience poles apart from the clear blue Mediterranean. Our land away exercises did however provide some entertainment, with visits to Amsterdam and Copenhagen.

Our arrival at the Dutch airbase of Valkenburg caused Air Traffic Control much consternation. We assumed we would receive radar vectors to controlled approaches, standard NATO procedure. Wrong. We were asked to hold over their NDB (radio beacon), and we would then be cleared for approach one at a time. The Sea Princes had only just had the ADF equipment fitted and no training had been carried out. A holding pattern did not appear to be any big deal, but we had no approach plates and just took a stab at it. Unfortunately there was 30 knots of crosswind and it just didn't seem to work out. There were four of us, all over the sky, basically doing a melée of figures of eight instead of the standard racetrack pattern. A report was filed and practice ensued on return.

We spent three nights in Amsterdam, enough said. The flight back was strenuous. We all had hangovers. There was a 60-knot headwind all the way across the North Sea and icing was forecast. Not having any anti-icing equipment, we had to fly below cloud, which meant through the salt spray at 300 feet. We kept an eye open for tall ships and oil rigs but were forced to land at Edinburgh/Turnhouse for fuel. The flight home took two hours longer than the flight out.

Ian Frenz and I became known as the "Terrible Twins" due to our party habits.

I was missing Janet very much, and the more we corresponded the stronger the feelings became, so I planned a trip out to Malta. My leave was approved and was due to start on the 28th October. As the flying programme showed I had days off on the 26th and 27th. Ken Sinclair approved my request to leave on the 26th. I booked flights from Aberdeen via Edinburgh to Heathrow and Malta. Then the word got around that I was taking early leave and Ken had to retract his approval. On the afternoon of the 27th I went by train to Aberdeen, flew to Edinburgh and then on to Heathrow, landing at 0130. I slept for a few hours in the terminal before catching the early flight to Malta.

After take-off I opened the paper and was confronted by a half-page photo of an aircraft accident. The flight I had previously booked for the 26th had crashed attempting to land in fog. There were no survivors.

I had been unable to inform Janet of the reversion to the original leave date. Thinking I was now lost, her friends had taken her out and got her pickled. My arrival at the nurses' quarters stunned Janet, who was angry that I had failed to notify her of my change in itinerary, but after the shock had subsided we had a great time. I hired a car from the guy in Birzebbugia...he didn't mention the burnt-out clutch.

Back at Lossie, apart from flying students around the Moray Firth and the Highlands we were sometimes asked to fly the "station barge" (a Sea Prince configured for passengers). These flights could be arduous, as at 150 knots flying down to Lee-on-Solent or Yeovilton and back took all day. Crew duty limitations were unheard of.

During one of these sagas I was carrying Admiralty top brass on an inspection tour. Ready to depart RNAS Brawdy in Pembrokeshire, it was about 10 pm, blustery and raining hard. The passengers arrived and I ushered them on board. While giving them the usual spiel prior to settling into the cockpit, I couldn't help but notice their nervous demeanour. I now realise that this was due to my childlike looks and the lack of a co-pilot.

I started the port engine, but the starboard one refused to fire up. I had my suspicions as to the cause, so I shut down and assured the passengers (now looking seriously agitated) that the situation could probably be rectified. I think they would have disembarked if it hadn't been for the late hour and atrocious weather. I sent the ground crew for some steps, dropped the lower cowling and struck the fuel valve solenoid with a screwdriver. Going back to the cockpit I casually said "should be OK now". When the engine started I felt a warm glow of satisfaction and turned round to give the passengers an encouraging smile. Their look of concern had changed to one of approval, which was great for my ego.

The next day Ken Sinclair called me in to his office and thanked me. I hope it enhanced his reputation, as he, being a recovering alcoholic, was under scrutiny from above.

Janet had now been transferred to Stonehouse Naval Hospital in Plymouth and we arranged to meet while on leave. She would be staying with her eldest sister in London and I was with my parents in Whitchurch-on-Thames. I found it very difficult to get hold of Janet on the phone, as her sister, jealous of our relationship, hung up on me. When I finally got through Janet told me that her sister was holding all her documents and cash and she felt trapped. I told Janet to pack and said I would be there in two hours. I reached their house in Dalston (London's East End) at midnight and tentatively knocked on the door. Janet, suitcase in hand, quietly opened the door and we got away unnoticed.

I introduced Janet to my parents, and Mum was very kind. We had a wonderful two weeks. Looking back it was obvious we were good for each other, but I was frightened of commitment. When Ian Frenz got married to Cheryl, we attended the wedding in his home town, Perth. Weddings being what they are I decided that if I were to marry anyone it would be Janet. I asked her if she could wait. She said yes, thinking that I was off to the toilet. We still laugh over that one.

We went on up to Lossiemouth, Janet staying on in the Frenz's caravan at Milltown, while I had to remain on station. During a "happy hour" in the Officers' Mess, Paddy Anderson and Simon Creasy, my ex 803 Squadron colleagues, called me aside and advised me that it was not a wise move to marry a "jungle bunny". He said that by the time they were 35 they would be fat and wrinkled and besides, past experience had shown that mixed marriages were doomed to failure. I knew from their body language that they had been asked to pass on this message.

My time in 750 Squadron was coming to an end, and I had been selected to train as an Air Warfare Instructor. I finally popped the question, and Janet agreed to marry me. Wow!

The Air Weapons ground studies were carried out at the gunnery school on Whale Island (HMS Excellent) in Portsmouth. Andy McMeekan and Dave Henry were my course mates. The wedding was to be soon after.

I was very aware of the life-changing moment about to unfold and felt nervous, but Janet took it all in her stride. We were to be married in church, to keep Mum happy. Having been raised in a mix of different cultures, Janet had to complete a Christianity refresher course with the vicar, Reverend Walmsley of nearby St Mary's. These briefings consisted of a fireside chat, afternoon tea and several glasses of sherry. Janet said it was very difficult to stay awake, but she was baptised anyway.

On the day, it was snowing. The vicar asked me and my brother Rob, the best man, into the vestry for a quick sherry. Before we knew it the bridal march was playing and we had to scurry out into position. Janet was already waiting at the altar. Goodness knows what was going through her mind.

The reception was held at my parents' place, Swanston House. After the wedding breakfast we drove in the snow and ice, full of champagne, to Dorchester. Snow jammed the windscreen wipers, forcing me to drive with my head out of the window, which caught the attention of the local police. Fortunately I was still in uniform, confetti still visible. The officer was sympathetic and told me to follow. The police car drove very, very, slowly all the way to the hotel, the White Hart.

Often featured in the *Midsomer Murders* TV series, this hotel is a romantic 16th century coaching inn. We had booked the honeymoon suite. The customers in the bar were a very jolly crowd who insisted on buying us even more drinks. We finally retired to our suite and a very grand four-poster bed. It had been a tiring day and we were already well acquainted, so we slept.

Breakfast was in the main bar, where the staff looked very much the worse for wear. I remarked on this to one of the waiters, who pointed at the ceiling above the bar. Through the ceiling came a length of string to which was attached an apple. "Your room" the waiter said, raising his eyebrows heavenward. The other end of the string had been tied to the bedsprings. Many had stayed late, waiting in vain to see the apple dance.

764 squadron operated the Air Warfare School at Lossiemouth, carrying out intensive training for its instructor candidates. Graduates served on all front-line squadrons, their task being to ensure that standards of weapons delivery and air-to-air combat were maintained or improved. The AWI would work with the CO and Senior Pilot when planning a strike.

Graduates from the school on exchange to the US equivalent at Miramar assisted in refreshing American naval fighter tactics. The Americans had allowed their previous skills in this area to lapse, due to the introduction of the air-to-air missile. During the Vietnam War their loss of aircraft forced them to realise that dog-fighting tactics remained a vital element of the fighter pilot's portfolio.

Not being old enough to qualify for naval married quarters, we moved on to the caravan site (trailer park) at nearby Milltown. I had bought a second-hand caravan and we moved in. Boy it was cold! First thing in the morning boiling water had to be poured down the sink to ensure the drain would not ice up. I had to exchange the Ford Anglia for a VW Beetle to ensure I got to work in the morning.

The "Top Gun" school was equipped with the Hunter GA11. I enjoyed the flying immensely but felt too young and not ready for the responsibility that went with the qualification. I felt trapped and began to suffer regrets. The CO of the AWI School, Mike Kennet, was aware of the problem and suggested a reassessment. After being questioned by various departments, by mutual agreement, I was reassigned. The fact that my weaponry was above average seemed to have been the sole criterion for my being selected as a candidate.

Having the benefit of the AWI school instruction put me in a good position to become a tactical instructor at the Operational Flying School. 738 Squadron was now located at RNAS Brawdy and equipped with Hunter GA11s. This was my next appointment.

I learned that there were good surf beaches around Brawdy, so I phoned around and discovered that the only surf board available was in St Agnes, Cornwall. I rang the shop owner and asked if he could hold it for me - no such luck, so we jumped in the car and drove down overnight. It took seven hours, but we were on the doorstep when the shop opened in the morning. We went straight to the beach. After slipping off repeatedly I realised that I should of course wax the board. Back to the shop, get the wax, back to the beach.

In those days "big gun" boards were the norm, and this one was 9 ft 6 in long and weighed 27 pounds. These boards got you up on even the smallest of swells, enabling a long ride. Turns were difficult, and only the pros could do fancy stuff. Newgale beach was half a mile away from Brawdy and I spent a lot of time in the water. At that time there were no wet suits available, and more than an hour in the water could bring on hypothermia.

Our caravan was relocated to Brawdy and the station cliff-top site. The autumn gales arrived and we got hit by 70-knot winds, gusting 90. Although the caravan was secured with extra rope over the roof, the walls began flexing in and out and the caravan threatened to implode. I grabbed some wooden beams from the woodshed and rigged internal bracing... we survived.

I ran the station surf life-saving team, and if the weather was fine this allowed me beach time during working hours. We won the local Surf Life Saving Trophy but failed dismally at the National Championships. We were unprepared for the more rigorous events. During the summer we manned Newgale Beach, saving one girl from drowning and rescuing another cut off by the tide. Both were embarrassed by their need for our services and seemed ungrateful - par for the course I'm told.

One weekend a big summer storm closed the beach, but the British holidaymaker is not easily deterred. In order to prevent a tragedy we had to man the beach and monitor the few who insisted on entering the water (not being employed by the local council, we had no authority to enforce the warning placards).

In the end, tempted by the monster waves, I cracked. The waves were forming well out to sea and promised a long ride. I advised the team that it would take a while to fight my way out and launched myself into the foam. The waves were about twelve to fifteen feet, which is enormous for the UK. They were not the type usually associated with surfing, being truncated by the strong onshore wind. They were building way out to sea and rolling in with their tops blown forward in a welter of spray.

The chop made for a hard and long paddle out. When I finally came back in it was one hell of a ride. The long board hammered down the choppy front face, needing a firm front foot to avoid lift-off. I still dream of that ride.

Janet and I teamed up with Ian and Cheryl Frenz on the party scene; Ian was now a QFI on 759 Squadron, Hunter T8s. We enjoyed the wild and sometimes outrageous parties thrown by the students (they were more our age). We didn't encourage the practice, but occasionally we gave in to entreaties from students and their WRNS girlfriends to spend the night in our tiny spare room. Roger Lockley and friend were frequent guests.

Approaching the eight-year break point, I decided not to extend my time in the Navy. I was restless. As a supplementary list officer my options were limited, and I was hankering for adventure and something different. In addition, one of our Rhodesian officers had made a racially-offensive remark in the wardroom. The Commander politely brushed off my demand for an apology. I now realised that our mixed marriage was tolerated but not accepted.

Most of my compatriots who had left the Navy had signed on with airlines, but I was not ready for "bus driving". I could not envisage being a co-pilot even for a few years. So I replied to an ad which said "Pilots required for the Zambia Air Force" and resigned.

We felt vulnerable having to fend for ourselves, for the Navy cares for its personnel. Now unemployed, we stayed with Mum and Dad in Whitchurch-on-Thames, awaiting a response from the Zambian High Commission.

Dad worked for the Thames Conservancy as a Navigation Officer, carrying out his patrols in a 100-year-old steam launch. This elegant vessel of varnished wood and brass slid up and down the river like a wraith, its deceptively quiet engine producing a remarkable turn of speed.

It being high summer, we helped Dad restore his Thames rowing skiff. Built by T. G. Tagg, the boat was a classic. It was double sculled and finely crafted of cedar and fitted with storage for picnic hamper and wine bottles. We enjoyed some idyllic trips on the Thames and its backwaters.

Finally I received a letter from the Zambia High Commission, telling me I should attend an interview. An ex-RAF type with a handlebar moustache inspected my logbook, asked one or two vague questions, and that was it. I was notified by post, air tickets enclosed, two weeks later.

Chapter Ten

THE ZAMBIA
AIR FORCE

January 1968 - January 1971

We flew out with British Caledonian on a Vickers VC10, landing first at Ndola, the country's only international airport at that time. Descending the steps on to the tarmac I was surprised by how cool and dry it felt. It was morning and the sky was brilliantly clear with just a hint of smoke close to the horizon. I remember the smell, the tang of the wood smoke combined with the heady scent of the bush, so different from the humid air of the Far East. Those in transit for Lusaka were required to clear customs and immigration at Ndola. Customs checked our bags out on the apron, then they were reloaded for the flight to Lusaka.

In the deserted terminal (it was Sunday) there was nobody waiting to meet us, so we asked around, to be told there was a telephone in the bar. We entered and were surprised to see a couple of uniformed Air Force officers, mugs of beer in hand. Peter Zuze and Martin Simbule were surprised at our approach but made us welcome. Martin drove us to the air force base on the other side of the airfield.

The duty officer installed us in the transit house, then took us to the bar in the officers' mess (where else) to meet the rest of the gang. They were a very mixed bag; ex Northern Rhodesian Air Force, seconded Royal Air Force, one or two contract officers like me and several Zambians. The white ex-colonials (the majority had left after independence) took great pains to explain that they were Zambians, thus drawing a line between themselves and us contract guys. It was a front. They could not hide their admiration of Ian Smith in Rhodesia and it was obvious they were in cahoots with the Rhodesians. Their days were numbered.

The RAF were needed to run things during the changeover to nationalisation. They managed the two transport squadrons and ran the Flying Training School in Livingstone. This bunch considered themselves a cut above the rest of us, God knows why. We contract chaps were a motley crew, but along with the white Zambians we were (mostly) pragmatic and capable operators.

The Lusaka ZAF Base was brand new, and our neat and practical bungalow was fitted out with basic furniture identical with UK government issue. The gardens were barren and the land was reclaimed swamp with the occasional tree or hillock. We had one such mound in our back garden full of snakes. We had three types, green tree snakes, spitting cobras, and the dreaded puff adder.

The joining routine started at Air Force HQ in downtown Lusaka. Registering and completion of forms at just about every government department took a week or two. During the time between appointments we set up home. Documentation complete, the Beaver DHC 2 conversion commenced.

No 1 Squadron was equipped with the DHC 4 Caribou and No 2 Squadron the Beaver DHC 2. The QFI, Flt Lieutenant Bob Page, carried out my flight and line training.

The current task of Nos 1 and 2 Squadrons was to provide support to the army units stationed on the borders with Angola, Rhodesia and Mozambique. Ian Smith in Rhodesia had recently declared unilateral independence to avoid handover of power to the blacks.

To give him his due, he knew the country and its people and could see the problems in store. Unfortunately for him it was too late to counter the winds of change. The Rhodesian infrastructure relied on the services of diehard colonials. With one or two exceptions the whites had excluded the blacks from positions of responsibility in both government and commerce, and this was resented. A smooth handover of power was no longer possible; UDI was doomed to fail.

Post UDI, the UK, under pressure from the UN, tried to establish an embargo on Rhodesia. A token squadron of RAF Javelins was based at Ndola, and a naval blockade was established off the Mozambique port of Beira (to stop supplies of oil). The Air Force and Navy went through the motions with a distinct lack of enthusiasm. Feedback via the armed forces grapevine confirmed that the sympathies of our military lay with Mr Smith.

The countries bordering Zambia all had insurgency problems. The fledgling independence movements in Angola and Mozambique had been hijacked by the Soviet Union and China as they vied for influence and control. The stakes were high, and having set their sights on the control of mineral resources these sponsors supplied arms to the various factions. The Portuguese fought back and as usual it was the civilian population that suffered. Both sides overran towns and villages, killing and looting, paranoia dictating that the residents had supported the other side.

Sometimes the fight spilled over into Zambia as the armed rebels ran for cover. Hiding among the villagers they looted valuable food stocks and abused the women. They had the guns and any show of resistance would trigger outright slaughter.

The Zambian military responded by positioning troops along the border. The OAU wanted Zambia to secretly support the guerrilla fighters, but there are no secrets in Africa. It would incur the wrath of the colonial states and encourage hot pursuit. In the end Zambia agreed not to incarcerate rebels if they surrendered their weapons - no chance, but at least this declaration maintained Zambia's standing with the OAU. The Portuguese army accepted the status quo, but the Rhodesians and South Africans took the fight on to Zambian soil, if only temporarily. They considered Zambia the enemy but did not want to provoke the UN by engaging our troops.

When on location in the field the Beavers provided non-stop reconnaissance and re-supply services to units positioned along the border. In order to avoid escalation of hostilities we were instructed not to fly into neighbouring airspace. This did not stop hotheads on the other side from taking pot-shots, and we occasionally sustained small arms damage.

Pilot and aircraft were on site for a week at a time, the handover done on location. During training pilots had been instructed to pass their movements using HF radio, as when en route to the border we got out of range of Air Traffic Control VHF. The only continuous HF coverage was that provided by South Africa. I assumed our movements were being tracked by the Rhodesian, Portuguese and South African military. These forces thus pursued the UNITA and MPLA guerrillas on to Zambian soil unobserved. I saw the horrific results of these forays across the border, not just collateral damage. Torture was used to gain intelligence from the hapless villagers. Caught in the middle, they suffered brutality from both sides. When I became the squadron CO I cancelled HF reporting.

In the early days of border ops the Beaver stopped overnight at the nearest airport, which allowed the pilot accommodation at a hotel or guest house. No matter how basic the establishment, a decent shower and proper food meant a great deal, as our days were long and hard. The southern section of the Angola border was monitored from a camp in Mongu, pilots staying at the Lyambai Hotel, a tourist hotel which was at a safe distance from the border. Cold beer and good food made for a good night's sleep so long as the mosquito net was tucked in.

The hotel was on a rise overlooking the Zambezi flood plain and during the rainy season the water reached to within fifty yards of the veranda. In the dry season it was nowhere in sight.

When incursions became more frequent, operations were transferred to Kalabo, the other side of the Zambezi, closer to the border. We stayed under canvas, bathed in the river and ate tinned food or badly-cooked game.

In the North West, Company HQ was initially located at Balovale, pilots staying at the Government Rest House. This ancient establishment was run by what must have been the original manager, who appeared to be about ninety years old. He was a lovable old guy who spoke perfect English. His housekeeper was a very shapely lass who had a habit of entering the room or bathroom unexpectedly. One time when I came out of the bathroom, she was on the bed naked. Those African girls! Just as well the operations were transferred to Chavuma. The Company camp site occupied a bluff overlooking some rapids, and the view was stunning. Just across the border, over the hill behind us, was a Portuguese fort.

On the other side of the country the confluence of The Zambezi and Luangwa rivers marked the intersection of the Zambian, Mozambique and Rhodesian borders. This was the focal point for monitoring terrorist activity, our heavily camouflaged camp was set in the jungle next to a tiny airstrip. Cross-border trade had been banned, and the once-busy little port of Feira was now derelict. Only a few determined smugglers and fishermen remained. The Rhodesians took pot shots at our patrolling Beavers.

Every morning we flew the Company Commander to inspect the various platoons stationed along the border, landing in the bush. A Land Rover would have previously driven up and down the selected landing site to flatten the elephant grass and check for termite mounds, potholes and tree stumps. Flying overhead we waggled the wings, which was the signal for the Land Rover to set off and drive at 30 mph for twenty seconds. If the driver managed to maintain direction and control, we could land. Sometimes it was very rough, so baggage and stores had to be well secured.

When we moved to the border, camp beds proved remarkably comfortable. The cuisine was another matter entirely, and depended on the Company Commander. Sometimes I reverted to corn beef and baked beans rather than take a chance.

The Beaver Squadron Commander at this time was Tony Baylee, an ex RAF Navigator who had taught himself to fly. He was a gentleman and we got on well. When he was transferred to No.1 Squadron, DHC Caribous, I took over as CO of No. 2. I was concerned about the increasingly confident Zambian pilots, who were the sons of politicians and other influential members of society. I expected them to be spoilt brats, unlikely to follow advice or instructions. I was pleasantly surprised however, and found the initial intake to be well educated and mature. These guys were about my own age, twenty five, and they had anticipated the difficulties I would face and could offer sound advice. Later problems were related to the mix of dinosaur expats and a fresh intake of younger rebellious Zambians. We managed.

One of the stalwarts, Martin Simbule, was the son of Ali Simbule, the Foreign Minister, who famously called the British Government a "toothless bulldog". Gilbert Chileshe eventually became the military attaché in Washington and Peter Zuze became a permanent Zambian rep to the UN in New York. Godfrey Mulundika was to become a very controversial MD of Zambia Airways and Joe Chisala (a James Brown fanatic) made it to ZAF Director of Operations. Others, like Phillip Lemba, faded into obscurity, while some met ignominious ends as a result of their challenges to the establishment.

In addition to the Caribous, two ageing DC3s were retained as back-up transport. During a resupply I was surprised to see Janet (now pregnant) disembark from one of these Dakotas. It turned out there had been a party in the mess the night before and the Departure being at 5 am, she had done a quick change and boarded the flight straight from the party. I assume she slept on the flight. After a quick hello I had to go, but Janet did have lunch under canvas before returning to Lusaka. No need to worry about Janet getting bored then. Shortly afterwards, the DC3s were donated to the Biafra Air Force.

We later acquired a battered-looking Brit, an ex-Nigerian Air Force mercenary who when asked to explain his lack of teeth told the following story. Following a Mig 15 sortie strafing the Biafrans he was returning to Lagos short of fuel. The weather had turned very bad, making landing at Lagos impossible, so the only option was to land on a road. Nigerian roads being what they are, the Mig 17 disintegrated after touchdown. The armoured cockpit, however, barrelled down the road, coming to rest in a ditch. How our man was rescued I cannot remember, but he suffered broken limbs and loss of teeth. He should have been fitted with dentures, but seemed oddly fond of his few remaining pegs (probably the cue for his story).

Back on the border, a more rapid response was required in support of patrols on the ground, so the army prepared more landing strips along the border. Some of these were decidedly dodgy. The expat COs were on their way out and some of the Zambian replacements lacked experience and sometimes proper training. After a few hair-raising incidents it became necessary to check out the strips on foot, which usually entailed a Land Rover trip of several hours across rough terrain. Fascinating scenery but tough on the bum.

When Kingsley Chingkuli was Kalabo Company Commander being on detachment was quite tolerable. As an ex-Sandhurst-trained officer, Kingsley was a committed professional. When he set up camp he did so in style. He installed proper showers to avoid public ablutions by the river and served Orange Pekoe in china cups poured from a silver service. I took my trusty radio and we listened to the BBC Overseas Service over a decent cup of tea... fantastic. Kingsley was eventually made Chief of Staff. I understand he is now the Zambian Ambassador to Germany.

During one detachment at the border, Tia, our daughter, was born. I was informed by radio, but they forgot to mention that the birth was by caesarean section. The current expat CO, Roger Hunt (six foot four, blond and with Hollywood good looks), decided a celebration was in order, and we would go out for a beer. I remarked that our camp was in the middle of the bush, but he winked and said "follow me". After half an hour and feeling weary, I asked how far we had to walk. "Just round the corner" he said. We were on a very faintly defined footpath through the elephant grass and could see no further than several yards ahead.

Then I heard the upbeat sounds of Congolese *soukous* music and the purr of a portable generator. Rounding a bend in the path, we came upon the bar. It was a grass shack with a couple of home-made tables set beside a meandering river. The scene was straight out of the movies. The generator managed to run a mini fridge and radio, and at night illumination was provided by the inevitable Tilley lamp.

We were well into our second drink when Roger said we should go. With at least half a mug of beer remaining I protested, as it would not be dark for a while. "You hear that?" he said. I could just discern the throb of an outboard boat engine. "That's the Portuguese patrol coming for their sundowner". "Does HQ know they do this?" I asked, thinking how lax his supervision of the border must be. Roger then informed me that we were about a mile inside Angola and we had best keep out of sight. I swallowed my beer in one gulp and set off, Roger chuckling behind. I later found out that he often made trips into Angola, exchanging Zambian beer for Portuguese wine. Roger was a fun-loving adventurer and had served in several foreign armies.

Taking some leave, I drove our little family down to Livingstone to see the Victoria Falls. We stayed at the Mosi-oa-Tunya (the smoke that thunders) Hotel. A short walk took us to the edge of the falls, and there were no guardrails. At the river bank the Zambezi, a mile wide, and in full spate, sped past, then curved over and disappeared into the void. It was disorientating, but exciting. The bottom and far side of the gorge were not visible, due to the clouds of spray that came speeding back up. Stunning.

Our QFI, Flt Lt Page, retired and was replaced by Reg Drown. A new pilot, Graham Nock, arrived; contract officers were gradually replacing the ex-Northern Rhodesian Air Force contingent.

Nock had come from the private sector but had somehow managed to convince the interviewing officer that his experience as a flying club instructor would bring a significant contribution to the ZAF. He was a Walter Mitty type but aggressive, so instead of just dreaming about his fantasies he tried to put them into practice. He was younger but chubbier than most of us contract types and came with an attractive "wife" who was in fact his girlfriend. Being a consummate bullshit artist, he had persuaded the ZAF to allow him married accompanied status and bungalow accommodation. We were not sure why the girl stayed, as she was often seen with fresh bruises. From limited conversations in the bar we surmised that she had been "rescued" from impoverished circumstances.

One day shortly after Nock's arrival, Martin Simbule came into my office and told me that Nock's briefcase was in the crewroom, open, with a 9mm Browning visible. I couldn't believe it. Nock was proving to be a fool on top of everything else. I called the armoury and they locked the gun away. Ten minutes later Nock stormed into my office saying he would have me charged for theft. I told him to go ahead, and he stormed out. Nothing more was heard, and the gun remained in safe keeping.

It was my job to fly with Nock and carry out his operational training. It was quite tiring as he spent most of the time trying to convince me that his methods of operating were superior to our standard procedures.

During one of these flights en route to Kalabo I was checking Nock's single pilot procedures and he had the controls. The weather was typical tropical convergence line stuff with embedded cbs (storm cells). As we tried to find a way through a series of thunderstorms in teeth-jarring turbulence, there was a loud bang and the top cowling broke loose. The rear fasteners had failed, and being hinged at the front, the cowling rose up, obscuring the forward view. Nock exclaimed dramatically "This is it, we're going down" and shut down the engine. We were in cloud, only 3000 feet above the ground, the terrain beneath, dense bush.

Two-crew procedures had not yet been implemented so I instructed "I have control". He refused, saying he could handle it. I gave the order again, this time in a bellow, and Nock handed over in surprise (as the quiet type I was not known to raise my voice). We were now descending in cloud, in silence. I restarted the engine, and Nock looked confused as power resumed. I checked the instruments and confirmed that the engine was running normally. Nock looked sheepish and said he thought we had blown a "pot" (cylinder). In those conditions, even if we had blown a pot, radial engines can deliver enough power to stay airborne. We yawed the aircraft left and right, but the cowling refused to separate.

Approaching Mongu airport, I took control again. The only way to land with no forward vision was to sideslip on final approach, straightening up just before touchdown. Although Nock was OK with basic handling, my name was the one in the tech. log, and I would do the landing. As it turned out, when I crossed the controls and entered a sideslip, the change in airflow tore the cowling off and a normal landing ensued.

114

The number of bush strips increased, but some had to be abandoned due to their impractical construction. The newly-graduated Zambian Company Commanders were on a steep learning curve and did not always appreciate the dynamics of aircraft take-off and landings – they even built one strip across the side of a hill. I encountered this when the troops on the ground were desperately in need of supplies. Normally a landing would not have been attempted, as the lateral slope exceeded limits. An exception was made, again. After touchdown I slewed the aircraft up slope in order to continue in the runway direction. As speed reduced, the aircraft required more and more deflection. We finally drifted to a stop, power on, heading uphill 90º to the runway direction. Having just been graded, the runway surface was soft and loose. If the surface had been hard we wouldn't have tried, as the tyres would have been ripped off.

The methods used to prepare these strips varied according to the terrain. On the Angola border it was all sand. Grass was flattened by driving a vehicle up and down. Where thick bush had been cleared the surface had to be graded, debris removed and the surface compacted. Our Beavers were equipped with large low-pressure tyres (high flotation) set at 27 psi, which enabled us to land on fairly soft surfaces. If the sand was too loose landings were risky and take-off distances became an unknown quantity.

New pilots were checked out for bush operations. Godfrey Mulundika was one of those guys who suspected us expats of holding back their progress to front-line certification. Approaching one of the new strips, he was at the controls. When we inspected the strip on a slow fly-by I thought the surface a bit soft, and to be on the safe side I said I would take control for the landing. Godfrey replied quite forcefully that he could manage, and I relented as he was a capable pilot under normal circumstances.

As we crossed the threshold and descended below the level of the trees, the prevailing crosswind disappeared. During the flare for touchdown we drifted left of centre, touching down with one wheel off the runway in the soft sand. The aircraft slewed toward the trees and Mulundika stood on the brakes. The wheels locked and dug in, the tail lifted and the nose lunged down. I cut the engine, expecting a flip over on to our back. The prop tips sprayed sand everywhere. Staring out of the windscreen, we watched the ground approach. Almost vertical and in total silence, we hung in our straps. After what seemed a lifetime we crashed back down on to all three wheels. We sat there trying to regain our composure as the Major charged toward us in his Land Rover.

After a visual check I restarted the engine and checked out parameters, which seemed OK (though the propeller tips were very shiny). I felt a bit uneasy during the next take-off, but there were no further problems.

Martin Simbule was cleared for solo operations and he flew out on detachment unaware that the prevailing wind had changed with the monsoon. Having taken off on a westerly heading for the last six months he carried out another in the same direction, but this time he was going downwind. Doomed to failure, he failed to get airborne and crashed into the teak trees. Fortunately they were the smaller scrub type. The wings and fuselage stopped at the tree line but the heavy radial engine forged on, dragging the cockpit behind. When Martin jerked to a halt he looked over his shoulder to assess the condition of his passengers. They stared back from fifty yards away, still strapped in their seats, unhurt.

The nearest we came to a bit of action occurred on a normally quiet Sunday morning. I got called out to carry out a recce of the Kariba gorge. The Rhodesian Army had crossed the river on to Zambian soil in hot pursuit of terrorists. Our task was to collect photographic evidence of the offending troops. In order to carry this out effectively I would have to catch them by surprise. If I flew along the gorge they would hear us coming, so I planned to approach the gorge at right angles, very slow with flaps down, and then drop over the edge. The speed increase would allow a sharp turn and operation of the sideways-looking camera.

The grid reference I had been given was accurate, and as I popped over the edge of the gorge there right below was an inflatable with soldiers scrambling to get back on board. After obtaining the evidence we ended up flying down the river at very low level. I now realised I was in Rhodesian airspace as the border was marked down the Zambian river bank and not as I expected, the median line. I instinctively checked my six o' clock and there coming over the edge of the gorge in a fast-descending turn was a Cessna (Lynx) Skymaster. These civilian light aircraft had been locally converted into the 0-2, a counterinsurgency version which could carry light machine guns or rockets.

I was concerned, as I knew how reckless that lot could be. I would normally follow the river until I had enough height to cross the side of the gorge. This time I decided to stay low, not being able to outrun the Cessna. I could not see behind, so I held steady until I reckoned he might be close enough to take a shot. I pulled up steeply, lowered the flap and eased the nose over to avoid a stall. In a steep climb at 50 knots, we turned over the edge of the gorge back into Zambian airspace. I never saw the Skymaster again, but back at base the ground crew pointed out a bullet hole in the tailplane. Whether the damage was a result of air-to-air or ground fire I never knew.

As Zambia was not on a war footing, the Rhodesians monitored our movements via radio transmissions. This sometimes suited both sides, as embarrassing encounters could be avoided. The Rhodesians became overconfident, assuming the Zambian military to be totally incompetent.

At Mongu airport curiosity led me to check out a Rhodesian-registered Cessna 172 parked on the apron. In full view on the pilot's seat lay a map marked with, among other things, the locations of our newly-constructed border strips. This might have been for his use as emergency landing sites, but when I mentioned this to our Company Commander he impounded the Cessna and informed HQ. They discovered that the Cessna belonged to the tsetse fly eradication programme. The UN was asked to instruct their contractors to refrain from freelance intelligence gathering.

Apart from funding the tsetse control programme, the UN investigated atrocities committed against civilians. I flew their team to a refugee medical facility near the border. I declined their invitation to accompany them as I had already seen the injuries sustained by torture victims.

Late as always, the UN guys returned to the strip accompanied by local villagers bearing sacks of vegetables. I explained that the Beaver would be overweight if all the produce was loaded. There followed some difficult negotiations, during which it became clear that the villagers considered the produce payment for UN protection. If the team refused the offering it would be an affront.

The sun was setting and tempers were fraying, so after pleas from the senior UN guy I relented and loaded the veggies. The passengers had to accept a cabin stuffed full of produce to avoid centre of gravity problems. I had meanwhile checked out the terrain at the far end of the strip. Although unprepared, it was flat with no obstructions, just a plot of cassava. The take-off was as expected, with slow acceleration. We were still on the ground as we went off the end of the runway, and the corrugated cassava field launched us into the air with some resounding thumps.

I hoped the shake out through the cassava was not lost on the passengers. I resolved to turn down requests for extra baggage but of course "special circumstances" have a habit of re-occurring. Our operations pushed pilots to the limit of their discretion.

118

One of my favourite spots was Sinjembele, where the camp by the river had been located in the shade of teak trees. The site overlooked an expanse of wetland with marsh and rushes, and the location was always cool. The drive from the airport into the village brought to mind *King Solomon's Mines*. Down each side of the track for a quarter of a mile, elephant skulls had been placed about ten yards apart. It was impressive and a little scary, as if the local poo-bah required a sacrifice to be made by all who entered his domain.

Sinjembele was close to the border with the Caprivi Strip and Angola. Colonel Dowling, an expat battalion commander, was carrying out a border recce and I received the message to go to the airstrip and await his arrival for departure to Lusaka. He said this would be late, probably just before nightfall. Knowing how this might turn out, I checked out the strip for an unlit night take-off. It was a bare grass and sand strip used as a base by the tsetse control DC3. Being both long and wide there was plenty of room for the small deviations a night take-off might incur. It was the dry season with considerable smoke haze, so an instrument take-off would be required. This is not too difficult, but previous experience is a must, as the tailwheel, radial engine, and direction indicator all present their own problems. I was fortunate to have covered blind take-offs during training on the Piston Provost, a similar type.

I marked out a line in the sand to enable line-up in the correct direction for take-off and awaited Col. Dowling's arrival. Sure enough he was late and it was night-time. He looked me in the eye and said "Can you do it?" I said yes and he quickly replied "Let's go".

After brake release, you focus on the direction indicator to correct any torque-induced turning. Never look out (there's nothing to see) to avoid disorientation. The take-off was OK but disconcerting.

There came another operational readiness inspection, this time on the Rhodesian and Mozambique borders. The Regimental

Commander Colonel Blunt, who was the spitting image of Captain Mainwaring, arrived late for take-off and the sun was setting.

Getting airborne from Feira airstrip, I knew it would be a close-run thing. The flight duration was twenty minutes. Our final landing for that day was at a farm airstrip unknown to me. Halfway through the flight the sun set and ground features became indiscernible. Passing the point of no return, I maintained calculated heading until time up. The guys on the ground said they could see and hear us. They had positioned a Land Rover, headlights on, at the far end of the runway and a guy with a signal lamp at the threshold. Only ten minutes' fuel remained and I commenced an orbit, searching the gloom for the lights. The guy on the radio said "Turn right… no no, the other way", his voice increasing in pitch and volume.

A few seconds later I spotted their setup and positioned for an approach. Distance to run and height of touchdown were ballpark figures. It was now pitch black with no horizon or lights visible, and I was frightened. We were in the classic "black hole" situation. I asked the guy with the lamp to wave it from side to side at arm's length, which would allow a rough estimate of distance. They told me that the distance between the signal lamp and the Land Rover was about 800 yards.

I flew on down toward the threshold lamp, monitoring the increasing separation between the two lights. As the lamp disappeared under the nose the landing lights picked out the grass surface and we landed with a bounce. My legs were so wobbly that I had a hard time taxiing up to the Land Rover.

We refuelled from drums in the back of the truck. I reckon my remaining endurance was only a minute or two. Colonel Blunt looked sideways at me on the drive to the camp, and he could see I was shaken. He seemed unperturbed. I suspect on his scale of dangerous moments, this might rate pretty low. I don't think he realised the implications of a forced landing at night.

The Zambian combined services held the usual exercises to improve communication and battlefield skills. In simulations of this type, the creation of live action scenarios resulted in an increased accident rate, usually bent Land Rovers. Hopefully the incidents are not lethal and lessons are learned.

There being radio silence for one particular phase, my task was to deliver maps and instructions to a platoon commander isolated in "enemy territory". The documents were placed in a canvas pouch, to which was attached a coloured streamer. This had to be dropped as close as possible to the recipients. The drop zone was at the edge of a clearing, the platoon remaining behind the treeline. If I'd dropped it directly overhead the target the chances were that it would have got hung up in the trees, so I flew in a tight curve across the clearing. To ensure accuracy, a low release was required. With my eyes fixed on the target I allowed my wing tip to occasionally brush the tops of the elephant grass.

Just before I dropped the message. a loud bang rattled the aircraft. Back at base I was inspecting the wing tips when the ground crew brought to my attention a large notch with embedded splinters half way along the leading edge. The damage report quoted "operational hazards".

On the same exercise the following day and on a reconnaissance flight with the Company Commander, we were weaving our way down a twisty gorge checking for "insurgents" when the engine unexpectedly spluttered and quit. We were below the surrounding terrain, with rocks a hundred feet below. The Beaver had a design weakness in that the two main fuel tanks were independent, so the fuel cock had to be switched to the second tank when the first was almost empty. Being preoccupied I had failed to notice the fuel state and the first tank had run dry.

I switched, but the fuel lines were empty. Frantically operating the manual priming pump with my left hand, the engine finally caught about twenty feet above the rocks. I gingerly coaxed the almost stalled Beaver up out of the gorge.

This exercise took place near Mpika in the middle of Zambia's right-hand "dumbbell". The CO of the company we were attached to was a Brit and had been exploring the surroundings. He had made a "find" and took me to see it. After running for a few miles through a eucalyptus plantation, the road fanned out into an open area beside a sizeable lake. Across the other side stood a dilapidated mock-Tudor mansion half hidden by flowering trees. The air was filled with the fragrance of citrus. The Major said the house had long been abandoned.

On the shore to our left stood a large shed, from which a dilapidated wooden jetty extended out into the lake. The shed had remained secure and padlocked, and the glass windows were intact but grimy. Using a torch, we could see that the shed was a combined workshop and store. On shelving behind the worktop were immaculate antique tools, and a row of one-gallon tin-plated cans of Shell oil which carried brass plates inscribed "Imperial Airways". Later research proved this lake to have been an emergency landing site for the Cape to Cairo flying-boat service. In the event of a precautionary landing passengers would have been accommodated at the mansion. In colonial times the estate was run by a British fellow to produce flowers for the perfume trade.

After this interesting interlude, back at ZAF Lusaka more new faces had arrived. The Zambian Government, being aware that they had no control over the RAF, was recruiting more contract officers to replace the RAF exchange personnel. We contract types came under the same ordnance as the Zambians themselves and could be held to account.

The post of Operations Officer was taken over by Tony Gostelow. Back in the UK, years later, I heard that Tony had admitted spying for South Africa. I don't know how true this was, but one of the Zambian pilots who had relatives in Rhodesia returned from leave reporting that he had been informally approached in a bar in downtown Harare. After being plied with beer he was among other things asked for details about me, by name.

Two of the newer contract officers, Barney Shannon and John Colerne, replaced the RAF pilots crewing the presidential Avro 748. During a mutual training session practising engine failures after take-off something went drastically wrong (neither pilot was a QFI). The 748 crashed half a mile from the runway and burst into flames.

In those days it was common practice to allow a certain number of deserving ground crew, office staff, and dependants on training flights. This occasion was no exception, but no one survived. On board were the son of the Admin officer, Squadron Leader Cathcart, the cheerful tea boy, "Coffee", and one or two of the technicians. Janet, now working as OC Flying Wing secretary and pregnant again, had thankfully not been offered a seat. It was a tragic lesson. Since then passengers have been banned from training flights worldwide.

I was nominated to keep one of the bereaved wives company and I stayed with her, morning and afternoon, every day until she could be repatriated. Aged only 25 I had no previous experience in assisting those suffering extreme distress. I did my best and the lady in question coped as well as could be expected, but we often lapsed into painful silence.

Back on the border, fun and games. A new young Company Commander in Kalabo proudly announced that they were going to be self-sufficient as far as meat was concerned. The wildlife was abundant, but these army guys knew nothing about hunting game. Suppertime arrived and I was presented with a stew concocted from tripe and offal. I had no idea whether or not this was normal Zambian fare but the smell was enough to send me off to the small store in town. I ate corned beef, baked beans and fried onions that night. Janet and I had tried elephant and hippo steak, available from the butchers, both of which tasted similar to beef but needed proper cooking. Army stew cooked in a cut-off oil drum didn't cut it.

The next day I was asked to land at their newly-constructed strip. The runway was positioned at 90 degrees to a river bank with the threshold at the water's edge. The strip ran uphill through cleared bush, ending abruptly at a wall of trees. Although of the correct dimensions, landings could only be made uphill and take-offs downhill. Carrying out an inspection from the ground had not been possible and the platoon stationed nearby was running out of supplies. Could I land there please?

I inspected the runway with a slow flypast and remarked that the brush, although well chopped up by the local villagers, had been left lying on the ground. I was worried about the brake lines being severed by trapped branches. "Don't worry, it's only woodchips" the Company Commander assured me.

The final approach was flown low across the river, flaring to land uphill. After touchdown I was shocked by the noise as splinters, twigs and branches thrashed up under the wings and tailplane. The aircraft decelerated rapidly on touchdown and a huge amount of power was needed to get to the end of the runway at the top of the slope. Once there we turned round and lined up for take-off before shutting down. Luckily the brake lines and tyres were undamaged. Checking the runway, I discovered that the mat of chopped wood served to even out the uneven surface of holes and stumps, and there was no option but to take off across the detritus. The take-off was less noisy and acceleration good. Descending the slope, a large rotation was required to avoid flying into the river. Rotations at this speed could not be sharp, otherwise a stall would ensue - it was a fine line to follow. I condemned the airstrip for future use and they eventually found a better site not far away, only 300 metres from the border. Unfortunately it could be seen by Portuguese army patrols.

Returning to Kalabo that evening the company CO came on the radio. Could I do a quick search for his intrepid hunters? They had not yet returned from an expedition out on the savannah. We followed their tracks through the grass and saw them just as the light began to fail. Their Land Rover was on its side, but they waved a thumbs up. The Company Commander said he would send a vehicle the next morning, as they would have taken food and water.

After their rescue the two explained that they had shot the biggest "cow" they could see, a male buffalo. This is probably the most dangerous animal in Africa, mean and aggressive. Once they had shot it they expected their target to drop dead, so they were surprised when the monster, weighing almost a ton, turned in their direction. Spotting the Land Rover, it launched into a charge, hitting the vehicle amidships and rolling it over. Fortunately the buffalo, suffering a headache and gunshot wound, staggered away. The weapon used was the British SLR, which delivers a high velocity round normally guaranteed to stop anything in its tracks. The Company Commander took note, instructing future marksmen to target small game. These, apart from being less dangerous, were less wasteful. Not being able to retrieve the buffalo carcass, the soldiers could only remove a leg or two.

While having a beer in a Kalabo bar I met a friendly South African schoolteacher who I gathered had left SA to escape race prejudice. He was of pale complexion but obviously of mixed race. I asked him how he could stay sane being out in the bush so far from his own. He pulled out his wallet and withdrew some photos to show me. They were of nude young girls, and I was surprised he was prepared to share. When he told me they were pupils from his school I was shocked. He even implied they were available. Without giving names or places, I mentioned the matter to some of my Zambian friends. Their only reaction was to shrug their shoulders and say it happened all the time. I later learnt that village girls in Africa usually lost their innocence at puberty; an uncle, friend of the family, or the village headman would be responsible.

Carrying out an early morning pre-flight check at Kalabo, I discovered that the battery switch had been left on. I blamed the co-pilot - that's what they're for. After shutdown and refuelling the power had been restored to check the fuel quantity, and the switch had been left on.

I asked the Company Commander to provide a length of stout rope and six soldiers. Tying a large knot at the end of the rope, I placed this over the propeller boss behind one blade and then wound the rope back over the knot about four times. Handing the other end to the six soldiers I climbed back into the cockpit and got ready. Instructions were given to the men to run and to let go when the engine fired. I had visions of the khaki clad six flailing round like some giant catherine wheel. Ready to cut the fuel should anything go wrong, I shouted GO! They ran, the engine turned over, we had ignition and start up and the rope was thrown clear.

However we had to fly up to Chavuma with a dead battery; it would not charge because there was no exciter current. At Chavuma we gave the battery to the local police MT section to charge overnight. All was OK on start up the next morning, saving me huge embarrassment.

The Chavuma camp was idyllic. It was sited on a rise, on a shoulder of some rapids on the east bank of the Zambezi. The river spilled over a ten-foot drop into a large basin with a sandy beach on each side. It was too rough for crocs, and I often swam there after work. A mission house stood further back on the top of the hill. The pastor had arrived sixty years before at the tender age of nineteen. He was still around, but I never met him.

One evening I had arrived back too late for a swim. I poured myself a beer and wandered down to the edge of the falls to admire the sunset. From the other side of the Zambezi I could hear lions roaring. It was one of those evenings that captured the quintessential Africa. I was mesmerised.

My reverie was interrupted by a tickling sensation inside the legs of my flying suit, I casually brushed my hand across my legs and they caught fire. I looked down and realised I was standing in a river of army ants.

The flying suit, being a one-piece overall, takes time to remove, and ants do not let go once their fangs are in. I dropped my beer and leapt off the rocky ledge into the water, about ten feet down. When I entered the water the relief was instant as the ants let go. I removed the overalls and threw them ashore, then rubbed off any survivors before I climbed out, finding most of them were still trapped in the flight suit. Now in only underpants I looked up to see Major Wightman and a corporal staring down perplexed, presumably relieved to know that tomorrow's flight would operate as planned.

The Major asked after the health of Flying Officer Nock. Surprised, I told him he was fine and asked why. His answer set my mind racing. Apparently, the previous week, Nock had sent a message to the Major saying he was unable to fly due to sickness. He had not appeared for duty for three consecutive days. Back in Mongu I enquired about his whereabouts and discovered that he had been making regular flights. Getting details from ATC, I learned that he had been delivering supplies on a commercial basis to various hotels around western Zambia. I was stunned. How could he not realise it was only a matter of time before his enterprise reached the ears of the authorities?

On returning to base I gave OC Flying a schedule of Nock's movements and a rundown of his activities. The army had not thought to check with the air force as to the validity of Nock's claim. OC Flying, Squadron Leader Dick Holloway (RAF), told me he would deal with the matter. Nock was given two weeks' continuous duty as Station Duty Officer, but returned to the squadron to resume flying duties. I couldn't believe it and confronted Holloway, saying I did not want Nock on the squadron. Holloway told me I had no choice in the matter. I said OK, but told him he would have to sign Nock's flight authorisations. There was a pause. Suddenly it was a different story. Nock was relieved from flying and reassigned to administrative duties in the Operations Centre. Nock threatened me with physical violence, which I hoped was bluster.

Nock had taken the initiative, but sometimes it was difficult to draw the line when asked to assist deserving causes. One day I was propositioned by a lady schoolteacher who wanted a lift from Lukena to Kalabo. When I apologised, she was annoyed at my refusal. I knew some of our guys helped the locals out, but it was the thin end of the wedge and being the CO I had to set an example – as I said, there are no secrets in Africa. I was unsure where I was to receive her favours, maybe in the cockpit.

Our squadron QFI, Reg Drown, was older than the average contract guys and considered me a young upstart. On one of the periodic checks we flew over to the old City Airstrip to carry out practice emergencies, he asked me to carry out a STOL (Short field take-off), which entailed a very steep climb out at 48 kts. At 200 feet he cut the engine and said "Engine failure, land ahead". I rammed the nose down to maintain flying speed and applied full throttle, the carburettor paused. Drown tried to pull my hands off the lever, but I knew that for a power-off landing the extreme rotation would cause a stall followed by a violent impact. The engine roared into life, and after an initial dive to pick up speed I pulled up and climbed away.

"You've failed, return to base" said Drown. After landing and much argument we both went in to see Holloway. Drown insisted that to pass the check I must successfully carry out the STOL engine failure drill. I countered that there was no recovery from such a situation. Holloway took the easy way out and told Drown to forget it and sign me off.

A few weeks later I was called to the office from home and told that

Drown and a young Pilot Officer (Simutowe) had crashed at Lusaka City airport while training. Drown was in hospital with suspected crushed vertebrae and the student was under observation. The Beaver was a total write-off, having pancaked from a stall. A week later I got the chance to talk to the young co-pilot, and found that Drown had done it again. Simutowe had previously received unfavourable write-ups from Drown, and I suspected personal animosity.

Drown was repatriated for further treatment. At the Board of Enquiry, I was asked to give a character reference for Drown. My attempt to raise the issue of the non-recoverable situation was instantly quashed. "Just give your assessment" was the curt response from Holloway. I said that Drown was "overconfident" and jaws dropped. I quoted my flight check and other incidents when asked for proof. The Zambian officer on the board looked greatly relieved. The RAF Chairman, stony faced, asked me to leave, their conclusions were never released. It seemed Drown had convinced senior officers that Simutowe was to blame.

I needed a break, so it was time for some leave. Janet and I took eight-month old Tia on holiday to Malindi in Kenya. My brother Rob, then flying helicopters from HMS Albion, had recently passed through Mombasa and had left my surfboard with East African Airways. One of my navy students, "Nosh" Skillet, was now an F27 captain and had agreed to bring the board up to Malindi. I met the flight at the airport and waited by the baggage hold. I was surprised when Nosh and surfboard came out of the passenger door. "Where did you store that, Nosh?" "In the aisle, the hostess is a good friend" he said. I raised my eyebrows, but he just winked.

Back in Zambia, on my next visit to Chavuma I was asked to take a new pair of boots for the rather serious Company Commander. On arriving at the strip I was met by a normally ebullient young lieutenant who asked for the boots. He seemed relieved when I handed them over, and told me the CO not only made him bear the cost of replacement but was deducting his detachment pay until they arrived.

I got the story. The rookie lieutenant had recently arrived from training at Sandhurst, where he was taken with the British Army tradition of practical jokes. Hearing of one such prank performed in Malaya, he bought some rubber snakes and brought them back to Zambia. He placed one of these under the CO's camp bed next to the boots. The CO, reaching for them early one morning, had encountered the fake reptile and fled, shouting "snake, snake!". The duty snake guard, with sawn-off shotgun, raced in and let loose with both barrels. The noise was deafening, but the destruction was worse. Boots and camp bed were shredded. When the smoke cleared, the prank was exposed. 100% success you might say, but expensive. The joker still reckoned it was worth the trouble. Never mind the penalties, he received free beer from his mates for some considerable time.

Back at home Janet was dealing with the real thing. In the evenings, the stoep or veranda retained the warmth of the day, attracting snakes. These were not the harmless rat or tree snakes, but spitting cobras. It turned out that the snakes had taken over the giant ant mound and were nesting underground. Pest control later cleared them out but meanwhile we had to deal with the problem. Their effective spitting range was around six feet.

Janet, being a Trinidadian, was not intimidated. Using a long-poled garden hoe she teased the intruders, and when their spit ran out Janet went in for the kill. Four cobras were despatched in this fashion. Puff adders were a different matter, as one bite could be fatal. We encountered one of these when Janet spied our cat Moggy leaping up and down in the cabbage patch. He was baiting the fat brown sausage-shaped snake by dancing around just out of range. When the cat judged the snake to be tired enough, he leapt in and delivered the *coup de grâce*. Cats may be cute and cuddly at home, but they are lethal predators when out and about.

I don't know about snakes, but in the local paper there was a report quoting that in that year the number of Zambians killed by lightning and crocodiles was the same, 76. Now wary of crocs, we nevertheless enjoyed our outings to see the hippos at the Kafue River.

Then Janet gave birth to baby Leon. On seeing him for the first time I blurted out that he looked like Winston Churchill. Janet was a trifle hurt, but had to agree. Fortunately his crinkly features soon smoothed out into a cute baby face.

Over lunchtime beer in the Lusaka Hotel, a Flying Club expat asked if I knew Les Ingham. , I nodded in the affirmative and asked why. "He's flying the Islander for the Zambian Flying Doctor service" he said. We never got to meet as he was based in the Copper Belt (in the north) but we did say hello over the radio. He joined East African Airways after his stint in Zambia.

Finally all RAF personnel at ZAF Lusaka had been replaced, the admin and executive posts taken over by Zambian ex-pilots. Basic training at ZAF Livingstone continued under their supervision for the time being, but eventually the RAF and their Chipmunks were replaced by the Italians and their Aeromacchi SF 260s.

The tenders went out for an intermediate light transport. This was narrowed down to the Shorts Skyvan and the Dornier 28D Skyservant. I reckoned the Skyvan a far more suitable aircraft, but Dornier offered the right people the right incentives and they got the contract. The aircraft arrived with the training team, who immediately set up shop in one of the huge hangars. The Zambian pilots were disappointed, as they had anticipated training at Oberpfaffenhofen with expenses and much fun in Münich. Never mind, the Germans brought a keg of Löwenbräu in each Dornier. There was much silliness in the officers' mess, but Münich would have been better.

Although not cleared for aerobatics, Johannes Mouwens, my

instructor, demonstrated how the Do28 could do a pretty neat loop, best not done with passengers. The Dornier had a finely-tuned engine, the IGSO 540, with a gearbox-driven supercharger. Great if you want to climb to 19,000 feet, which it could, but not the best machine for bush work. With the rough handling sometimes required, the supercharger drive would shear, a real pain. Another drawback turned out to be the tyre pressure. The Beaver came with high flotation tyres as standard (27 psi), but the Dornier tyre pressure was more than twice that. When we started to operate them in the bush, the simple act of braking tore out grass by the roots, so this left the soft Kalahari sand like a ploughed field. The strips became unusable if used regularly. In soft sand, take-offs and landings are unpredictable and dangerous.

A minor hazard pointed out during the conversion course was that failure to positively check that the pilot's seat is locked for take-off might result in the seat sliding back on application of power. Being a tailwheel aircraft, the cockpit and cabin floor sloped down toward the rear at an angle of approximately ten degrees, hauling the seat back up against the slope and acceleration was not possible. This might not be serious in a two crew situation, but with a single pilot, if you couldn't reach the controls at full power... Murphy's Law rules.

Joe Chisala, being a bright but laid-back sort of chap, was not as thorough with his checks as he should have been. Flying as my co-pilot, his casual approach to pre-flight preparations was highlighted in dramatic fashion. The Dornier was configured for freight, no seats in the cabin, no payload, Joe's take-off. Normal procedure for STOL piston-engined aircraft was to apply full power before brake release (in order to confirm engine parameters). Being very light, the aircraft shot forward, and Joe's seat shot back, left the tracks and ended up against the rear bulkhead. Joe suffered bruises and a strained neck. It took him a while to live that down. Imagine that single pilot!

When the Tan-Zam railway project was inaugurated we flew Presidents Kaunda and Nyerere and the Chinese foreign minister to the junction town of Kapiri-Mposhi. As the airport was too short for regular aircraft, they had to use the Dornier. Although the new aircraft was new and shiny, they were not impressed by the cramped utility seating.

The Dornier, not being as robust as the Beaver, suffered accordingly. During a pre-flight inspection at Nsumbu game lodge (Northern Zambia), I discovered damage to the wingtip faring and navigation light. I complained to the park warden, who explained that an elephant had used the wingtip as a back-scratcher.

The ZAF was growing fast. Aeromacchi MB326Bs and a competitor, the Soko Galeb, were delivered. Augusta Bell Hueys were delivered to Lusaka. Gilbert and Martin managed to crash one of these in a swamp down by the Kafue River. I heard they were trying to prod a hippo with the skids when it reared up and flipped them over.

The Portuguese and South Africans assumed that Zambia was secretly supporting guerrilla activity. I wasn't aware that any of the company commanders were turning a blind eye, but the colonials sure thought so and took drastic action.

I got an urgent call to collect evidence that would be presented to the UN. One of our Land Rovers had been blown up at Shangombo on the Angolan border and investigations uncovered anti-tank mines along some of the border roads. I landed at Shangombo strip and the CO was there holding an example of this ordnance. It was of Chinese origin and would have been originally laid in Angola by UNITA.

I asked the CO where this incident had occurred and he pointed to a Land Rover tyre hanging in the tree nearby. I caught my breath. "Did you check the strip?" I asked him. He shook his head. I then told him that we would return to Lusaka the next day and meanwhile his guys should check the strip thoroughly.

The next morning the CO informed us that they had indeed found three more mines down the centre of the strip. The South Africans must have been responsible, as only they had the nerve.

The government required the mine in Lagos, where it would be shown as evidence. We were to deliver it ASAP. The CO assured me it had been defused. I smiled and added that he was on the same flight. We did not have decent cargo nets in the hold, so I told the CO that one of his men must hold the mine in his lap, just in case.

Later I was told that back at the barracks the mine had been dropped, killing the bearer and taking out the corner of a barrack block.

Approaching the end of my contract and contemplating my future, I received a phone call from a chap with a pronounced South African accent. He calmly informed me that I would be putting the safety of me and my family at risk if I renewed for another term. I had to assume this threat credible, as speculation surrounding the deaths of two Brits on contract to the Zambian government was rife. They had been mysteriously killed in a road accident, with no other vehicle involved.

It didn't help that an RN Buccaneer pilot, Fred Secker, had joined the South African Air Force. He and some others went along with the aircraft that UK sold to the SAAF. Fred had married Maggie, Janet's best friend from her nursing days. Janet and Maggie were corresponding, and their mail always arrived opened and re-sealed.

Now with two kids, and bearing in mind the threatening phone call, I needed to plan my next career move. I had started a correspondence course to prepare for examinations for the Airline Transport Pilot's Licence. It was impossible, too many distractions, I would have to go back to school. Being totally out of the civilian aviation picture I booked the CPL course as a primer, to be followed by the ATPL course and the Instrument Rating course at CSE Kidlington, Oxford. This belts-and-braces strategy would swallow most of my end of contract gratuity but should do the job.

Chapter Eleven

UK AND UGANDA

January 1971 – September 1972

We arrived back in UK in January, to find it freezing. Swanston House was the ideal family home, with plenty of room. Mum of course was delighted to meet Tia and Leon. I started my course with CSE in Kidlington, staying at a B&B but coming home at weekends. It was boring but it kept me out of the Greyhound pub in Whitchurch.

My youngest brother Roger, now in between jobs and a real tearaway, also lived at home, and he introduced us to his social scene. Every weekend it started Saturday lunchtime at the Thames riverside pub, the Swan, and carried on non-stop until the Sunday "hair of the dog" lunchtime session. Rich Cole, the exuberant "roadie" for Led Zeppelin, was one of the bunch. We never met any of the band, but Rich threw some outrageous parties at his converted barn in Tilehurst.

The friends we made in Pangbourne were a totally different breed from those we had socialised with in the military; it was like entering *Alice in Wonderland*. Strange people with even stranger habits frequented our weekend world. Mum was only too pleased to look after the kids, which allowed us the freedom to enjoy ourselves to the full. During the week I focused on my studies at Oxford while Janet had fun with Tia, Leon and new toys at Swanston House.

Friday nights remained conventional. The Greyhound, just a few yards down the road, was the haunt of a more mature crowd. That's not to say they were any less fun loving, but they tended to finish their drinking in situ rather than relocating to party. The regulars came from across the professional spectrum and included a chap from the Foreign Office and a charming but ageing couple who were seriously hard-drinking writers, one from The Times, the other from the BBC . We initiated a regular darts match, Flexmans versus the Yarrow family from across the road. We even had a trophy.

I passed the CPL exam and obtained my Instrument Rating. Feeling more confident, I commenced the ATPL course. It was now summer, so I opted to drive to Kidlington and back every day. Under pressure from the crowd at the Swan I bought a complete new wardrobe, kitting out with all the latest trendy gear. Looking more like a member of Sergeant Pepper's Lonely Hearts Club Band than a professional pilot, my outfits drew disapproving looks from the blazer-and-flannel brigade.

The weekend parties were exhausting, and if nobody was hosting we drove to Skinners, a disco on the Maidenhead-Henley road. The breath test had not yet come into force; it was a miracle we all survived.

At a lunchtime session at the Black Swan we received a verbal invitation to a barbecue thrown by the Goring and Streatly Rugby Club. The barbecue was held at the Yacht Club premises on the banks of the Thames. That evening Rich Cole led our motley crowd up to the gate, where we were asked to show our invitation cards. Rich explained that we had been personally invited that lunchtime. When names were mentioned we were allowed entry. The evening progressed with the rugby crowd way ahead on beer consumption - they had a reputation to maintain.

There had always been a cultural divide between the music freaks and the macho crowd. When the latter observed that their girls favoured our company, the hosts changed their minds and asked us to leave. They nominated a suitably belligerent monster to confront

Rich. Rich knew that refusal to leave would result in a less than stylish departure and politely asked if he could first find his dog. The mutt was by now investigating the river bank. The bully sneered "What dog?" and Rich raised his arm to show a chain link dog leash wrapped around his fist. This was misinterpreted, Rich's leather jacket was grabbed by the lapels and he was hoisted off the ground. I pushed my way between the two, trying to explain and calm things down. Rich was dropped as the "heavy" saw an easier target. He picked me up and threw me across the tables. Being of the folding variety they collapsed, cushioning my fall. Hollywood couldn't have staged it any better.

The scattering of tables and chairs mixed with the crash of breaking glass got immediate attention. Macho man looked very proud of himself, until Janet beaned him with a full wine bottle. Pole-axed, the "hero" fell to the ground, bleeding from a scalp wound. His friends escorted him to the toilet to clean him up. When asked what happened he replied, "You won't believe it but a little girl bashed me with a wine bottle".

Our gang melted away in the confusion and drove off on a high to reconvene at a small cottage in the middle of nowhere. This place always welcomed partygoers no matter what time of day, as the tenants were hopeless dopers. The police showed up around 2.30 am. They were polite and cheerful, and after noting who was present they said "Take it easy" and went on their way.

Rich Cole took us to the Reading Festival, prime seats, wow! We saw Wishbone Ash, Genesis, Ralph McTell, Lindisfarne and for light relief, Sha Na Na. The back stage scene was a revelation, as when not performing these guys seemed just like you and me. I was overawed by the star count, but when Rich told them I flew for a living they all wanted to hear flying stories, so that's all we talked about. It's a boy thing I suppose.

One of the Swan crowd, Bob Cooper, threw a champagne dinner

for his girlfriend's birthday. Bob had booked the whole of a Greek restaurant in Reading for privacy. One of our girls had been known to do impromptu striptease, and by the time dessert was served calls for her to perform overcame normal conversation. The erstwhile stripper was having none of it, as if she was going to strip it had to be on her initiative and not to order.

Sitting opposite me, she pointed in my direction and called "strip!" The idea caught on - in those days a male stripper was a novelty. There was no way out, so I wove my way out on to the dance floor as the band struck up with the appropriate music. Finally down to my briefs, I whipped them off and turned away from my friends and towards the band. One of the musicians had a beatific smile and blew me a kiss.

Bob Cooper was a local Reading lad who made his fortune leasing juke boxes. He now sells medical equipment, lives and works in the Seychelles and likes to be known by his full name, Robert Gaines-Cooper.

For old time's sake I took Janet to see my original home town, Wokingham. When we entered the Rose, one of the ancient pubs in the market place, the only two people at the bar stared at us and exclaimed "I know you". They then looked at each other in surprise. It turned out they both knew me, but for wildly different reasons. The guy I had met on one occasion only. He had been a visiting RAF officer from RAF Kinloss attending a function at the mess at RNAS Lossiemouth. We had literally bumped into each other during the rough and tumble of after-dinner games. He was now engaged to the girl, who was the daughter of the bursar at my old school, RHS Holbrook. They were passing through and had stopped for lunch. Calculate those odds!

Surprisingly, I passed the ATPL exams at the first attempt (we were allowed to use slide-rules but not calculators) and it felt good to hold the coveted licence in my hand. The end of that summer and the early autumn were delightful. Exams over, we behaved as families should, showing the kids around the English countryside. Children's zoos and bird parks seemed pretty tame after the big game in Zambia, but it was fun.

I applied for some of the more interesting vacancies. The only position immediately available was in the Uganda Police Air Wing. The advertisement was placed by the Overseas Development Administration. I applied, and after the usual medicals and interview received a ticket to Entebbe. The ODA explained that I should get settled in before the family joined me. Those were the rules - no exceptions.

Now having a future in sight, I splashed my remaining cash on a hi-fi system recommended by Rich Cole, A Quad 30/303 amplifier, Tannoy Lancaster speakers and a Goldring Lenco turntable. Mum thought I was insane, but Janet was won over by the stunning sound. The system was shipped insured, but I was worried.

Clearing customs at Entebbe, the officer on duty would not release my bags until I had signed a declaration that nothing was missing. The flight had been overnight, I was tired and now this unusual request raised my suspicions. A brief check assured me that the important items were present so I signed. Checking the arrival hall meet-and-greet crowd I was not surprised that my name did not feature, and got a taxi to the Lake Victoria Hotel. Unpacking in my room I realised that my new tropical suit was missing. The bulk shipment would be delivered to my door, thank god.

I hadn't been briefed about the lake flies, which looked like small mosquitoes. The walls of my room, although air-conditioned, were covered with these tiny pests. Most were dead in spider webs, but I was concerned about what night-time might bring. The next morning I was surprised not to have been bitten. At breakfast I noticed that the UV bug-busters around the terrace had mounds of these insects dead underneath.

That afternoon I was directed to look out over the lake at plumes of "smoke" rising out of the water. They were newly-hatched lake flies, which were heading in to shore. When this happened, windows were closed and everyone ran for cover. If you were caught in the open, the best thing was to cover your head with a towel or your shirt. If this was not an option then it was best to cover your mouth and nose with a handkerchief and close your eyes.

After breakfast and a nap I phoned the Police Air Wing. Sure enough I got the response, "Oh… you're here!" Transport was sent, and after a ten-minute drive, crossing the equator, I arrived at the hangar. I was impressed by the number of aircraft the Air Wing operated. A Caribou, a Twin Otter and a Turbo Beaver were complemented by five helicopters, two Bell 212s, two Westland Scouts and a Bell 206.

The boss, Superintendent Bill Hutchings, greeted me formally as I entered his office. His questioning gaze bored into me as he tried to figure me out. He then bluntly asked "Why on earth did you decide to come to Uganda?"

I tried to explain, but it appeared that he considered me a threat. He could not come to terms with the fact that an experienced pilot with a new ALTP had chosen to end up in what he considered a dead end. After questioning me in depth regarding previous experience, I could see he would treat me with caution. He needn't have worried, for I have never envied the reins of power. I preferred to enjoy the flying without the burden of management.

I was introduced to the other pilots. White-haired John Dodgson, the fixed wing QFI, was cynical with a dry sense of humour. The helicopter QFI, Robin Vaughan-Johnson, was warm-hearted, refined and a gentleman of the old school. Robin differed from my experience of Australians, not having the blunt, up-front mannerisms one normally expects of those from Oz. The other Beaver pilot was a very old guy called Fenn whom I rarely saw, and there was a young Ugandan pilot who flew the 206. The engineer in charge had been a chief technician on 803, my old navy squadron.

The Air Wing flew some security patrols and assisted the game parks with anti-poaching surveillance but most of the flights were for the benefit of government ministers. Occasionally Idi Amin was flown on visits to his home town of Arua in northern Uganda.

Life at the hotel had been fun as it was the international social centre for Entebbe. 16mm movies were shown on Sunday evenings. The Hutchings, the Fenns and some other Brits favoured the Entebbe Club, which had retained its colonial style and drinking habits. Status ruled. A local alcoholic drinks producer, Waragi, made substitutes for brandy, gin, and rum, I'm not sure about whiskey. These beverages were cheap and consumed with gusto, but did weird things to your insides. Club and hotel toilet facilities were best avoided on Saturday and Sunday mornings.

The British Caledonian flight crews stayed overnight at the "Lake Vic". Those evenings could be quite lively, although most of the action took place at room parties. I occasionally had breakfast with them on the terrace, but their captains could be extremely protective of the girls and openly discouraged them from talking to outsiders. I suspect this was for personal reasons rather than for the welfare of the crew.

I recount the following as evidence. At about 1 am I was awoken by a soft but persistent tapping on the door of my room. As I was groggily shaking sleep away, I thought maybe one of the stewardesses had taken a fancy to me. But no, a quiet but gruff "I know you're in there sweetie" startled me. For a moment I was dumbstruck, until I realised he had the wrong room. I opened the door. There stood the porky, white haired, B-Cal captain, unsteadily eyeing me up. After a momentary look of rage came the realisation that he was at the wrong door. He quickly lowered his head, mumbled an apology and shuffled off.

My opinion of B-Cal captains went down a couple of notches. I went for breakfast early and sat at the B-Cal table. I knew the girls would be there and related our little night-time episode. The senior girl thanked me and said she would write a report, as this guy persistently harassed the girls. The captain had breakfast in his room.

The local flying licence was issued by the East African Civil Aviation Authority in Nairobi. John Dodgson and I flew down in the Twin Otter with the additional purpose of picking up dog food for the police kennels. I took the Type Rating and Air Law exams the next day. The flight back to Entebbe was made in fine weather across the incredible scenery of the savannah and the Great Rift Valley - awesome.

John Dodgson completed my type rating on the Beaver. The PT6 engine transformed the Beaver, which now had extraordinary performance for a nine-seat (including crew) single-engine aircraft. Empty, it could climb at 7000 feet a minute, and with its high idle setting and reverse thrust it could, when empty, stop within forty yards of touchdown - take into account the fact that Entebbe was at 3800 feet above sea level, giving reduced engine performance. Short landings were assisted by the selection of the high idle setting, which maintained high engine rpm when the power lever was pulled from forward into reverse. Full stopping power was then instantly available.

The Twin Otter conversion followed and the final proficiency test or "base check" was carried out at night and at maximum weight. John had arranged for all the passenger seats to be occupied by burly airport firemen. Remembering the ZAF disaster, I reminded him that this was a training flight. He replied "OK, find eighteen sandbags and load them!"

It was obvious that these firemen exceeded standard passenger weights used for load calculations, so I thought John was a bit mean for throwing that at me. Just at rotation (The moment of lift-off) John chopped an engine. Climb rate after that was barely 100 feet a minute, but we had Lake Victoria ahead of us, no obstructions until we reached Tanzania, about 200 miles away.

We were allocated a house in the government residential area. It was in a delightful setting, the garden being fully mature with a full complement of tropical fruit trees. Ibis strutted about the lawn and monkeys ate the fruit. The house itself was desperately in need of renovation but the balmy climate called for no heating or air-conditioning.

Amazingly, there was a telephone installed. Phones were rare in Entebbe at that time and lines were difficult to acquire. It was not connected, so back at the office I asked the secretary to arrange this with Telecom. I was impressed to be told that a technician would call the next day. But when he arrived he took the handset and disappeared, I never got a line.

Hutchings briefed me on the security situation, which seemed pretty bad. Armed gangs from the Congo were operating around Kampala and Entebbe. They specialised in vehicle thefts, so I bought a second-hand modified Volvo. This vehicle not only had fortified suspension but a dual fuel supply. The normal system could be bypassed, allowing an electric pump to operate a parallel fuel line.

The gangs would lie in wait outside your front gate, T-junctions, or even at traffic lights downtown. Pointing a gun at the driver, they would instruct him to get out, leaving the keys in the ignition and the engine running. In the Volvo the electric pump could be turned off by a small switch under the driver's seat, next to the handbrake. This allowed the carjackers to drive out of range before the engine died.

My neighbour, not having this feature in his car, had his Peugeot 504 (an African favourite) taken at his front gate. By some miracle he was able to telephone the police checkpoint on the causeway, the only road out of Entebbe. Fifteen minutes later he received a phone call from the police to say "We have your Peugeot". I was not at home when he got a lift to collect his car. At the checkpoint he found his car semi-submerged in Lake Victoria, riddled with bullet holes and full of dead Congolese.

Throwing the keys away was the wrong move. Some nuns driving their newly donated minibus were caught at the lights in Kampala. They threw the keys into the storm drain and were shot dead.

As a police officer with a warrant card, I was asked if I wanted to carry a gun. I turned down the offer, as the only thing the robbers prized more than vehicles were small arms. If you had a gun, they shot first.

After some repairs the bungalow seemed habitable. Janet was sent tickets and arrived on an ancient 707 belonging to some second-rate charter outfit (trust HMG). Janet liked the house and the kids loved the climate and were excited at the thought they could swim every day.

Janet was entranced by the size of the fruit and vegetables. The climate was perfect, there was no dry season and we had a shower every afternoon to cool the day. At 4000 feet it was never too hot or too cold. Trees flowered, fruited and shed leaves with wild abandon, even having one branch out of sync with another. At the market a huge basket of fruit and vegetables would cost only ten shillings (about $1). At the meat market a good quality whole filet of beef could be bought for the same. It was fresh if you arrived on time and could stand the noise of the cow being killed and butchered on the other side of the wall.

Our houseboy, who lived in the quarters at the house, turned out to be a real pain, so he was replaced by a girl from Fort Portal. Her name was Praxida, she was married and lived with her customs-officer husband in government accommodation. These girls from the Ruwenzori were known for their beauty, and she was no exception.

Praxida noted my fondness for drinking tea and suggested we try the Ugandan variety. We agreed, and the next day I enjoyed a few cups of this strangely aromatic tea. Not long after while listening to the BBC world news I got a fit of the giggles. Janet, who was preparing the dinner, came into the lounge to find out what had caused this rare event. We realised that the tea was neat marijuana. Praxida revealed that it was available in the market at a shilling for a polythene bag the size of a football! She also pointed out that there was plenty growing in the garden, although this was of poor quality due to the shade.

Back at the hangar, everyone trooped outside to witness the arrival of the Otter, returning with a victim of communal violence. After parking, the door opened and the patient was assisted down the steps. He had a hatchet buried in his skull. He walked slowly but steadily to the waiting ambulance, not wanting to disturb the implant in any way. The victim, a villager from the Karamoja district in north eastern Uganda, had been defending his cattle from Karamojong rustlers. This tribe believed all cattle were theirs by divine right. Not recognising national boundaries, they roamed between Uganda and Kenya avoiding the security forces. The Karamojong have always been a problem to peace and stability.

Part of the Police Air Wing duties was to support the anti-poaching effort in the north east. I have not been able to verify the facts of the case, but I was reliably told the following story. After a previous anti-poaching purge a few years before, the game warden persuaded the police wing guys to stay for a drink or two as he missed expat social life. The pilots had brought their wives and the occasion was an enjoyable one. Unfortunately the choppers, two Westland Scouts, were needed for tasks the next day and the decision was made to fly back that night. For a lark, each pilot flew back with the other's wife for company. One chopper crashed on the way back to Entebbe. I was never told the outcome of the enquiry, and Bill remaining tight-lipped on the matter.

Meanwhile my line training on the Otter continued. John briefed me regarding use of the tail strut when loading passengers. Picture this aeroplane; the nose is supported by the nosewheel, the main wheels support the wings and engines, the tail is unsupported. The entrance to the cabin is at the rear, and passengers are instructed to climb the steps one at a time and immediately move to a seat at the front of the cabin. Failure to comply may result in the Otter tipping back on to the strut, or if not fitted, its rear end.

This had happened before my arrival when President Idi Amin and half of his cabinet ignored John's instructions (or chose not to listen to them). The co-pilot was in the cockpit calling for start but had failed to position the strut. John had met the VIPs in the terminal and was escorting them across the apron. Following third-world tradition the ministers arrived first, VIP last. Several corpulent members of the cabinet were on the steps or bunched in the doorway wondering where to sit. Bang, the Otter suddenly tipped back on its tail, throwing all in a heap. They were not amused.

Flying hours were limited, which allowed us an active social life. For sports recreation I joined the boat club; John had sold me his Dory with outboard motor and water ski kit.

Other friends included a couple of teachers, Paul McCoy and his girl friend Carol, who were also employed under the umbrella of the ODA. Paul was a competitive swimmer and taught our kids to swim. Paul and Carol occasionally accompanied us for leisurely picnics out on the islands. On one of the trips bad weather was building up and we set off back to Entebbe, but unfortunately it overtook us. The heavy chop made for slow progress and high fuel consumption. The fuel ran out as it was getting dark, but we were only two hundred metres from the shore and used the standby paddle. The yacht club members saw us waving for help, but they just laughed. It was exhausting and slow progress in the rough water. The club members watched our slow progress, grinning over their gin and tonics. Bastards.

The hi-fi arrived in good working order. Paul and Carol were great lovers of contemporary rock and came over with friends for impromptu parties. One of the gang was a Congolese saxophone player who always had a stash of pot with him. His weed was powerful stuff and after suffering some quite extraordinary hallucinations we decided to lay off completely. The following morning, still high, I wandered into the kitchen to make tea. Filling the kettle and gazing out of the window, I realised I was staring at a large and fierce-looking grey bird perched on the pole supporting the washing line. It stared back with beady eyes set in a lemon yellow face. I almost freaked out. It turned out to be an African harrier hawk, not a drug-induced fantasy.

When International Aeradio were contracted to operate air traffic services at Entebbe we became friends with one of the controllers, an ex RN observer, now married. One evening when we had been invited round for dinner we got lost in the dark and inadvertently drove through the open gates into Idi's palace grounds. After about a hundred yards we were surrounded by soldiers, all aiming their weapons at the Volvo. The gates had shut behind.

I tried to wind down the window, but the soldiers started screaming "Stop, stop!" They signalled for us to remain still and wait. After five nerve-wracking minutes an English speaking officer arrived, and after questioning our intentions he said he would guide us to the address we supplied. He stopped his Land Rover outside the house, signalled for us to wait, then went to the door and asked our hosts one or two questions. Now satisfied, he beckoned us over. We gave our thanks. "My pleasure" he replied, and disappeared. The pre-dinner drinks went down pretty quick.

Idi was justifiably paranoid and after landing he often climbed into a nondescript vehicle rather than his Rolls-Royce. On one occasion he swapped places with an army colonel he no longer trusted. Sure enough that officer was shot during an ambush. This may have been a setup or maybe not. I heard there were several attempts on Idi's life that year.

Late one night John Dodgson and I were flying Idi back to Entebbe from his home in Arua. We noticed a large trim change, and sure enough he loomed into the cockpit. Being tall, he had to duck, and as he did so his head knocked off both generator switches on the overhead panel. John Dodgson and I both jumped when the master warning sounded and red warning lights flashed. Seeing our consternation and ignoring the alarms, Idi came to his own conclusions. "Where are you taking me?" he demanded. After John calmly stated "Entebbe" he told us that we must turn 40° to the right. When told that this direction would take us to the Congo he said "I know my country, go that way". Outside was totally black, there were no lights on the ground, but we turned. Arguing with Idi could be fatal. The radios, most of the instrumentation and all the illumination faded as the battery drained. We had not dared to ask Idi to back off.

Finally he returned to the cabin and power was reinstated. We cautiously used the rudder against ailerons to slide the aircraft back on course and regain our original track. After landing he came back to the cockpit. "I told you" were his few terse words. Idi had thought we were delivering him to his arch enemy Milton Obote in Tanzania, in which case his change of direction would have been correct. We wondered if he would take any action but events of greater significance kept him occupied.

Idi promoted the commander at Gulu and asked us to fly his tailor to the airbase in order to fit the guy with a new uniform. After landing I taxied to the apron in front of the air force hangar. There being no one to meet us, I went into the hangar in search of a phone. The hangar was full of Mig 15s and 17s, some covered with dust, one or two appearing ready to fly. Finding nobody to ask, I located a phone and told the tailor to ask for the duty officer. Transport arrived, and we drove on to the base.

The new CO was in his office next to the operations room and the tailor set about his business. One of the deputies asked if I would like refreshments. Expecting to be sent to the officers' mess, I was surprised when he said we would eat together in the ops room, but first he would show me around. He was proud of all his new communications equipment. I got the guided tour, including a demonstration of the SSB HF link direct to Idi's bunker in KL. He wanted me (and thereby the UK) to know they were ready for all comers. Taking notes was out of the question. I tried to memorise the frequencies on the green LED panel, but failed. The lunch was almost inedible. The meat, being cooked for the African palate, was tough as old boots.

When I told Hutchings, he was shocked that I had parked on the Air Force apron, thinking it dangerous. Being ex-military myself it had seemed the obvious thing to do. I then realised that Hutchings and I operated on different wavelengths.

Idi had arranged a conference, which was really more of a mutual admiration session for two murderous dictators. This took place at Murchison Falls Game Lodge, and the guest was the diminutive president of the Central African Republic, Colonel Jean-Bedel Bokassa. We flew them up on the Otter. After landing at the Falls airstrip we taxied to where the guard of honour was waiting and lowered the door, which also served as the steps. Wearing five-inch heels and topped with a ridiculously high peaked hat, Bokassa descended toward the waiting reception committee. Medal upon medal formed a sort of chain mail apron that reached to his waist. Monty Python couldn't hold a candle to this clown.

As he reached the bottom of the steps he turned his back on the guard, now presenting arms, and peed toward the aircraft. There's a photograph out there somewhere, taken by the Game Lodge manager, with me at the top of the steps looking on with disbelief.

After Murchison the VIPs requested a flight across to Paraa (it took many hours by launch). I had been told that the grass strip at Paraa was OK when checked six months previously and decided to give it a try. If the strip was not up to it, we would have to go back. Idi and Jean-Bedel accepted the plan. When we arrived I did a low flyby, to find that it did look a trifle overgrown, but with my previous bush experience and huge respect for De Havilland of Canada, I thought it worth a shot.

On short finals I had second thoughts, as the bushes and vegetation appeared higher than expected. There was however a meandering set of wheel tracks roughly up the centre, so I continued. On landing I had to do a sort of slalom, which must have been very uncomfortable for the passengers, especially those at the back. Disembarking, their relief at arriving at their destination outweighed any other consideration. They actually said thank you. I left them there and returned to Entebbe.

Amin finally "lost it". In order to gain popular support he devised a new economic plan which included the expulsion of Ugandan Indians. Some say he had a fit of pique when he was denied the daughter of a prominent Indian cotton merchant. Planning to take the girl as another wife, he was outmanoeuvred when the family secretly left the country. The outcome of his plan, although popular with indigenous Ugandans, was the destruction of the economy.

The exodus was painful to watch. Hoping to take most of their belongings, the deportees packed their possessions in huge bundles. These soon filled the cargo sheds and the remainder was stored out in the open. When there was no more storage space available at the airport the overflow was stacked in the botanical gardens. Most of this cargo was never shipped, but perished in the sun and rain before finally being disposed of.

Road blocks were set up to ensure no Indians remained. Life became difficult for us, as Janet, being of Asian complexion, was treated as suspect. Several times the soldiers poked their guns through the car window while they questioned us. It was upsetting to hear Leon, in the back seat, asking if we were to be shot. My police warrant card saved us on most occasions.

As Amin had often insulted the British he became concerned about retribution. This fear spread to Ugandans in general, and we were often asked at the roadblocks how strong the British army was. I always replied that the British troops were "very fierce".

Our sole Ugandan pilot disappeared. He was known to dislike Idi's régime, being of a different tribe. Bodies started to appear in the lake. I had used the dory for water skiing, but it now became a distressing experience out on the water. The crocodiles swarmed. The town swimming pool, on a low bluff by the lakeside was now a place to be avoided. Headless bodies could be seen while you were admiring the normally idyllic view. Distracting kids became a futile task. They caught on quick, and would scream and shout with glee at any new discovery. For the sensitive, it was traumatic.

Amin's security goons inhabited the beer halls and bars. If they heard loose talk demeaning Idi, those responsible were shot within minutes of leaving and were left by the roadside as a lesson to others.

Because of the shortage of foreign exchange, the Air Wing ran out of spares for the aircraft. Finally, when Idi called for another flight to Arua, he was told that there were no aircraft available. Shortly after we were informed we were to be deported, Hutchings was told that Idi suspected us of sabotage. It was quite a relief to know we were going home.

Information seeped down from police HQ in Kampala of atrocities committed during the extermination of dissidents. To save on ammunition, the practice was to line up the victims handing a machete to the second in line. He would kill the man in front before handing the weapon back to the guy behind, and so on, until completion. Failure to comply would result in an even more gruesome fate.

It was definitely time to go. The British High Commission intervened on our behalf, insisting we were given six days' notice. This was good news as it allowed me time to sell the boat and car. Expats were not buying, as they were all nervous about what the future held.

The Volvo I sold to a customs officer for a ridiculously low figure, but the boat I managed to sell to the Wildlife and Fisheries Department. I got the "as new" price, as they had no hard currency and were desperate for replacements.

We had to be out of the country by midnight on the given date. The flight was due to depart at 11 pm and we were all checked in when the public address announced that the flight was delayed. With midnight approaching, the armed escort ushered us through immigration to wait in the departure lounge. It was now past midnight and we were wondering if we would end up camping at the airport. It was a great relief when we heard the Tannoy announce the arrival of the B-Cal VC10. Meanwhile the guards, stony faced, monitored our every move. When Tia needed to go for a pee (the restroom was outside the departure lounge), she and Janet headed in that direction, but a guard blocked the way saying "No".

I had Leon to look after and was filling in forms when I observed the confrontation from across the hall. Janet, in her usual no-nonsense style, informed the guard that no way was she going to pee on the floor and marched through into the toilets with Tia. The guard tried to follow, but she slammed the door in his face. Putting on a brave face, the guard smartly turned round and stood guard, while other passengers chuckled nervously. It felt great to finally get airborne for the UK.

Me and my sister Liz (in front of the air raid shelter), 1944 I think

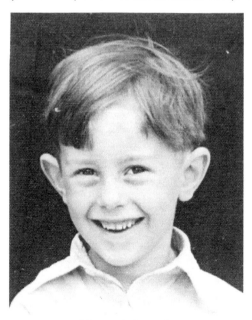

Me aged about five

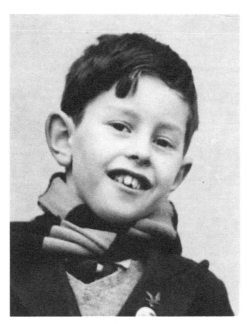

Me and those teeth

The main entrance to the Royal Hospital School, Holbrook

The RHS dining hall, classroom block and gymnasium,
taken from the St Vincent dayroom

Me and Rob Outred after Sunday "Divisions"on the
RHS parade ground (I'm on the right)

The two aircraft that sparked my schoolboy imagination

The ad that kick-started my career in aviation

H.M.S. THUNDERER

"VENGEANCE" 89(P) AND 47(O) TERM AIR CADETS - JOINED 16th OCTOBER, 1959

The Air Cadets, HMS Thunderer 1959

Cadet Flexman dressed for dinner. HMS Thunderer, Plymouth October 1959

Two "Hunting Percival Provost" aircraft,
Linton-on-Ouse, 1969-70

Provost T1 ab initio trainer

A Seahawk FGA6

A French Etendard using the ground-based catapult at RAE Bedford

736 Squadron Scimitar

Early photo of the squadron aircraft being cleaned.
Note their size (and boring tail logo)

On the flight deck of HMS Hermes (R12)

A Scimitar ready for launch

For launch the Scimitar rests on main wheels and tail skid

Just after launch - note the wire strop falling away

I took this picture using the aircraft's F94 photo- recce camera

The flight deck edge catwalk saved this Scimitar from
the sea The rookie pilot never flew again.

This still from cine footage shows a Scimitar
which applied power too late after bolting

Getting ready for the next sortie. Note the "Palouste" external HP air starter

Officers of 803 squadron on the HMS Hermes quarterdeck.
Front row - Ben Bosworth Chris Wilson, myself and John Middleton

Captain O'Brien & Simon Creasy cutting the cake for the
1000th deck landing of the commission

Missing the arrestor wires is termed a "bolter"

Simon Creasy, John Middleton and myself on the
"goofers" platform. HMS Hermes 1962

Simon Creasy had to take the barrier when
the hook damper (shock absorber) failed

HMS Hermes at speed 1963

The huge Forrestal class carrier

Compare our deck to the vast acreage of USS Ranger

The 803 squadron CO Freddie Mills (giving me the evil eye)
and Brian Wilson, the Senior Pilot.

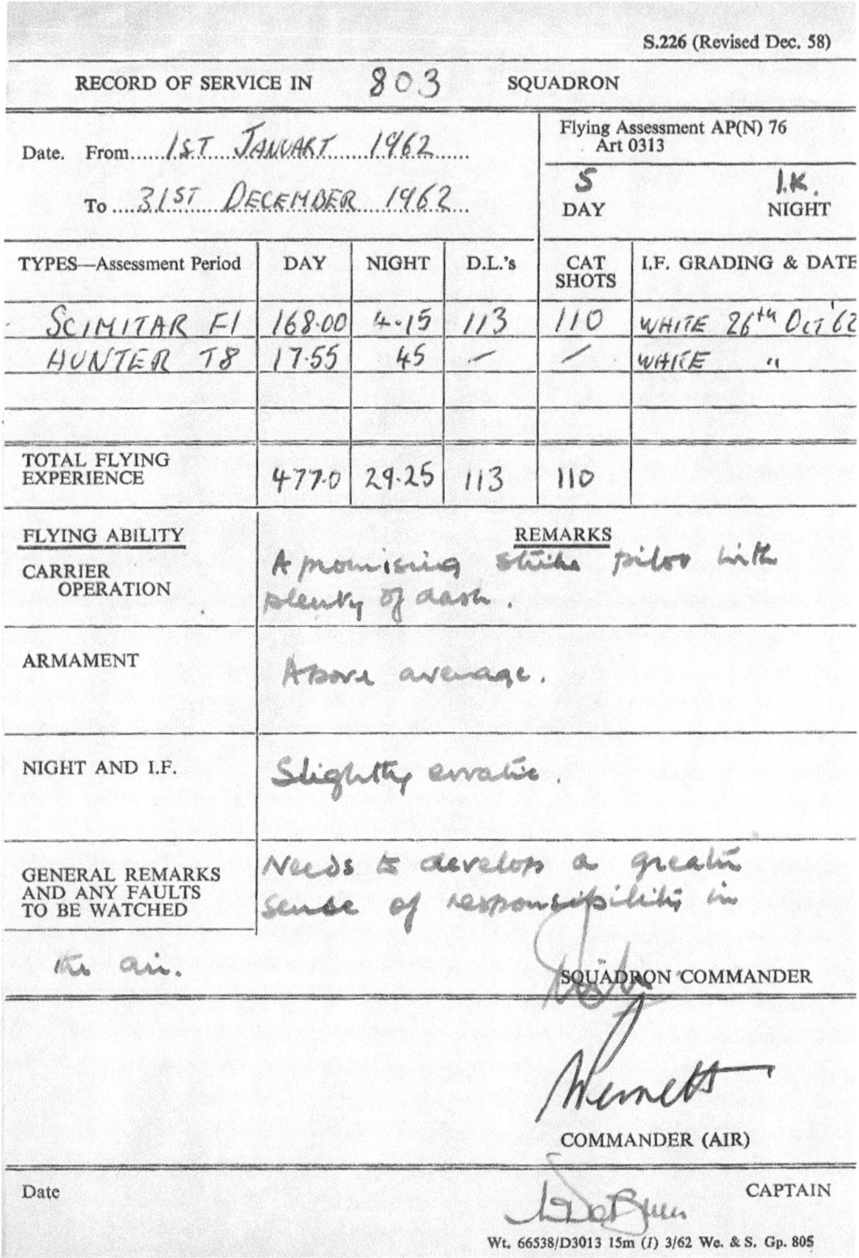

S.226 (Revised Dec. 58)

RECORD OF SERVICE IN   803   SQUADRON

Date. From......1ST JANUARY 1962......

To ....31ST DECEMBER 1962...

Flying Assessment AP(N) 76
Art 0313

5	1.K.
DAY	NIGHT

TYPES—Assessment Period	DAY	NIGHT	D.L.'s	CAT SHOTS	I.F. GRADING & DATE
SCIMITAR F1	168.00	4.15	113	110	WHITE 26th Oct 62
HUNTER T8	17.55	45	—	/	WHITE ''
TOTAL FLYING EXPERIENCE	477.0	29.25	113	110	

FLYING ABILITY   REMARKS

CARRIER OPERATION   A promising strike pilot with plenty of dash.

ARMAMENT   Above average.

NIGHT AND I.F.   Slightly erratic.

GENERAL REMARKS AND ANY FAULTS TO BE WATCHED   Needs to develop a greater sense of responsibility in the air.

SQUADRON COMMANDER

Bennett

COMMANDER (AIR)

Date   CAPTAIN

Wt. 66538/D3013 15m (I) 3/62 We. & S. Gp. 805

The squadron CO, Freddie Mills, gave me this double-edged assessment

Launching in heavy seas
can be hazardous

During typhoon Polly the crane broke
loose and rammed a Sea Vixen

HMS Hermes was involved in joint exercises with the
US Navy on several occasions.

This is what happens if you shut down in strong winds

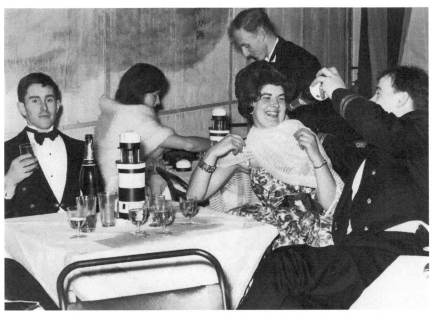

At the Hermes decommissioning ball with Fred and girlfriend

This picture, taken a few months after we met, was taken with a large wooden box camera. The three-second exposure was achieved by removing the lens cover

Janet at RNAS Culdrose (Cornwall UK) prior to being posted to Malta

Sea Prince of 750 squadron on the apron, RNAS Hal-Far, Malta 1965

The FAW22 DeHavilland Sea Venom

St Marys, Whitchurch-on Thames, April 1966

Janet with Leon, 2 months and Tia, 15 months

Major Kingsley Chingkuli posing by the Beaver. Mongu, Zambia 1969

Chingkuli relaxing under canvas, Kalabo 1969

With Tia, just home from work as CO of No 2 squadron Zambia Air Force 1969

Janet and Tia in the back garden, ZAF Lusaka

Our married quarters at ZAF Lusaka, Tia wandering up the drive

With president Kenneth Kaunda, Independence Day Review 1970

At Kalabo waiting for fuel

The UN Tsetse fly eradication aircraft flew from this"base"
at Sinjembele Zambia

Tia and Leon in Uganda

The Uganda Police Turbo Beaver

Me (on the right) with Tony Baylee 1974

A Baylee Piper Aztec sporting the later colour scheme. That's me in the cockpit.

At Southampton airport with Tia and Leon 1973

Janet in the garden of our Aberdeen "Scottish Special"

The Sikorsky 61 used to ferry workers out to the North Sea rigs

Standing next to the B212 - note the "North Sea Rig" apparel

A 212 approaching the Treasure Finder (attached to the Brent "B")

It sometimes got rough out in the North Sea

It gets pretty cold too

Inside the Treasure Finder hangar out in the Brent Oil Field

Tia & Leon in front of 14 Princess Drive, our Aberdeen "Scottish Special"

Portland House, Chagford, Devon, 1979

The Bristow 125 400 on the apron in Miri, Sarawak, 1980

Me standing by the 125 400 at the old Bintulu airport. Note the small intakes

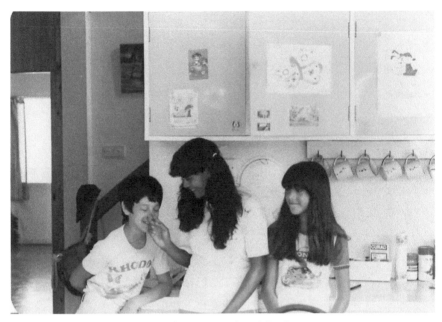

Janet & kids in our first Miri house

Bibi, Gerald and Angela, Miri 1980

Luak Bay, Miri 1980

Janet sporting her new Miri hairdo

A bunch of the Miri brats, early years

Sundays we spent on the beach with Mark and Ann Salmon

The Suzuki with the Phantom attached prior to 1st launch. Miri 1983

The home-built "Phantom" on the beach in Miri

Sudden storms can spoil your day - Miri 1983

The "Tarzan" pool at Lambir National Park, Miri

Leon and Mr Mapan on the way to the Longhouse Niah Sarawak

The girls, further up the river on the way to the longhouse

The Iban still keep trophies from their head hunting
days - these are Mr Mapan's

Andy Rice attempting the Ngajat traditional dance
while family Mapan look on.

Later we struggled to sleep on that hard longhouse floor

"The Residence", our second home in Miri

Tia (with ponytail) sketching at Clayesmore

The 125 700 arrived at Miri with Mr Bristow

The Bristow Residential Complex at Isolo Lagos
was approached along this road

The Bristow Complex viewed from Lateef Salami Street

The car port at the Bristow Residential Complex, Isolo, Nigeria

The infamous "Crocodile Bar", Isolo

Karl and Nancy Sauter, proprietors of the "Crocodile Bar", Isolo, Nigeria

The beast at the Crocodile Bar, Isolo, Lagos

The Bristow hangar, Mutala Muhamed airport, 1986

The Bristow Mitsubishi Solitaire (MU2) on the General Aviation Apron,
Port Harcourt

And with the Twin Otter

Janet sparked some interest when she joined the Chagford bowls team in 1986

The oak trees in Estcots Park after the hurricane of 86

Janet surveying the aftermath of the hurricane. East Grinstead

With Val and Tom Frost (I blinked)

The Turbofan 125 700 somewhere in Spain or Portugal

Doing the tourist thing with Jan, our regular cabin attendant

Dapper Hong Kong CAA guy with his wife
and friends on the apron at Santiago

A Learjet 35 similar to the one operated for Loftur Johannesson

Flying the Learjet, we spent many of our precious weekends away in Périgueux

Chateau de la Roque des Peagers, Loftur's home in Perigord, France

Reykjavik general aviation airport

Mafoluku, the way to avoid the traffic to Lagos airport

Our maid Abigail and driver Levinious at Abeokuta Nigeria 1991

This picture taken during a five-hour Hash run
(The "hare" screwed up laying the trail)

A welcome beer after Hashing at Lekki Beach

The IHHH girls taking a dip. The name of the girl in the blue bikini is "Love"

The Dornier 328 Bristow support team, Lagos 2000

Myself, Ken Spears, Martin Duck, Frank, Janet & Donnie

Tea time at Tarkwa Bay, Lagos 1994

Janet putting out on a "brown" at Ikeja Golf Club

The Ikeja Ladies Golf team (Janet in the pink)

The Dornier 328 Jet on the apron at Abuja, Nigeria

The Bronco, ready for battle on Lagos roads

Rush hour traffic, downtown Lagos

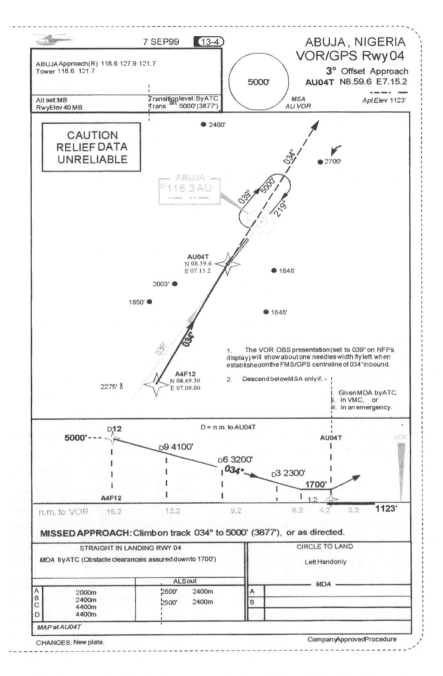

The homemade Abuja chart was safer than that published by the state

The Dornier 328 prop version outside the hangar at Oberpfaffenhofen

And disembarking passengers outside the Bristow Hangar

The D328 parked on the apron at Principe

Captain Wosu

The last type on my licence, the Dornier 328Jet

Cabin attendant Ade

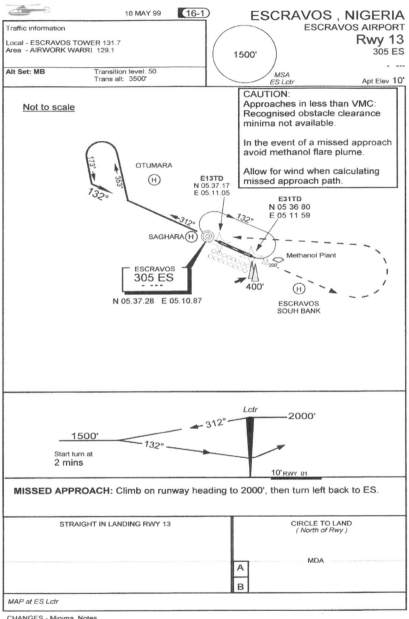

ESCRAVOS , NIGERIA
ESCRAVOS AIRPORT
Rwy 13
305 ES

Traffic information

Local - ESCRAVOS TOWER 131.7
Area - AIRWORK WARRI 129.1

1500'

MSA
ES Lctr

Apt Elev 10'

Alt Set: MB   Transition level: 50
Trans alt: 3500'

Not to scale

CAUTION:
Approaches in less than VMC:
Recognised obstacle clearance
minima not available.

In the event of a missed approach
avoid methanol flare plume.

Allow for wind when calculating
missed approach path.

173°   353°
OTUMARA
(H)
132°

E13TD
N 05.37.17
E 05.11.05

E31TD
N 05 36 80
E 05 11 59

312°   132°

SAGHARA (H)

Methanol Plant

ESCRAVOS
305 ES
- - ---

N 05.37.28   E 05.10.87

200'

400'

(H)

ESCRAVOS
SOUH BANK

Lctr
312°   2000'

1500'
132°

Start turn at
2 mins

10' RWY 01

MISSED APPROACH: Climb on runway heading to 2000', then turn left back to ES.

STRAIGHT IN LANDING RWY 13		CIRCLE TO LAND (North of Rwy)
		MDA
	A	
	B	

MAP at ES Lctr

CHANGES - Minima, Notes.

One of the "Jungle Jepp" approach charts I made for the "Delta Operators"

One of the many explosions that took place when the old army dump went up

The back garden of our house in Melaka 2004

The morning coffee spot

Inside our pad in Melaka

Chapter Twelve

BAYLEE AIR
CHARTER UK

January 1973 - April 1976

Mum and Dad were very relieved to see us, as the UK media had given the impression that in Uganda everybody was at risk. Being on an ODA contract we would receive all monies due as long as we completed all the claim forms.

Dad had been reassigned to the upper reaches of the Thames and was now based in Oxford. Their new house, in Standlake near Whitney, was new and had none of the charm of Swanston House. I set about getting another job immediately, as living with the parents was not so easy now they had downsized.

Out of the blue I got a call from Bill Hutchings saying I should expect a call from military intelligence. He said he had advised them that I had information which they might find useful. This referred to my visit to the Ugandan airbase at Gulu. Would I co-operate? I said OK. Bill had set himself up with the Hong Kong Police Air Wing. Shortly after putting the phone down it rang again and I was told there was a car on the way to collect me.

The services intelligence centre was an unimpressive and nondescript group of buildings hidden by trees. I passed on my information to an RAF chap, who said Gulu was being considered as an option for evacuation plans. After the debriefing I was invited for beer and lunch, not in the mess but at a nearby pub. No problem, with car and driver to take me home it seemed a pleasant idea.

The lunch was most enjoyable and by the time it was over the host knew more about my career than my family. Just as we were about to leave the pub the phone rang. It was for me! The American guy on the other end asked me if I remembered our conversation in Hong Kong. After mentioning the bar in Kowloon, it clicked. He said a chap with my sort of experience was a valuable commodity and I could be employed immediately on extremely good terms, ie a six-month contract for $60,000, renewable. In 1972 that was a fortune. The details followed. The task was to fly for Air America, operating the STOL Helio Courier in and out of jungle clearings in Laos. I asked what the life expectancy was. "One year, but it's worth a shot isn't it?"

I liked excitement, but the offer had come too late. I loved my little family and had to turn it down. When I came back to the table the RAF guy raised his eyebrows and I shook my head. He smiled, and nothing more was said.

I remembered that Tony Baylee of No. 1 Squadron ZAF had spoken of starting his own air taxi business in the Channel Island of Jersey. I called him up, and after updating him with our Ugandan episode he confirmed that he was indeed in business and just happened to need another pilot. The job was mine if I wanted it. I flew over to Jersey immediately and signed on. It was a real mom-and-pop operation run from the conservatory of Tony's house near the airport. The "office" was manned by his wife Lorraine. Tony checked me out on the PA23 Aztec and briefed me on the procedures for operating around the Channel Islands.

Until accommodation for the family was found I stayed in a guest house and drove myself to and from work. The roads in Jersey are notoriously narrow and winding and I wasn't prepared for the appalling behaviour of the local drivers. One morning I was involved in a minor collision and had to present myself to the Local Centenier who is an elected honorary constable or sheriff. The other party, a local and not in attendance, was patently guilty, but the Centenier said if I insisted he was responsible I would be charged, have my car impounded, and would have to go to court. As the accident was only a minor insurance job, I gave in. I subsequently discovered that the Centenier's "enquiry" was not legal, as a neutral witness should have been present.

Permission to reside in Jersey was much sought after. Tony arranged for me to be granted essential service status, but the sky-high price of property meant buying a house was out of the question. I settled for renting a small semi-detached house in Mont à L'Abbé. The owner turned out to be the entertainer Max Wall. He had married a cute young thing and it didn't work out. Max no longer used his little hideaway, and as his work was a tad unpredictable the extra income came in handy. Janet and the kids soon joined me and we set up home. Max had left some of his stuff in the house, and he occasionally dropped in to collect or deposit stage material. Janet always offered him a cup of tea, which he greatly appreciated. He told jokes and performed his "funny walks" for the kids, sending them into fits of laughter. Max was well known for these antics years before John Cleese.

The other pilots with Baylee were a mixed bunch, a retired British Airways captain, Ian Le Gresley, a young Jersey lad, Clive Parkes (enjoying his first employment), and a young ex-RAF transport pilot, Terry McCarthy. At that time we operated single crew. To give him credit Tony was thorough, and the line training, although expensive, was extensive. The main task of Baylee Air Charter's three Aztecs was to deliver live crab and lobster to the surrounding French towns. The shellfish was farmed in the old U-boat pens. Granville, Dinard and St Brieuc were about ten minutes away, while Cherbourg, Morlaix, Quimper and Brest were only a little further.

It was hard work, with up to ten sectors a day. Loading and unloading half a ton of shellfish on each outbound sector began to take a toll on my back, as inside the cabin one could only crouch while stacking the boxes.

Flying the wealthy on their various excursions provided much-needed relief. During March of 1973 my logbook shows 110 sectors for 52 hours flying. During the half hour turnaround, apart from loading and unloading, pilots were required to complete all the EU import and export forms, file the flight plan, check the weather and supervise refuelling. To maximise payload minimum fuel was used, which required a refuel after each delivery. The fuel uplifted was calculated to be enough to arrive back at base with the fuel required for the next departure.

The fuel gauges in the Aztec were next to useless, being even less reliable than the average family car. The fuel uplift was estimated by the pilot, errors could accumulate through the day, especially when sector fuel was consumed by delays at the holding point (waiting your turn for take-off). Murphy's Law caught up with us.

Fuel gauge errors varied between aircraft, and some were dangerously misleading. It was late afternoon, last flight of the day, and the sky was gin clear. It was company practice in these conditions to operate these short ten-minute sectors under visual flight rules. Using VFR rules far less fuel is required, as there is no allowance for instrument procedures and diversion; this of course allowed a greater payload.

Half way back to Jersey at 1000 feet the starboard engine spluttered; it was running out of fuel. Hoping it was only the right-hand fuel gauge that was in error I flipped open the cross feed. Now both engines were running off the left hand tank and I was getting that tickly feeling at the base of my spine.

Jersey airport sits atop a cliff, so if the fuel ran out at the wrong time the consequences would be dire. Jersey is a busy airport and aircraft operating under visual flight rules are asked to hold clear if instrument traffic (the airlines) had commenced an approach. I was so instructed, but under the circumstances could not accept and requested a priority landing. Reasons had to be given and I was asked to report to the SATCO with my licence. Fortunately Tony Baylee was informed, and being the straight-up guy he is, took the blame. How much fuel did I have left after parking? About half a gallon. Company procedures were revised. The fuel tanks were now to be physically dipped before every sector.

I was learning the mechanics of civil aviation fast, as at this time air taxi services were still allowed to operate in and out of the major international airports. In 1973 the Civil Aviation Authority (CAA) exempted Air Taxi operations from normal public transport regulations. We operated single crew if the autopilot was working and used home-made flight navigation logs. It seemed normal performance criteria were not enforced either, as some of the strips we were asked to land at were no better than cow pasture.

To simplify turnarounds the smaller general aviation airfields were used at major cities, but when passengers were connecting with international flights they would insist on landing at the main hub. Going into the big airports was an eye opener. We were briefed of course, but the first time was an ordeal. It was not feasible to be checked into each and every one by a training captain. It was especially tough going on single pilot ops.

Arrival and departure procedures are published in pilots' manuals (in our case Jeppesons) stored in the cockpit. Current approach and landing instructions were broadcast on a different radio frequency to air traffic control. Imagine trying to respond to ATC on one radio while copying information transmitted on another. A late change of arrival procedure meant a frantic search for the appropriate pages. These instructions were required to set up radio and navigation equipment, London Heathrow had about fifty pages to sort through, all in fine print.

The other hazard for light aircraft was wake turbulence. At that time awareness of this problem had not sunk in and I was caught on final for 09R at Heathrow. I had been given a chance to beat the build up of traffic if I could tuck in VFR behind a Lockheed 1011. This I did at a distance of one mile. Passing five hundred feet, the Aztec suddenly rolled over to the right. I had seen these vortices while waiting at the holding point and realised that using the controls would have no effect and most likely cause the aircraft to flick (a one-wing stall) and crash. I let the nose drop and the speed pick up before barrelling out close to the ground. The tower asked if I was OK, so I just said "Yep, vortex". Jelly legs again.

There were three other air taxi operators at Jersey airport, and to maintain a competitive edge Baylee did not permit the use of costly handling agents. This meant that after landing, pilots had to escort passengers through the terminal, pay the landing fees, file the flight plan, get the forecast, and arrange refuelling. At major airports the various offices concerned could be a long way from the parking areas. At Frankfurt for instance, it was about one kilometre.

When I first joined Baylee we didn't even have uniforms and I got arrested at Le Bourget trying to get back on to the parking apron. The main handling agent at Le Bourget must have been in cahoots with air traffic control.

Here's an example of how difficult they were. After the chore of attending to all the above I escorted the passengers out to the aircraft, we boarded, and I called for start. "Call back in thirty minutes" ground control advised. It was winter and freezing cold. We were parked on the General Aviation apron adjacent to the handling agent's office and passenger lounge. My passengers could see other passengers cosy and warm at the bar or in plush seating, eating snacks and reading. "We'll go inside and wait" they said. I had to explain that we had not paid for the use of these facilities but we did have our own bar and told them to avail themselves. They did so, but asked for heating. I had to start one engine for that, which was OK as long as we didn't have to wait too long.

I finally got start clearance and was told to taxi to the holding bay at the end of the runway and await departure instructions. We held there for another twenty minutes as night fell. The next call from ATC told me that as it was now dark I should return and pay the night lighting surcharge. As far as I know I have never suffered from high blood pressure, but I'm sure it went up a notch. I probably taxied back to the ramp at excessive speed. The passengers were well into the liquor and did not complain too much. I had to shut down of course, and ran the half mile to the main terminal. I paid the dues and ran back. Technically I should have taken on more fuel, but by now the passengers were grouchy, and although a bit short on reserves I had more than enough to get back to Jersey.

This time I was given start and departure clearance simultaneously and told that I had only five minutes to depart. otherwise I would lose my "slot". My taxiing speed was now definitely excessive, as ATC knew it would be. They advised me that my company would be notified. Fearing further provocation, I did not answer. Is it any wonder us Brits regard the French the way we do?

After much pleading by his pilots, Baylee finally agreed to issue uniforms and allow use of handling agents at major airports.

The company recommended deliveries of shellfish to Spain, which is a long haul from Jersey. Lobster cannot survive at altitude, so we had to fly at 6000 feet or below. On the return journey we used portable oxygen packs and returned at 17,000 feet. Much fuel was saved, enabling us to undercut the competition. The O2 packs were Mickey Mouse stuff and we had to constantly check the little non-return valve (red, in a clear plastic tube); if it got stuck, anoxia would set in. Thanks to the early demonstration in the chamber at Lee-on-Solent, I recognised the symptoms when it happened to me.

Tony warned us about the need to obtain accurate weather forecasts. He had endured a nerve-wracking incident with icing over the Bay of Biscay. When Tony started the company it was just him, Captain Le Gresley and an old Piper Apache. Returning to Jersey at 8000 feet in winter, he entered cloud, the Apache started to accumulate ice and lost power fast. There was no anti-icing on the engine air intakes and the build-up was restricting engine aspiration. The freezing level was at 2000 feet. Tony descended at maximum speed, hoping the cloud base was not too low. He broke out at about 1500 feet, but the ice did not clear. Noticing that high winds were whipping the sea into high waves and spume, he descended just above the waves entering the salt spray. As the aircraft speed decayed, the ice slowly started to dissolve and the power gradually increased. After landing back in Jersey, Tony traded in the Apache for an Aztec.

Spanish importers linked up with fish farms in Cork and Tralee to supply lobsters to Bilbao, Santander and Santiago, sometimes Lisbon. It was hard work with very early starts, and flying could total up to eight or nine hours a day.

Some of those lobsters did not give up. Hearing noises from behind I turned round and could see that one of these beasties had managed to push hard enough to unstick the packing tape and get halfway out of the box. I had to unstrap, turn round, push the creature back in and load another box on top. Fortunately they were packed with their claws secured by rubber bands.

Thomas O'Dowd, the exporter from Tralee, was a rogue. After one hair-raising take off from Shannon airport he was warned of the implications of false declarations of cargo weight. I should have aborted the take-off and returned to the ramp, but I was still relatively green in the business (and behind schedule) so I continued the take-off. In general aviation the learning curve is steep.

Flying hours were nothing remarkable, but in my first six months I flew 669 sorties. At least half of those of those involved the manual loading and unloading of half a ton of shellfish.

It wasn't all heavy duty stuff, and some of the charters could be hugely enjoyable. Billy Walker, the former boxing champ, had retired to the Channel Islands and become a successful property developer. His dad, a builder, used Baylee occasionally and on 22 May 1973 I flew him over to London to watch the John Conteh/Chris Finnegan title fight. Walker got me tickets to watch the match at Wembley and invited me to a private dinner with the boxing fraternity in the East End of London. The table was set Louis XIV style with candelabra and gold plated cutlery. The room, decorated with crystal chandeliers and purple-carpeted walls, looked set for an orgy. The drinks flowed, but with an early start the next day I had to restrain myself. I sat back and observed these incredible characters letting their hair down. The waitresses in their cute outfits were very attractive young ladies, and I was told these girls were available for hire. I excused myself when some of the more edgy characters started recounting their exploits - best not to know.

On the flight back to Guernsey Mr Walker helped himself to drinks from the small bar, ending up in quite a jolly mood. When I had parked and was about to open the door he stuffed a roll of banknotes into my hands. His minder tried to grab the roll but it fell on to the cockpit floor. If the guy had asked politely I would have handed it back in toto, but he had annoyed me. I peeled off a few notes and handed back the wad... he didn't argue.

Pilots carried out all their own flight planning and preparation. Filing the day's flight plans at AIS (Air Information Service) in the Jersey control tower, I witnessed an argument between the duty officer and Douglas Bader, the wartime fighter hero. I revised my opinion of him immediately. Flying his own Piper Apache he had been refused start-up clearance for not having filed a flight plan. Bader had lost his temper and was trying to verbally beat the duty officer into submission. He failed and had to comply with the regulations, but he was now struggling with the flight plan. I helped him out. I would have thought that as an ex-head of Shell Aviation he would have been able to cope, not act like a bumptious, hot-tempered old fart.

Tony arranged contracts with insurance companies to operate air ambulance flights. If the rear seats and rear bulkhead were removed, stretchers could be loaded through the rear cargo hatch. It was an awkward process and not the slick operation seen on TV, but lives were saved. I had flown badly-injured soldiers in Zambia, but the sight of hastily patched-up girls and young kids came as a shock. Patients were mainly car accident victims from rural France and were flown home to almost every city in Europe. Some patients died on the way, so to avoid complications the certificate always stated the location as the country of destination.

Our social life varied greatly. Sometimes we were invited to functions hosted by wealthy customers, but more often to simple get-togethers at Tony's or the Flying Club. There were wilder parties, where anything went. After one of the latter I got taught a hard lesson. Having had a quick smoke of someone else's joint I thought no more about it. It was Saturday and I had a late start the next day, just one short flight to Dinard. Setting up the flight progressed as normal, but once in the air I suffered a flashback. This was ten times scarier than that beery flight from Gibraltar. Drifting off into a dream, it became next to impossible to get back to reality. Nothing seemed real. I had to bite hard on my lower lip; the pain and taste of blood were just enough to bring me back to the job in hand. After landing I went straight to the airport cafe and stoked up on espresso. That was the second and last time I ever flew under the influence.

Jersey was getting claustrophobic and we needed the assurance of owning property. When the chance came to transfer to a new operation on the mainland we jumped at the chance, less lobster-loading too. An Aztec was to be based at Exeter Airport. The frequency of requests for charters originating in Devon had increased and Baylee could now justify a locally-based aircraft.

Janet and I had a lot of fun looking for a house. We eventually settled for a small end-of-terrace place in Millway Gardens, Bradninch. It was ideal. The village primary school was just around the corner and the neighbours were all first-timers with small kids. Although small, the house was modern and well designed with a lovely view over the valley. Our furniture we obtained cheap at auctions or jumble sales.

We had been introduced to Bradninch by Paul and Glen, Baylee's Exeter operations staff. This lively couple lived together in a cute 300-year-old oak-beamed terraced cottage. They were well versed in charter operations, having previously worked for South West Aviation, another small charter outfit.

The flying programme was much more relaxed, although we did our share of shellfish flights. Most were from Ireland to Spain, but some were long haul from Benbecula (in the Western Isles of Scotland) to Paris.

Ford Motors became a client. When their assembly plant in Germany ran short of nuts and bolts etc. we flew these from Plymouth (then a grass airstrip) to Saarbrücken. Again using portable oxygen, we flew high, causing cries of alarm and panic from a British Airways crew. "I've just passed a light twin at 17,000 feet" he shrieked. "He's under our control" ATC replied. In the silence that followed I could feel the question marks all across the FIR (regional airspace).

Nothing wrong with Saarbrücken - it was a smart little airport - but I had two incidents there, both at night on final approach.

The weather seemed benign; there was high pressure with no cloud apart from a thin veil of stratus close to the ground. It was winter and very cold. Descending through the layer of cloud on the ILS (Instrument Landing System), I started to pick up ice. The Aztec was only equipped with de-icing and the current thinking was to allow a moderate build-up before switching it on.

But before I knew it, the accumulation had increased unbelievably. Over a period of about thirty seconds power had to be increased to maximum, but even this could not prevent the Aztec from slowly descending below the glidepath. Breaking cloud was a huge relief - I was going to make the runway. I would be short of the proper touchdown point, but thankfully on the runway, not in the approach lights.

The Aztec thumped into the ground. The ground handling staff could not believe the amount of ice. I blew all the profit for that trip on the de-icing service.

Saarbrücken again. The weather was similar, misty with a lower cloud base but no ice. Descending on the ILS again, I saw the approach lights just as I reached decision height (the height at which if nothing is seen, diversion to an alternative airfield becomes mandatory).

Just as I caught sight of the runway lights, the airfield blacked out. The view out front now consisted of a wall of mist illuminated by reflection from the aircraft landing lights. I applied full power, called "going around, missed approach" and climbed straight ahead - no reply from ATC. Climbing away, I established contact with Frankfurt and told them I was diverting to them. I was well on my way when Saarbrücken ATC broke through, repeating my call sign with some urgency and advising me to call them back on their frequency. It turned out that they had problems starting the standby generator after grid failure. Would I please return to Saarbrücken, as Ford was waiting? I had no time to recalculate fuel reserves and told them to ask the Ford guy to arrange collection of their parts from Frankfurt.

At Frankfurt the General Aviation Terminal was closed. Normally late night diversions are parked overnight. Ground control got themselves into a tizzy when I requested an immediate turnround, but they jumped into action when asked if Frankfurt was indeed operated on a 24-hour basis. The guy in AIS needed much prodding to obtain the weather and we had to wake up his colleague to pay the airport charges.

To be fair all regular operators held an account, while ad hoc flights were required to pay cash. A phone call to ATC at Exeter got an extension to opening hours for my return. This was far cheaper than taxi fares and a hotel in Frankfurt. Back at the aircraft the fuel truck and a van from Ford had arrived. Refuelled, unloaded and much relieved, I called for start-up.

En route I learned that most airports in southern England were closing due to fog, and only Exeter remained open. The lack of alternative airfields was a cause for concern, but Exeter has its own microclimate and under the conditions prevailing should remain clear. I landed at 3.30 am, tired but satisfied.

Not having toilet facilities on board sometimes caught our passengers unawares. I have had to divert for pee stops once or twice, but on one occasion over the Alps this option was not available. The poor guy was forced to pee in one of the sick bags in front of his colleagues and to make things worse, the bag started to leak. I was unaware of all this until I received a tap on the shoulder; could I please dispose of the bag. They had observed me using the small document port in the cockpit side window and pointed to it. It would be a tight fit, but the vacuum effect might help. I opened the flap and pushed it out. In an instant the bag exploded. It was horrendous. The passengers, showered and shocked, were quiet for the remainder of the flight. I wondered how their reception in Geneva went. From then on all our Aztecs were equipped with pee bottles.

One of our regional TV stations arranged for Reinhold Eggers to attend a Colditz veterans' reunion in Torbay. Eggers had been the security officer at this high-security prisoner of war castle during the war years. He was well respected for his fair and proper dealings with the internees, and they wished to show their appreciation.

Baylee was chartered to fly Eggers from Friedrichshafen to Exeter. Eggers spoke perfect English and asked if he could occupy the other seat in the cockpit - no problem, we had quite a conversation on the way over. He asked me a few questions regarding my time in the military, but he had far more interesting stories about the pilots previously under his care.

Being an old gentleman, he needed a pee about halfway through the journey. To save him the indignity of using the bottle I landed at Reims and took the opportunity to buy some duty-free champagne. After landing at Exeter Eggers presented me with a signed copy of one of his books (written in English); unfortunately this has long since disappeared.

One of our best customers at Exeter was Don Tidey, a senior manager for Associated British Foods. At that time he lived in Exeter and managed all their supermarket business from there. We flew him two or three times a month to most of the airfields in Ireland. Some of them, like Galway Airport, were of the "cow pasture" variety. When Mr Tidey eventually became resident in Ireland he was kidnapped by the IRA. His rescue, involving a shootout and the use of grenades, makes interesting reading. I never encountered any problems with security in Belfast but I did hear gunfire while having lunch at the hotel.

Posing as a member of the IRA, a taxi driver in Galway (he knew my next destination was Liverpool) asked me if I could deliver a large package to a "friend" who would collect outside the terminal. He had me fooled and worried until he burst out laughing. I felt like smacking him round the head, I was never a fan of practical jokes.

Mr Tidey never knew, but as we arrived at Dublin one morning the shortcomings of our maintenance contractor at Exeter became dangerously apparent. On short finals half a mile from touchdown, rearwards movement of the controls was prevented by some unknown restriction. I could not reduce to the normal touchdown speed by pulling back on the controls, and if I reduced power we would enter a dive. Not being able to flare for touchdown, I had no choice but to drive the Aztec on to the runway at speed, checking the rate of descent with just a short burst of power. We thumped down, using the whole length of the runway to stop. I could feel Mr Tidey's eyes on the back of my neck. After shutdown he said "Not like you Flexman, that landing". "Windshear" I replied with a smile. More jelly legs.

The radio mechanic at Exeter had removed a VOR control box for repair, leaving the multi-pin plug dangling behind the instrument panel. The twin control yokes were joined just forward of the avionics by an arrangement of chains and cogs. Not properly secured, the plug and cabling had flopped into this gearing. For the return flight I strapped the plug out of the way myself. I should have written an incident report, but the avionics guy was the only one available to us in Exeter and I didn't want him out of a job. I did however go to see him and his boss. They didn't know what to say and were very red faced.

On one of Mr Tidey's trips Dublin was fogged out and we diverted to the Isle of Man. After spending an hour or so chatting in the airport lounge, Tidey said it was not often he was forced not to work and that he greatly enjoyed our conversation. Coming from widely different lifestyles, it was interesting for both of us. As an ex-army man he was interested in my military exploits, his parting shot being that I should polish my shoes more often!

In order to visit one of his turkey processing plants in Ballyfree, just south of Dublin, Mr Tidey asked if I could land in a field nearby. He found out the length of the strip and said it had on occasion been used by the local flying club. It seemed OK on a low flyby, so we landed. I have never stopped so quickly in an Aztec, and I didn't even touch the brakes. The lush green grass was about eighteen inches high. While we visited the farm and factory their Land Rover spent half an hour driving up and down the field, making it fine for take-off.

On July 13th 1974, I had a surprise charter to take James Hunt, the racing driver, to Silverstone. He was to race Lord Hesketh's new F1 machine. I was invited to lunch with them in the VIP tent. It was a great meal, but not being a motor racing freak I could only listen vacantly to all the tech speak. The atmosphere was terrific, but even in the best seats you only got to see a bunch of extremely loud machines every few minutes. It would have been better on TV. I suppose nowadays the big screens will be up, enabling better coverage.

As an air taxi pilot one has to be prepared for just about everything. An 800kg cylinder head for a ship's engine had to be shipped urgently from Groningen in Holland. The weight and loading parameters could be met OK, but getting the damn thing safely on board was a different kettle of fish.

The item had arrived crated, and no way was it going to fit through the relatively small entry door. After breaking open their very smart piece of carpentry, it took a good half hour of juggling to finally get the thing on board. We used a forklift, a jerry-rigged sling and boards and rollers. The whole process had to be monitored closely. The agent used the shipyard's men rather than expensive air cargo handlers - big mistake. The DIY sling broke. Fortunately the cargo only dropped about an inch on to the door sill, but even so it left a dent. The door would close, but it failed to form a proper seal. The leak provided an annoying whistle all the way home. I had called ahead to ensure provision of men and suitable lifting gear at Exeter. Thankfully the unloading process proved uneventful.

The doorsill was straightened out, but it was never the same and the door had to be closed firmly and with care. During a subsequent charter I had dropped the passengers at Gloucester/Staverton and was climbing out en route for base when the damn door popped open. The aircraft yawed awkwardly. The sudden increase in noise made radio calls impossible as the airflow held the door open rigidly at about four inches.

Reaching across and pulling with one hand proved futile. In order to get both hands on the door I had to unstrap and move across to the right hand seat. To overcome the suction a considerable reduction in speed was required before I could successfully slam the door closed. The autopilot would not engage, so the whole thing was a trifle precarious. Don't get the wrong impression - the vast majority of flights for Baylee were carried out without incident... honestly!

My experiences flying light aircraft led me to develop a personal warning system. The more points any particular flight clocked up, the more dangerous it became. The following table shows how it worked:

1 Point	Night flight	Bad weather	Common cold	Hangover
	Loss of a radio	Loss of one Nav	Icing	
2 Points	Fatigue			
3 Points	Lost generator	Hydraulic failure	Low oil pressure	
6 Points	Engine failure	Landing gear problem	Fire	

Points could be accumulated by any combination from the table. The following action was advised:

1 Point: Focus.
2 Points: Check options.
3 Points: Inform base, possible change of route.
4 Points: After next landing resolve any problems before continuing.
5 Points: Precautionary landing at a suitably equipped airfield.
6 Points: Declare emergency and land at nearest airfield.

Accidents will occur when more than six points are accumulated. (If simulator training is used on a regular basis then the threshold can be as high as 8 points). This contingency plan served me well. I passed on the idea and it was well received, but I never knew if anyone else had found it useful.

Meanwhile back in Bradninch, the hippy life continued. Our little community thrived on self sufficiency, recycling and mutual support. Maybe it was due to financial restraints, but it made for a great social life. Our garden was on a south-west facing slope and was highly productive. The very laid-back weekends were spent visiting each other for good music (the Moody Blues were favourite), fine food and the occasional joint. If the weather was fine we preferred a meandering walk through the woods with the music and food on return. Others in the village also smoked the weed and several members of the local branch of the Liberal Party were busted for possession.

Unfortunately Baylee had been unable to afford to give me a pay rise for some time. To save money we became mostly vegetarian, occasionally eating eggs and fish to supplement the kids' diet. Avoiding the expense of petrol, we took the kids on long country walks, learning the names of birds, wild flowers, and herbs. It was a very healthy life.

Baylee decided to open up a base in Aberdeen to cash in on the oil boom. Until the business gained a secure foothold, pilots were rotated from Jersey and Exeter. Initially only one Aztec was based there, but the new station manager, Richard Ross, was building the client base so quickly that larger aircraft were being considered. Richard asked me round for dinner. He revealed that he was actually employed by Bristow Helicopters as a co-pilot! If there was any confliction of duties he paid other Bristow co-pilots to operate flights on his behalf. Baylee seemed happy to turn a blind eye to this as long as the business kept rolling in.

Ross either had inside contacts or was an extremely persuasive salesman. He continually obtained charters from most of the oil companies and their contractors. Baylee's enthusiasm increased, as we seemed to be well ahead of the competition.

A charter came in from a major American oil company to carry a drill bit to Sfax in Tunisia. The drilling rig was shut down for the want of this part. Baylee accepted the charter. I would carry the bit and the oil rep down to Luton, and from there a sub-chartered McAlpine Hawker 125 would take over.

Some seats were removed and an improvised load spreader made to support the cargo. It was the middle of winter and icing was forecast. Flying down to Luton took just over an hour; the de-icing worked OK but ice snapped off one of the VOR aerials.

Checking in with McAlpine, I learned that they had been unable to get diplomatic clearance for the flight. Airlines receive block clearance for flights, but non-scheduled charters need individual permission. This clearance is not required in Europe, but African and Asian countries need to approve flights into or over their territories (the issue of diplomatic clearance can also be a handy tool for extorting bribes).

By now the oil company rep was getting agitated. He told McAlpine that the oil company would arrange clearance and that they should depart now. McAlpine refused, the rep then turned to me and said "let's go". I asked where, "Sfax".

Sfax was in Africa and outside of our permitted operating area, I did not have the charts and was minus one VOR aerial. I explained this to the rep, who immediately called his boss, who called Baylee threatening our company, saying it would be blacklisted if we failed to deliver. I agreed to go if approvals and exemptions were arranged and the operations department completed the planning for the onward flight from Jersey. I could pick up the charts and documents while the VOR aerial was being fixed during the fuel stop.

We got airborne for Jersey. The turnaround there went as planned and we were soon on our way to Marseilles, where we would spend the night. After just a few hours' sleep we returned to the airport, but when I tried to file the flight plan it was refused. Without proof of diplomatic clearance the flight would not be allowed. The rep instructed me to carry out the pre-flight on the aeroplane and said that meanwhile he would work on the clearance.

The rep arrived back on the apron and said we were OK to start. While we were taxiing, the flight clearance was given to the limit of French airspace only. I knew I would have to obtain onward clearance from Tunisian Air Traffic Control and this worried me somewhat, as it was a long flight for the Aztec and if clearance was refused I would have to divert to Cagliari in Sardinia or Palermo in Sicily.

Tunis cleared us on to Sfax, the oil company having obtained the necessary approval. Embarrassingly the charts provided ended just South of Tunis and I had to ask ATC for the appropriate radio frequencies for our destination. We landed after a flight of four hours and fifteen minutes with only the minimum of reserves. The drill bit was whisked away.

The rep had assured me that all facilities for a quick turnaround had been arranged, and sure enough the airport staff met us on the apron. I filed the return flight plan right there. Landing fees were already taken care of, the only problem being… no fuel. I had 45 minutes to dry tanks. Djerba was twenty minutes away, but guaranteed to have fuel. Dipping the tanks proved I had just enough, but the gauges were very close to empty. I hate these tricky decisions.

Flying to Djerba with so little fuel gave me that horrible tickly feeling again. My arrival took the airport authorities by surprise, but I had cleared customs and immigration at Sfax and now only needed a quick refuel. I paid all fees in US dollars and skedaddled out of there before any smartarse could dream up an excuse to extort more. It took four and a half hours to get back to Marseilles; accurate fine tuning of the fuel mixture achieved the necessary range.

As we parked, the aircraft was surrounded by police. The rep went off under escort and I was taken to a bare locked room above the handling agent's office. The window overlooked the apron and I could see a team of technicians and police taking the aeroplane apart. All the panels came off and the carpet was removed. I hoped these guys knew how to put it back together. My armed guard remained stony faced and would say nothing. I was given a bottle of water and was there for an hour and a half. Finally I was told I could go. The handling agent told me that the police team were part of the famous Marseilles drug squad. The agent then handed me a terse note from the oil company rep saying that I was free to return to base without him. I flew to Jersey, where the aeroplane was required to help out. I then slept for twelve hours solid.

At Aberdeen Richard Ross had walked out on Baylee, taking most of the customers with him. It seemed he had copied the files and bugged the phone. Ross had worked out a deal with Fairflight while still employed by Baylee. Fairflight, a Biggin Hill-based company, would provide an aircraft and crew until the new subsidiary obtained its operating certificate. This new company would be called "Air Ecosse".

On hearing the news Tony flew up to Aberdeen and went straight to the office. He called the Industrial Espionage Agency and asked them if they could fly up right away. They said no, balking at the expense. The investigators would travel on the overnight train.

Unfortunately Tony had used a bugged phone to notify the agency. The next morning he found that the office had been broken into and the bugs and other documents had been removed. When the investigators and the police sent their reports they advised that there was insufficient evidence to connect Ross or anybody else to the affair.

Meanwhile I had seen an ad in Flight magazine for a financially attractive position in Nigeria. I applied, was accepted and handed in my resignation. Tony understood that I had been forced to make this decision for financial reasons.

The three years with Baylee had been extremely valuable. With so much hands-on experience I had gained considerable knowledge of the practical side of air charter operations and my self-confidence had increased immeasurably. In the military, as long as you carried out your duties, the system took care of everything else. I had operated into 132 different airports in Europe and carried everything from shellfish to showbiz celebs and heavy machinery. Janet and I had also made lifelong friends during our time in Bradninch.

Tony continued operations at Aberdeen, but having purchased the extra aircraft and lost most of his customers to Air Ecosse it wasn't long before the company went into liquidation. Unfortunately Tony had borrowed money from friends and acquaintances in Jersey. His hair turned white. Under no obligation to pay back his loans, he nonetheless managed to do so after employment with Saudi Airlines. His honour restored, he retired from aviation, tried Australia, then returned to Jersey to run a guest house with Lorraine.

Chapter Thirteen

DELTA AIR CHARTER NIGERIA

May 1976 - May 1977

Delta Air Charter was based in Lagos and Port Harcourt. The pay was more than that of a regional airline captain in UK and was tax-free to boot. My ticket arrived in record time and I was told to fly out immediately. Being of a suspicious nature, I went to the Nigerian High Commission in London, applied for my visa and checked out the companies' credentials. They were OK, being owned and subsidised by the River State government.

As the British Caledonian DC10 taxied into the terminal I began to realise why the pay offered by Delta was so high. Crowded and bustling with activity, the airport terminal and its surroundings were shabby and patched up DIY fashion. The whole setup was sorely in need of maintenance. Zambia and Uganda seemed smart by comparison.

By the time we had collected my bags, I was drenched. I realised that my previous experience of Africa had been gained in sparsely-populated countries several thousand feet above sea level. Lagos was a totally different ball game. I booked a taxi for what I thought would be a long ride round the airport, but it turned out it was just around the corner, about three hundred yards. Even so I wasn't sure the dilapidated vehicle was going to make it.

The Delta Head Office, although in need of re-decoration, was surprisingly well equipped, and I began to feel more positive about my new employment. While waiting to be introduced to the MD, I was shown around the hangar and workshops. My mood improved further as I was shown the maintenance and test equipment, which was superior to that of Baylee. I was told that the River State Government managed the company finances from Port Harcourt. Cash, including the payroll, was flown up in our aircraft when required.

A new Piper Chieftain and Aztec F had recently been added to the complement of two Aztec Es and a Navajo. The Pipers replaced two Piaggio P166s and a DC3, now rotting on the apron. On the other side of the taxiway sat derelict Russian classics of the Nigerian Air Force. Mig 17s, an Ilyushin 28 Beagle and a Yakovlev 25 Flashlight were scattered in the long grass. I was told not to take any photos, because if spotted I would be arrested as a spy.

Delta actually had a radio engineer who was also qualified on autopilots, John Nti. John had been trained and received his qualifications in UK while working for British Airways.

The Chief Pilot, Bob Ogden, was a tall and skinny Mancunian of dour aspect and cynical disposition. The disparaging remarks he frequently directed at his Nigerian colleagues amused those on the receiving end, because he tinged his barbs with dry humour. Bob had stayed with Delta through thick and thin, observing the endless parade of expats whose tolerance had expired. He received the Beano children's comic by air mail and at Sunday evening cinema at the Country Club he fed stray cats.

The immigration service insisted that all potential work permit holders be issued return tickets by their respective companies. A lot of these tickets were used to return to country of origin within weeks, sometimes days and in a couple of occasions the disenchanted caught the same aircraft on its return flight. Delta's policy of not pre-briefing potential employees on local conditions was based on the assumption that it was better to retain the odd blind success than deter the well-informed.

Exposure to Africa often resulted in culture shock for newcomers, but Lagos in the seventies was in a class of its own. Even old Africa hands were stunned by the appalling state of the infrastructure and the failure of most of the utilities. The streets were lined with monsoon drains blocked with garbage. They contained the outflow from buildings erected without proper approval. Cesspits were built, but the effluent often exceeded soakaway capability. In addition to normal household liquids the drains had to cope with industrial waste, often toxic.

Contemplation of these vile surroundings was unavoidable. Passengers had nothing else to do as traffic inched along in the "go slow" (traffic jam). It was quicker to walk, but due to the heat and dust this was an option only considered after failure of the air-conditioning. I tried this and arrived at the hangar with a sweat-soaked uniform shirt, covered in a thick film of dust.

The airport was in Ikeja, about eleven kilometres from downtown Lagos. Originally a well-planned light industrial zone with adjacent residential areas, Ikeja's unregulated urban sprawl and fast-growing population had overwhelmed the existing road services. This had been recognised and existing arteries were being widened and new highways were being constructed, all adding to the general chaos.

Most government offices and company headquarters were in Lagos itself. Senior managers who had appointments downtown had to depart Ikeja before 7 am if they were to have any chance of attending an afternoon meeting. Sometimes the traffic was so bad that if the halfway stage had not been reached by midday they would give up and turn back.

While unaccompanied, and before being allocated permanent

accommodation, the Delta Guest House would be home. From there it was possible to walk to work in twenty minutes, but in order to arrive with one's uniform in a presentable state, company transport was provided. Journey time was normally one hour. A bonus of residing in the guesthouse was its proximity to the Airport Hotel and its Olympic swimming pool. Only minutes away and reached across a couple of empty lots, it provided a cool oasis of calm. The pool was still maintained to a reasonable standard and allowed us to hang out in comfort when on standby. A runner from the guest house would advise us if we were required to fly.

The hotel was home for a large number of expatriate businessmen, most of whom were unaccompanied. This attracted many young ladies, who frequented the poolside clad in impossibly skimpy bikinis. Care had to be taken after consuming the beer brought to your table by courteous staff. Some of the girls were of course "on the game", but most were aiming for an expat boyfriend to act as sugar daddy. These often extremely well-endowed creatures were a distraction, as I was studying for the Nigerian Air Law exam.

We could acquire the local flying licence on the strength of our UK ATPLs but first had to pass this one additional test, and I studied diligently. Bob Ogden told me to relax, saying the DCA might not even mark our papers. "Just be very polite to the invigilator and you should be OK" he said.

There were two other Brits who had joined Delta at the same time. They did virtually no studying, as they had fallen under the spell of some of the poolside beauties. We all passed, with I suspect some added under-the-table assistance from the management. Bob of course knew all along, and the week's flying program was already out, printed with our names.

Now that I was settled into the job, Janet and the kids flew out to join me. Meeting them at the airport, I was amused by the kids' hand luggage, which was two dustbin bags full of teddy bears. I wondered where they had been stowed during the flight.

It was an uphill task pushing Delta to provide a house. After we had rejected many sub-standard apartments they realised that as a family we were entitled to the bungalow now occupied by a long-time employee, now unaccompanied. The ageing Swedish pilot, "Andy" Anderson, was a Lagos legend. Originally he had been accompanied by his wife, but she had had enough and was long gone. Andy was over seventy, but still flying. He still occasionally rode his motorbike to work, doing the maintenance himself in the front room.

Andy was re-located to the guesthouse and we set about getting the house fit for habitation. The floor of the front room was severely gouged and soaked in engine oil, and the premises needed a thorough clean before redecoration. When the decorators arrived they started painting over the dirt and grease, so I sent them away and requested a cleaning team. When nothing happened, I told Delta I was too busy cleaning to fly aeroplanes. When the house finally got smartened up, a battle over the air-conditioning commenced. We moved in when two of four units were fixed.

One day when I was flying the Aztec, I returned to the airport at Port Harcourt to find some AGIP passengers waiting by the Navajo. Andy, their pilot, had walked right past them and was inside doing the pre-flight checks. They asked if I was the captain. I said no and pointed to Andy now struggling down the steps to meet them (they had thought he was the cleaner). Their jaws dropped as this stooped old fellow now wearing captain's bars approached to greet them. They fled, leaving Andy with no passengers.

That was Andy's last flight for Delta. Up to then no one in the company had had the nerve to give this venerable institution his letter of termination. The poor guy could not believe his working life had finally come to an end, he refused a leaving party. The Delta bosses were kind enough to award him a very handsome gratuity. Imagine everyone's surprise and horror when after a month back home he returned for work.

Back at the ranch, the company supplied us with a "nightwatch" or security guard, who would arrive around 10 pm and establish himself in the garage. He had armed himself with a home-made pistol that could be loaded with a single 9 mm round, but I had doubts as to his ability to defend us against armed intruders. Richard the gardener (an ex-Biafran army sergeant) said we should not be concerned, as sufficient help was readily available. He could see we were unconvinced, and said that if I was prepared to provide a couple of crates of beer he would provide a demonstration. Intrigued, I agreed, and the next evening with the drinks on hand I told him to go ahead. He blew several loud notes on his army whistle. Seconds later the front garden was filled with about thirty villagers armed with machetes, spears, axes and more home-made guns.

The vigilantes, keen as mustard and hoping for action, were a trifle disappointed when Richard explained that it was only a practice drill, but they lightened up at the sight of the beer. During the ensuing "garden party" we were introduced to the volunteers, who were Igbo easterners, as was Richard.

During our year and a half in that house, with no front gate or alarm, we suffered no intruders. The exterior of the bungalow had not been redecorated and the place seemed derelict. In a society that flaunted wealth and status its appearance promised little return for would-be burglars.

Further down the road in the exclusive GRA (the old government residential area) they were plagued by regular break-ins. Windows were fitted with bars and wooden doors replaced with steel. Robbers would then come in through the roof, or trucks would pull out the steel grilles, casement attached. The nightwatch would be held as hostage, maybe even colluding with the burglars.

Since the Biafran war many weapons had remained unaccounted for, and the problem never dissipated. Sometimes off-duty police would be responsible. Despite all of this mayhem, expats, lured by generous tax-free salaries, kept on coming.

Our windows were of the louvred type and we had to hang sheets until the curtains arrived. Our water supply had been disconnected, as road widening was in progress. Not to worry, the bungalow had two underground storage tanks. Deliveries by tanker were unpredictable but Richard, being full of Nigerian ingenuity, tapped a pressure relief valve on the still-intact 24-inch Lagos water main. The folks from across the road soon cottoned on to this amenity. A long queue of plastic bucket and jerry-can-wielding villagers became a permanent feature outside our front gate.

The centre of Ikeja expat life was the Country Club. Now in the middle of town, it nevertheless provided an oasis of calm. Tia and Leon had been enrolled into the International School next door. The poolside was an ideal afternoon hangout for mums with kids, and this, the bar and the other club amenities were an essential ingredient of the Lagos resident's plan for maintaining sanity.

My attempts at obtaining my own driving licence failed dismally. I had struggled to the front of the crush at the licensing office, but on reaching the window had been totally ignored. Apparently, on reaching the office compound, one had to find and employ an unofficial agent, but it had to be one recognised by the issuing officer. When I mentioned this to Bob Ogden, he told me to use the company in any dealings with bureaucracy, otherwise it would cost me a fortune. I was learning.

Having experienced the standard of driving and seen many examples of Ikeja vehicle maintenance, the only sensible option was to buy a new model. Imports were extremely expensive, so it had to be a locally assembled Peugeot or Volkswagen. The VW Igala specs seemed pretty good. The design originated from VW Brazil, and it could carry my newly-acquired surfboard internally, so I bought one.

The sights and scenes we witnessed while driving beggared belief. There would be many more lanes of traffic than the road was intended for, with traffic on the sidewalk or unmade verge. The potholes were so deep that suspension and engine sump were at risk. The "go slow", although tedious, was a road safety factor, as the reduced speed meant that frequent minor bumps and dents were the only damage suffered. On weekends, when the pace quickened, the number of serious accidents rose alarmingly. The results of new accidents could be seen each day. Vehicles without doors or windows were common. Not only were cars occasionally seen travelling without a tyre on the rim, I once spotted one without a wheel at all - no kidding.

Burnt-out VW minibuses were a common sight. The VWs were turned into time bombs during fuel shortages. The driver would carry a plastic can of petrol in the luggage space over the engine. Hours of queueing at the petrol station would mean serious loss of revenue. Many died as the result of leaky containers.

Hit-and-run victims were left where they fell. If dead, their bloated corpses often remained at the roadside for days. If they were alive, casualties would be extremely lucky to receive any assistance. Some survivors who were unable to move were later hit by other vehicles. It was painful, but nobody stopped. Those who tried to help were often attacked as culprits or made victims of extortion.

Flying provided a welcome respite from the stress of urban life. For the first few weeks I flew the milk run to Port Harcourt, carrying oil company staff. The weather was an eye opener, for it was the start of the rainy season and thunderstorms were a constant threat. The Aztecs had no radar and extra fuel had to be carried to allow for large detours. Long lines of thunderheads often blocked the way, leading to inadvisable attempts to thread a way between the cells.

The Navajos were fitted with radar, but it was rarely serviceable. In those days the unserviceability of the radar could be logged as an acceptable defect and repairs deferred. In Zambia, flying the ponderous Beaver, there was never much point in operating anywhere but underneath the weather. Now, operating the Pipers at around 7000-8000 feet on airways, it didn't cross my mind to go down and dirty. Murphy's Law rules.

Flying with duff radar, I was tempted to fly between towering cumulus. I found myself flying up a canyon formed by rows of fast-growing storm cells. Reaching a dead end I reversed course, but found the cloud had closed in behind, so I entered the least threatening section and tried to thread my way out of the trap by heading for the brightest area.

I expected moderate turbulence, but this time it was so severe that my head kept hitting the cockpit roof, despite my being strapped in. The impact jarred my teeth and I worried that the cantilevered engines might be shaken loose. A spine-jarring impact sheared all the rivets along the bottom edge of the windscreen and sheets of rain came pouring in. I switched off the battery master switch and flew using the standby instruments. At this stage I was not concerned about the lack of radio communication. Expecting the aircraft to disintegrate at any moment, I suddenly popped out into blue sky and calm air.

I was drenched, but the radios and instruments had been sheltered by the combing. When I switched the battery back on, the master warning panel showed both door and baggage hatch warning lights. Luckily they remained closed, if not secure.

Repairs to the Navajo were extensive and it was out of service for some time. Fortunately the airframe had only flexed, not distorted, otherwise it would have been a write off.

The Bristow guys, flying Britten Norman Islanders, recommended flying under the weather. They flew to Warri and Port Harcourt under VFR (visual flight rules) at a thousand feet, saying they avoided problems by being below cloud. OK - I would use this technique when required, but even so it was not foolproof.

After one month I began flying off airways to other destinations in Nigeria. my previous Navy and ZAF experience of navigating by deduced reckoning (DR) proved invaluable. Only the main regional airports had beacons, and finding the many local airstrips had proved too great a challenge for most of the charter companies in Lagos. All pilots are trained in map reading and DR during basic training, but only military low-level navigation could hone these skills to the fine edge required.

During the months of harmattan (The dust-laden wind from the Sahara) visibility can be reduced to as low as 500 metres. If you are not familiar with DR and low visibility prevails, finding the way without navaids is impossible. DR nav. requires a plastic-covered map pre-marked with tracks and distances. Using a chinagraph pencil to plot progress, it is possible, using simple formulae, to accurately navigate to distant destinations.

Delta was able to accept charters other companies had turned down and business picked up. Bookings came mostly from government departments surveying for infrastructure projects. The World Bank and the IMF required visits to monitor how their money was being spent. Agricultural feasibility studies were undertaken by any number of eager contractors.

These charters could take us to parts of Nigeria that hadn't changed since colonial times. Some of the airstrips reminded me of bush operations in Zambia; often neglected or hastily improvised, they were a stimulating challenge and not for beginners.

Mokwa, where a company from Pakistan had an agricultural research station, had been carved out of the bush by a grader.

Normally quite safe, it became a skating rink after heavy rain. After a downpour the laterite dust turned into a skidpan of tomato ketchup. Although it was long enough to let you come to a stop, directional control could be lost with injudicious braking.

At Jalingo the airstrip was just a straight stretch of the laterite main road which had a steep camber designed to shed water. While braking, any deviation from the crown of the road would take the aircraft into the monsoon drain. It was essential to remain dead centre until down to walking pace.

Other strips gave access to sites of interest due to the local history. Lokoja, at the confluence of the Niger and Benue rivers, had been the capital of Nigeria during early British administration. The old town centre had retained the trappings of its past and was still graced with quiet shady streets lined with mature trees. With large gardens and well-separated lots, the old brick and wood buildings presented a calm and peaceful oasis away from the chaos of recent development. The guesthouse where I preferred to have lunch had the original framed sepia photos on the panelled walls of the dining room.

Finding the way to Mubi in the far north east of the country was especially difficult during the harmattan. Chartered by a team of Brazilian surveyors, we refuelled the Piper Chieftain at Kaduna and launched off into the thickening dust haze. At 9000 feet the haze was so thick that I lost sight of the ground. Initially navigating by Nigerian Radio transmitters, we eventually had to descend and pick up a landmark for map reading. From a bend in the river I was using DR to find Mubi.

Hearing raised voices from the cabin I looked back to see the passengers, all with maps spread out, hotly debating our position. We had passed a giant monolith, which had attracted the attention of the cartographers because it was not on their chart. I was aware of this omission, but could not convey this to the Brazilians. Their representative was sent up to the cockpit to express their collective conclusion that I had overflown Mubi and was now deep inside the Cameroon. They justified their conclusion by pointing to a spot height that marked another outcrop across the border. I pointed at my watch and said "ten minutes more" and they became extremely excited.

When the time was up and Mubi was nowhere in sight, I began an expanding orbit search. If Mubi was not found in the next five minutes I would have to divert to Maiduguri. The visibility was only around 1500 metres and my confidence was beginning to wane. The passengers were near hysterical and now feared for their lives.

Finally I saw the airstrip. After landing, their consternation continued unabated, because they were convinced that I had landed in the Cameroon and that we all faced imminent arrest. When a Nigerian government Land Cruiser turned up with their man on the ground they sheepishly loaded their equipment, avoiding eye contact.

At Mubi I was taken to meet the chief. His palace was an elaborate mud structure like nothing I had seen before. The building was circular in shape and about thirty feet across, with the conical thatch soaring forty feet to its ventilated peak. Two sentries on white chargers stood guard outside the entrance. These horsemen were wearing chain mail under colourful tunics; their turbans were decorated with a swatch of feathers. Inside, the floor was laid with locally-produced tiles and the throne was covered in leopard skins.

By this time the temperature outside had reached around 40°C, though inside it remained cool. I was asked to sit and given mint tea. After waiting for an appropriate time, about twenty minutes, I was introduced to the chief, who entered in flowing robes and turban. I was gently questioned about my background, all the while given local tid-bits - it was surreal. Meeting over, I was escorted back to the guest house. The antique chain-mail armour worn by the guards had apparently been made by Arab craftsmen and was a reproduction of those worn by the crusaders.

Unserviceabilities away from base required unusual solutions. Delivering a VIP to Bida I had been marshalled up to the red carpet for disembarkation. I was then asked to re-park away from the reception area, but the battery was dead. A willing crowd helped me push the Navajo across the apron.

Fortunately the airport manager was as concerned as I was regarding the return of their minister to Lagos. I asked if he could obtain a battery matching the aircraft power requirement. After consulting with the Air Traffic Controller he told me to wait; a battery was being arranged. My concern increased as time began running out.

When a farm tractor and trailer slowly approached the aircraft, I was surprised to be told that the battery had arrived. I looked into the trailer, and lo and behold it contained an array of very large glass jars filled with liquid and connected by electrodes. The chap accompanying the battery informed me that he was from the local radio station and that this was his emergency power supply.

I opened the panel on the left side of the nose and told him the power settings. He juggled with the wiring and we hooked it up. The readings in the cockpit were good. I knew that the aircraft battery was finished and would have to start both engines using the external power.

I was now concerned about removal of the jump leads and closure of the panel. The panel was immediately in front of the left-hand propeller. I would be unable to leave the cockpit when both engines were running and had to explain to the tractor driver how the disconnection should be carried out and the panel secured. I emphasised with theatrical demonstrations the harmful effects of contact with the propeller.

We had a couple of dry runs and then awaited return of the passengers. When they arrived, the minister eyed the tractor and raised his eyebrows at me. "Bida ground power unit" I volunteered, and he seemed happy with that. It all worked OK and on disembarking in Lagos the minister thanked me with a knowing smile.

On a flight back from Benin, the hydraulic warning light came on. I thought it best to sort the problem out early and about fifteen minutes out of Lagos lowered the landing gear. Sure enough it failed to operate properly, unlocking but only half lowering. The next course of action was to operate the hand pump on the cockpit floor. I pumped away until my arm ached, but all my efforts only extended the gear a trifle.

Now my only remaining option was to use the emergency air bottle. This cylinder would add its high-pressure air into the system, theoretically forcing the gear down and locked. It was a one-shot solution. I pulled the toggle and wham, the nosewheel and right main gear slammed into position. The left gear continued to dangle uselessly. I did not want to land one wheel up as this would cause major damage.

In the co-pilot's seat was John Nti, our radio engineer, who had been maintaining our Benin-based Aztec. He was a short but tough and stocky chap, so I told him to pump the standby hydraulic lever as fast as he could. The air bottle had blown most of the hydraulic liquid out of the system, but I figured that any pressure that could be added would help. I also told him what might happen if we landed with one main wheel unlocked.

John went crazy, and the gear slowly responded. In the remaining five minutes until touchdown he maintained his constant rapid pumping. The gear looked OK, but a red warning light remained. I had briefed the Lagos emergency services and they followed the aircraft after touchdown. Touching down as gently as possible, first on the right main, then the nose, I stopped the port engine and gently lowered the left wheel on to the runway. It held. After I had gently rolled the aircraft to a halt, the engineers applied a mechanical brace and we were towed back to the hangar.

Flat tyres were another hazard when landing at untended strips. This only happened to me once, but it certainly created a problem. The charter was for one of our regular customers, a state-run sugar producer. The cane fields and factory were on the banks of the Niger River at Bacita, about two hundred miles north of Lagos. After landing at the grass strip the passenger dropped me off at the company guesthouse, where I could get a bite to eat and a room to rest. A small swimming pool was available, which was great for cooling off.

When we arrived back at the strip late in the afternoon the Aztec had a flat, and as there was no immediate solution the passenger stormed off back to the office. I started an engine and tried to use the HF radio to call base, but there was no reply. I trudged across the road to the guest house and could not get through on the phone there either. What to do? The only option seemed to be a taxi back to Lagos. The manager arranged one from nearby Jebba. When it arrived I was surprised that it had made it to the airport and was alarmed at the price. No other taxi would accept the job, so the driver had me over a barrel, but the company would pay.

Off we went. Nigerian taxis are something else, not only did the doors not close properly but it became apparent that the transmission, shocks and steering were extremely well worn. The engine seemed OK, which meant that we set off at great speed with much rattling and lurching.

Turning south on to the Great North Road I realised that this was going to be one hell of a ride. The road at that time was unpaved, and large potholes and occasional rainwater gullies pitted the surface. Eighteen-wheeler behemoths thundered along raising immense clouds of dust. We and other vehicles careered into the dust, it seemed to me, in blind ignorance. As night fell things improved, the headlights of oncoming vehicles gave greater advanced warning.

There was no chance of sleep, even on level graded laterite. The natural frequency of vehicle suspension triggered by some bump or other produced a vibration that the wheels transmitted to the road surface. The resulting washboard texture of the road was further amplified due to feedback. Hammering of the suspension was tolerated as the alternative meant a considerable change in speed, either by reduction or an increase. Either way was unsafe (think driving in fog).

On average there seemed to be three or four roadside wrecks per mile which had accumulated over the years. No abandoned vehicle was allowed to remain unmolested. Whether the result of an accident or simple unserviceability, untended machines were soon stripped of usable parts. If the crash was fatal, the bodies often remained in situ for days, sometimes for ever. Nature's scavengers would reduce them to a pile of bones..

At three in the morning, after eight long hours and 200 miles of dust and nail-biting tension, I was delivered home. Janet had assumed I had an unscheduled stopover and was horrified by my dishevelled appearance. After sluicing myself down I unwound with a beer or two before sleeping heavily.

We had no telephone, so when I finally showed up the next morning I was asked where I had parked the Aztec, which was required for a flight. "Bacita" I replied and explained the situation. The company had no idea what had happened. I flew an extra pilot, a spare wheel, two engineers and Janet up to Bacita in the Navajo. Janet and I had a picnic by the club pool while the wheel was fixed.

Telephones in Nigeria were a real problem. The standing charges and calls were cheap enough, but only companies or the very wealthy could afford the kickbacks required to keep the service connected. Janet arranged her social life either by calling in person or by meeting friends at the club.

The Ikeja Country Club had a very lively atmosphere. During the daytime the pool would be surrounded by wives and children. In the evening the bar was jammed with the chaps seeking solace from the trials of their working day. As Richard the gardener was accommodated in the servants' quarters adjacent to the bungalow, he willingly acted as babysitter, allowing Janet and me to socialise. Janet served on the committee as Ladies, Entertainment and Catering member.

The club was situated on the Airport Road, which was then being upgraded by Petra Monk. This outfit, a joint venture between British and Lebanese companies was staffed by a gregarious bunch who spent much time in the club bar. One of the workers, Roy, was an amiable northern giant, standing seven feet tall. His current task was to prepare the newly-constructed carriageway for surfacing with tarmac.

Roy's problem was that impatient taxi drivers had removed the barriers and sped across the freshly-rolled ballast to bypass the "go-slow". In just a few seconds several hours of preparation were undone. Roy had had enough of this and stood guard, waiting for the spreader to arrive. Eventually he was challenged by a taxi that had sneaked on to his virgin surface. Roy held his ground, holding up a warning hand, but the taxi continued a slow approach. When it became apparent that it intended to continue, Roy reached down and picked up his weapon of choice, a six-foot length of steel reinforcing, and adopted the pose of a baseball batsman ready to strike.

The long queue of stalled traffic beheld this frozen tableau. Roy upped the stakes by raising the steel bar above his head. The taxi driver, having studied the look of fury on the face of his adversary, suddenly careered off in reverse. Roy received the cheers of the onlookers with a big grin.

One, however, was not amused. The window of a big black Mercedes was wound down and a strident voice informed Roy that no foreigner should threaten a Nigerian. The steel bar was raised again and the window quickly closed.

Normally there would be no flying on weekends and recreation was vital; the seaside was favourite. There was Bar Beach, Tarkwa Bay and Lighthouse Beach in Lagos and an hour's drive west down a newly completed highway lay Badagri, a quiet, palm-tree-lined idyll.

Facing the Atlantic, Bar Beach fronted Victoria Island, an urban setting. It sported many sun shelters (essential) and traders of great entrepreneurial spirit (tiresome). The atmosphere was lively, but could be wearing if you were not trained in the art of fending off vendors of drinks, fruit and dry goods. The way to avoid their attention was to act as if they did not exist. Look up or in any way allow eye contact and you were committed. Among added attractions were street performers, dancing, performing animals and of course the inevitable bikini girls.

Execution days were a no-no, as these would attract thousands of onlookers and snatch thieves. Normally the shelter owners ran a vigilante scheme to protect their customers, but for these gruesome events numbers overwhelmed any attempts to protect patrons.

Firing-squad victims were tied to stout wooden poles concreted into oil drums. Last rites were performed by priests and mullahs before the firing squad of fifteen opened up for a fusillade lasting minutes. Robbers, politicians and rebellious army officers were all unwilling participants of the "Bar Beach Show".

Swimming in the heavy surf was perilous. Rip tides were an unpredictable hazard, there one minute, gone the next. These currents, narrow as they were, could sweep the unwary swiftly out to sea. Fighting the current was futile, so extrication by swimming sideways was the only answer. Drownings were an all-too-frequent occurrence, as there were no restrictions, warnings, or advice. Being an ex-surf lifesaver I knew the problem and warned many of my friends.

Sure enough, during one of our days at the beach I was fooling about in the surf when I spotted a young local lad struggling out beyond the break, caught by a rip. He was furiously swimming against the flow and tiring himself out. I knew that if nothing was done he would become another statistic. My conscience forced me into action and I swam out to get him.

When I reached the lad he was going down and gulping water. Gripping him by the standard hold, I swam out of the rip before heading backward toward the beach. Progress was good, but we had to enter the break, where the surf was huge. I knew I would not be able to retain my charge. Suddenly we were lifted up, flipped over and trapped in the rotor vortex. I lost him. It seemed to last for ever.

Finally, lungs bursting, I broke the surface, only to be rolled over into another maelstrom. I had only managed a partial intake of air and tumbled over and over, totally disorientated. I realised my air supply was exhausted and prepared to die. Then I hit the bottom and planted my feet in the sand preparing to make one final attempt to launch up to the surface. With my feet still on the ground the water level suddenly dropped, leaving me waist high in the foam. With my lungs screaming I staggered out of the water and collapsed on the beach. No one came to help, as all were attending to the boy. Thankfully he had been pulled out of the water by onlookers and survived. I vowed never to attempt a solo rescue again.

Tarkwa Bay was on the other side of Lagos harbour and was reached by a pleasant ride in a water taxi. Its main attraction, the calm water, made it a favourite with families. The local villagers were charming; they cleaned the beach and provided shelters and refreshments.

Lighthouse Beach had the heavy surf, but it stretched for miles and was mostly deserted. This beach was favoured by those seeking solitude and those with "girlfriends". It was not advisable to consort with a "pick up" as there were several cases of chaps going into the bushes for a quick one, only to be relieved of everything, and I mean everything, by accomplices.

Badagri was way down the coast. The old slaving town was separated from the beach by a twenty-mile lagoon. Again with heavy surf it struck a compromise, not busy and with the provision of just enough refreshments to make a good day out. Cotonou was just across the border and fresh baguettes were available there.

Having aviation contracts with NNPC, Agip, Elf and Willbros meant that our operations down in Port Harcourt were thriving. The Lagos-based Aztecs and Navajos were kept busy ferrying passengers for the helicopters and floatplanes to distribute to the oil installations offshore and in the Niger Delta, a vast network of rivers and mangrove. I had always dreamt of flying a boat or float plane and I tried very hard to persuade Delta to give me a conversion. Unfortunately neither of the two Canadian pilots was instructor qualified, nor was the DCA prepared to allow the course to be carried out in Nigeria. Never mind, I would wait.

On day stops in Port Harcourt I normally went for lunch at the Presidential Hotel, where I could spend time by the pool. After lunch and a sleep on one of the sun beds, a quick swim was a refreshing way to prepare for the return flight. The pesky girls were always present, but if treated in the same fashion as the traders they would inevitably cease their advances.

Dantata, one of the richest men in Nigeria, was staging a wedding for one of his family and needed ten of his wives (harem) flown from Lagos to Maiduguri way up in the north eastern corner of the country. His HS125 captain, a Brit named Penrose, arranged the charter. Delta only had the Navajo Chieftain available, which had eight passenger seats. "Never mind, two can sit on the floor" I was told.

As it was the dry season with no chance of turbulence, I agreed. We landed at Maiduguri after a refuelling stop at Kano and were marshalled to the side of the apron. I soon realised why. Three extended C130 Hercules landed in short order and after parking disgorged a cargo of Cadillacs and other impressive wedding presents. They had flown in from the US via Dakar, and left immediately after unloading. I saw no customs officers anywhere.

Although invited by Dantata and staying overnight, Penrose informed me with his nose in the air that I was not to attend the wedding and would leave with the "wives" the next day. We had been sub-chartered by him, the pompous old fart.

Back in Ikeja Janet had been discussing the ever-increasing piles of garbage with the other wives. Were they, and the companies their husbands worked for, interested in a garbage collection service? The state equivalent had long ago failed due to the culture of zero maintenance. The word got around and it became apparent that good money could be made by such an enterprise.

Not being able to become legally involved in commerce, Janet sought out locals who would be willing to assist. Our operations officer, Augustine, and the radio man, John Nti, were keen, and registered a company as Sword Refuse Collection, purchasing a stripped-down VW Kombi. Our gardener Richard drove the wagon and also collected the refuse. Plastic bags were distributed to all the customers and the business took off. Encouraged by good references the number of customers continued to rise. Eventually a further two Kombis were bought. The crew was increased by the addition of a collector to pick up the bags. Janet acted as honorary operations officer and treasurer.

Any successful business in Nigeria attracts the attention of the greedy and powerful, and sure enough a fleet of hi-tech garbage trucks now arrived. "Sword" was shut down, permit revoked, and the big boys moved in. A few months later all the new trucks were unserviceable, and garbage again accumulated on the streets.

Delta itself was becoming profitable. In any normal economy this would be great, but the directors of Delta Air Charter did not want to lose the subsidy from the River State Government. The profits could be siphoned off in time-honoured Nigerian fashion, but who gets what? The directors fought amongst themselves and the issue went to litigation. Court cases in Nigeria rarely reach a conclusion, as it is not in the lawyers' best interests.

When it became time for the annual renewal of the Air Operating Certificate the question of ownership remained unresolved. Delta was forced to cease operations. I flew the last flight, returning a grounded Navajo back to Lagos, where it was parked in the long grass with the rest of the fleet to join a host of other relics; sad really. Having seen this coming I had applied for a job with Bristow Helicopters, flying their BN2 Islanders. Their operation was just two hangars down from Delta Air Charter. It helped that the Chief Pilot was one Les Ingham, ex-RN course mate, ex-Scimitar, ex-Zambia Flying Doctor and ex-East African Airways pilot.

Chapter Fourteen

BRISTOW HELICOPTERS, NORTH SEA

September 1977 - May 1979

Bristow accepted my application and I was flown back to the UK. I completed the joining routine at Redhill Aerodrome, the Bristow HQ. Unknown to me, the helicopter pilots in Aberdeen had threatened industrial action in support of their claim for union recognition. Alan Bristow would not countenance any such thing. The pilots were divided, and the outcome of this highly-politicised dispute was that only non-union crew were retained. Bristow Aberdeen lost roughly half its complement of helicopter pilots.

The story goes that when Alan Bristow addressed the pilots on the apron at Aberdeen he asked those wishing to unionise to take a step forward. When they responded he told them "keep walking, collect your kit on the way out, you're fired".

When I walked through the door to sign up at Redhill, John Cameron baldly informed me that the job in Nigeria was no longer available, but they could offer me a position as a helicopter First Officer. My consternation, obviously apparent, caused a hasty upgrade of my status to Senior First Officer with third-year captain's pay. I accepted. Flying helicopters had not crossed my mind, but I now found the idea quite stimulating.

I returned to Lagos to complete my leaving routine. Janet and the kids flew back early while I packed, sold up and closed my accounts. I got invited to several farewell dinners, celebrating right up to the time of departure. I boarded the B-Cal flight still dressed in party gear, a white suit and red silk shirt. I slept all the way back and awoke with a fearsome hangover. God knows what I looked like, not having shaved for several days. I donned dark sun glasses to cut the glare and had to wear my favourite straw hat, which would not have survived packing.

Approaching the "nothing to declare" channel at Gatwick airport, I was called over by a young customs chap with a huge grin spread across his face. On reaching the counter he was surprised to hear fluent English. He explained (still chuckling away) that it was more than his job was worth to let me pass without examination. My baggage did not contain much, apart from an electric kettle and a toaster.

The helicopter course at Redhill was fun, my instructor being the legendary Bill Barrel. With his flaming red mane and beard, Bill, an Australian, was a well-known feature of the surrounding pubs. He was an engaging character of easy manner and old-world charm. When Bill taught you, you never felt you were under instruction.

Janet and the kids moved back into the house at Bradninch and I came home at weekends, a 200- mile drive.

I am often asked which was the most difficult to fly, aeroplanes or helicopters. They are totally different and not really comparable, but I wouldn't say one was more difficult than the other. Quick reactions are needed during fixed-wing flying, as one more often becomes committed to a specific course of action. With helicopters there is more time to think, the exception being the engine-off forced landing. My brother Rob, being a career helicopter man, had always joked that I would never be able to hack helicopter flying. I couldn't restrain a broad grin when I told him of my new profession.

The conversion to helicopters, including the ground school, only took three months as opposed to the *ab initio* two years. It felt good to have a helicopter licence. I drove to Aberdeen and arrived in early January 1979 in sub zero temperatures. Bristow, keen to get me online, completed the Sikorsky S61 course ground school in two weeks and the flying conversion in four days.

Finding somewhere for a young family was difficult in boomtown Aberdeen. Cheap and cheerful "Scottish Special" housing was provided for those employed in the oil industry, and we were put on the waiting list. Meanwhile I had arranged short-term rental of a picturesque granite farm cottage in Kintore. Janet flew up with the kids and joined me in the hotel, and after a few days buying the essentials we moved in. The granite walls were cold-soaked, you could feel the stone leeching the warmth from your body.

We had bought a gas heater to boost the one pathetic portable electric fire. Only one problem - it made the walls stream with condensation. The open coal fires were effective but needed constant attention. At night the banked-up fire in the bedroom roared into action just after midnight and then died away around three. We replaced the covers discarded an hour or so before.

Getting up for an early start was painful, but a steaming bowl of porridge worked wonders and made the process of sitting in my freezing car tolerable. The VW always started first time, but it took the half-hour drive to work to reach a comfortable temperature.

The Bristow S61 carried 25 passengers and a cabin attendant, its task being to ferry oil workers to oil installations up to 180 miles out to sea. It was a steady old bus, good natured and easy to fly. Safety equipment and procedures were well implemented, as was the impressive standard of maintenance.

Being a North Sea helicopter pilot was an exciting new experience. Flying out to the offshore platforms reminded me of my time in the navy, but only slightly. The weather in this region could be a challenge, for it was rarely benign. Strong winds and low cloud were the norm and fog and driving rain were frequent. Ice and snow were a problem during the winter. The immersion-style flight suits had improved considerably since my Navy days, being much easier to get in and out of. With extra fancy fittings and bright orange colour they looked pretty cool too.

Navigation assistance was provided by the Decca Navigator, a primitive system based on low-frequency transmissions. The cockpit presentation was a rolling map and position pointer. I never felt comfortable with this system, and most of us just headed out in the right direction relying on the weather radar to locate the platform.

Bristow had the BP Forties Field contract, just 80 miles north east of Aberdeen. This route was the "milk run" and guaranteed a good wholesome meal at lunchtime. Impoverished co-pilots often ordered a meal at each touchdown, ensuring a well-stocked fridge. When a gay steward brought the meals, co-pilots got extra treats. Mobil operated the Beryl Alpha way up north, east of the Shetlands, a boring two hours out and two back.

On the domestic front, about a month later a Scottish Special unit in Dyce became available. These small but functional terraced houses were warm. Our kids' new school was huge, with 1100 primary pupils. Many of the pupils were the offspring of oil workers and had been raised in the toughest parts of Glasgow. Our kids had only ever attended village and private schools. I had to brief Tia and Leon about bullying, as their complexions and diminutive stature made them a sure target. I told them that the first time any of the kids picked on them, they should without hesitation punch the offender on the nose, assuring them that the bullies would then cease to bother them.

I asked Janet how the kids had found their first few days at Dyce primary, "Fine, they have already made new friends" she said. Leon had carried out my instructions to a T. The headmaster was not amused and invited me for a chat. When asked if Leon had a history of aggression, I asked the headmaster if the victims were known bullies. He paused before finally replying "You have a point". The bullies remained subdued.

Our new location in Princess Drive proved quite sociable, as we were surrounded by the Bristow crowd. Two consolations of life in Scotland were porridge and excellent kippers. Unfortunately I am not a whisky drinker.

Aberdeen was a grey, cold, and windy city, but the countryside was stunning. During our year in Dyce we had two weeks of sunny weather, when we took the opportunity to explore the surrounding hills and forests.

The social life was an eye opener. Scottish pubs are not for the sensitive and the hotel bars could not quite pull off a convivial atmosphere. Bristow parties filled the gap. The ex-Vietnam vets were a very lively contingent and made dinner parties a hilarious event. Bringing their equally extrovert wives and a collection of heavy music, they guaranteed an enjoyable evening. Luke Bartelotta and Doug Palermo led the pack. Mike Moran next door pretended to be a hippy - I'm not sure his wife approved.

Meanwhile we had sold the empty house in Bradninch and had jointly purchased (with my Mum and Dad) a Victorian country house in Chagford, Devon.

At the end of the year I was told that Bell 212 co-pilots were required on the Brent field and asked if I was interested. Definitely. The contract was two weeks on, two weeks off, with the opportunity to commute from Chagford. Before moving I attended the 212 conversion course in Inverness. I preferred to swot in the evenings rather than join the training captain, Rod Good, and fellow students in the bar. Good thought me an irritating anti-social twit and he chose to make things difficult on my final check ride. I managed.

For the end-of-course celebration we booked a table at the hotel pre-Christmas dinner dance. My course mates, Brian Teeder and Mike Fooks-Bale, were joined by Austin Omerigie, a large and jolly Nigerian pilot. Austin had been boogying away with one of the local girls and brought her back to the table. The girl enjoyed our company, but her raucous laugh got the attention of her previous companions, now well into the whisky. One of their number staggered over to our table and directed some loud and insulting remarks in Austin's direction.

None of us could understand a word, but Austin got the message. The hall fell silent. In order to retain face, Austin knew a response was required, but he also realised that sympathy would switch if he beat the crap out of this guy. Austin stood up, large and broad shouldered, and the crowd held their breath. Grabbing the offender's shirt front in one mighty fist, Austin hoisted the fellow into the air, swung him back and then skimmed him, ten pin bowls style, across the dance floor. He crashed into the table and chairs across the other side unhurt. The crowd approved, and Austin received his ovation with a gentlemanly bow.

After spending Christmas with the family in Chagford we hired a truck and drove up to Dyce to collect our stuff. On the M9 near Sterling we encountered icy roads. It was quite eerie - one moment the road was wet and black, then with one puff of wind the surface instantly turned white with frost. I was suddenly in a predicament, as we were travelling at speed through a gentle left turn. Trying to round the curve and maintain control was impossible, and the truck swung from side to side. We waltzed down the highway for about 150 yards before encountering an offside gravel trap. This caught us very nicely before damage was done, but it was impossible to extricate the vehicle. We had been driving for ten hours or so and the temperature was now well below zero. There being no such thing as mobile phones then. We stood by the roadside to try and hitch a lift.

Miraculously the first vehicle along was an HGV recovery vehicle on the lookout for clients. We reached Dyce about 1.30 in the morning.

We loaded up the following day, planning to start the drive south early the next morning. Snow was forecast, with advice to stay off the roads unless travel was a matter of urgency. We decided to give it a go, otherwise our schedule would be in disarray.

We departed in heavy snow. It took four hours instead of 90 minutes to reach Perth, when the snow eased off. Warnings of another blizzard approaching from the south west came over the radio, and we ran into more snow around Gloucester. By the time we were passing Bristol, only police patrols were still moving. I knew that it would become difficult after leaving the highway, especially the last few miles into Chagford where the roads were the sunken lanes of Dartmoor. Only wide enough for one vehicle, they were provided with passing bays every few hundred yards, but these lanes accumulated drifting snow. As we turned off the highway and on to Dartmoor I put my foot down, thinking slowing might cause wheel spin. If there was conflicting traffic I would see the approaching headlights, but we would be trapped.

I discovered that cornering in the snow allowed higher speeds, as any tendency to skid sideways was prevented by a build up of snow, so I put my foot to the floor. Our journey ended at Easton Cross, a mile and a half from Chagford, where an abandoned car blocked the way. We continued on foot, getting overheated from struggling through the snow. We finally knocked on the door of Portland House at 3.30 a.m. When Mum opened the door she burst out laughing - we had icicles hanging from our hair.

The village was cut off for three days and we had to place heaters under the fuel tanks to melt the diesel, which had by then turned to jelly. When I phoned the truck rental company to apologise for the late return, the dispatcher was relieved to hear that the truck was OK.

No extra charge - several of his customers had ended up in ditches.

The kids were relieved to be back in a village school and Janet was kept busy with redecoration and improvements while the house was divided for two families.

I flew back to Aberdeen and on out to the Treasure Finder, a semi-submersible accommodation rig attached to the Brent "B" platform. This was to be my other "home" far out in the North Sea. It was now January with only a few hours of daylight, not the best time to be learning the new job. The weather was wild most of the time, the difference from high summer being a just few degrees.

The Bristow offshore bunch was an eclectic mix coming from wildly different backgrounds. Ex-Royal Marine and ex-Royal Navy pilots were mixed with ex-military pilots from Germany, France, Austria, as well as the inevitable Vietnam vets. Bristow employees were thankfully allocated individual cabins with showers. When not working, eating or sleeping we hung out in a Portakabin crewroom, playing the board game Uckers and watching movies.

Uckers is played on a common Ludo board. Adopted by the navy, it was developed into a game combining both strategy and luck. Bristow preferred the Fleet Air Arm version with advanced rules, ie cheating was allowed, it being the players' responsibility to spot the culprit and award penalties. Excitement increased as the game drew to a close, when critical decisions had to be made and calculated risks taken. The final outcome could never be accurately forecast. Sudden changes in fortune often caused upturned boards and scattered counters.

The movies supplied to the oil rigs tended to be of the sex-and-violence type, only occasionally appealing to the intellect. At that time they were provided on 16mm cine film, which made them vulnerable to deviant collectors who physically removed the sex scenes. This caused many of us to be hugely disappointed when the movie jumped the edit. Some only turned up to see the "action".

The catering, as on all offshore facilities, was of a very high standard. An impressive array of fine food was on offer 24 hours a day, and the temptation to overindulge was ever present. When my waistline increased by an inch or two I backed off the grub and spent more time in the gym.

Our two Bell 212s were protected and maintained in a heated double hangar adjacent to the helideck. As the 212s had skids rather than wheels, they were transported in and out of the hangar on mechanical bogies that ran on tracks. A motorised turntable on top of the bogie could then be turned into wind for start up and take-off. The average wind over the deck was around thirty knots. Wind speed had to be monitored closely to avoid exceeding the 40-knot limit for start-up and shut-down. This limit was set to avoid blade sailing and possible contact with the ground or tail boom. In a blade strike, all hell breaks loose and fragments can be thrown a long way.

In helicopters the engines are started with the rotor clutch disengaged in piston engines, or with the rotor brake on in turbine aircraft. After power is adjusted the rotor is allowed to wind up.

Our main task was to ferry the morning and evening shift change, when the riggies were taken to and from work on the rigs. The many platforms in the Brent Field were in close proximity, so we had a take-off and landing on average every ten minutes. Rotors were kept running throughout passenger boarding/disembarking and refuelling.

Pilots were rostered for either the morning or evening shuttle service, which at that time of year mostly took place in the dark. Carrying out the pre-flight inspections in the cold wind was a painful business.

I enjoyed the challenge of the final landing back on the bogie. The turntable was an oblong built to accommodate the 212 skids. Accuracy was essential, as there remained only about a four-inch margin on each side. If the wind direction meant the Treasure Finder was in the lee of the main platform, the turbulence could be extreme and a good touchdown difficult, so it was very satisfying when achieved in short order. If the wind strength had increased beyond limits and a shutdown was not possible, a relief pilot would be called to take control until the wind abated. If the forecast predicted no early reduction in wind strength, the 212 might have to be flown ashore, either to Stornoway in the Shetland Islands or Bergen in Norway (wind strengths onshore were normally less limiting).

On the rare occasions when there was no wind we faced other problems. With the oil companies demanding maximum payloads, less nose-down tilt could be used for take-off. With less forward speed, going over the edge of a helideck presented another hazard, because at the edge the loss of ground cushion and resulting sink could result in a tail rotor strike. To counter this a sneaky technique was developed to bounce off the cushion of air before the deck edge. You had to make sure you got it right.

During night take-offs a quick transference to flight by instruments was essential. Leaving the brightly-lit helideck to fly into total darkness could lead to disorientation, especially if it was snowing. Because of the initial nose-down attitude the snow produced an optical illusion, giving the false impression of a steep climb.

The challenges were stimulating. A diving support ship was anchored in the Brent field, which not being particularly large was prone to pitch, roll, and heave, all of which presented landing problems. There did not seem to be any limits for heave (up and down) but the pitch and roll limit was set at 4º. Not being able to carry out the end-of-tour crew change presented the operators with a whole host of problems and resulted in understatements of limiting conditions. As a result of this it was often left up to the pilot to decide if a landing was possible.

Both skids were supposed to be flat on the ground while boarding passengers. Trapping a foot or leg underneath would surely lead to injury and the pilot would be held responsible. The trouble was, if the ship was rolling out of limits and the 212 was flat on the deck, neither the pilot nor the anti-skid net would be able to prevent it from sliding. If the pilot decided to pick up passengers, it was easier to continue flying, just maintaining deck contact.

I calculated that during one pickup the deck was heaving about fifty feet. The only way to approach was to fly alongside the ship's helideck, then hover at the height of the highest point of heave. Judgement of the correct time to move across and touch down was critical. I'm sure MS Flight Simulator could use this.

During renovation and maintenance on the Treasure Finder, both 212s were transferred to Sumburgh. Crews were accommodated in a bed-and-breakfast inn at Sandwick, a few miles north of the airport. Being out of the way and the bar being open all hours was a temptation for some. One of the Vietnam vets, Roger Olds, served an amazing selection of "cocktails", which he presented a gallon at a time in a red plastic bucket. They tasted unusual, but pleasant enough. Roger would not divulge recipes and some were strangely addictive.

I'm pretty sure a hangover contributed to the departure of one of our team. Back out in the Brent Field he had landed on the wrong helideck, a real bad move. After waking up one day with a particularly fierce hangover I swore not to attend "cocktails" and took up running instead. My plan was to take part in the Two Hills Race in Chagford, I practised daily during my two weeks at home. In the end I never participated.

One of our 212s was fitted with a winch for emergency rescues, required a pilot to be on standby in the hanger at Sumburgh airport. During my weekend stint I was sent a curry lunch from the airport restaurant. Two hours later I suddenly suffered vomiting and stomach cramps which were so severe that I was unable to use the telephone. When I finally managed a call fifteen minutes later, I was told the doctor and ambulance were busy with six other victims. Could the police help?

By the time the Bristow duty operations officer arrived, I had recovered. I hate to think what might have happened if I had been called out. The restaurant was operated by a well-known hotel group. In retrospect I should have pushed them for a free weekend in London.

After a short spell out in the Thistle Field stationed on the Gulnare I had enough hours to qualify as a helicopter captain and went to Redhill to complete the Command Course. The flying side was carried out on an ancient Westland Whirlwind (WS 55) and the chirpy little Bell Jetranger.

Unfortunately, after I had completed the course, Bristow were unable to place me on a contract as oil companies required considerable helicopter command experience. I had heard rumours that a Shell contract in Malaysia had been tendered for and that this contract included fixed-wing aircraft. Failing to understand why Redhill had not got in touch, I nosed around the top floor offices. I struck gold in Bob Roffe's, for open on his desk was a folder with a summary of Bristow pilots with fixed-wing experience. My name was absent, despite being more qualified than everyone on the list.

The summary had been prepared by Dave Collinson. Previously a helicopter pilot, Collinson had inveigled his way into his position in charge of Bristow Fixed Wing Operations. It was blatantly obvious that he saw me as a threat and was keeping me out of the picture. I cannot understand why these guys get so paranoid, I just enjoy the work.

Bob entered the office and quietly asked what I was doing. I explained that I had heard rumours regarding the Miri contract and considered myself a HS125 candidate. He glanced at the file.

"Have you got a fixed-wing ATPL?" he asked. I nodded. "Do you have any jet time?" He paused, realising I had plenty. Bob knew my history from his Fleet Air Arm days. Giving me a form to fill in he murmured under his breath "Collinson!"

Chapter Fifteen

THE HS125 AND MALAYSIA

July 1979 – January 1985

I attended the 125 introduction course at Hatfield, which was something else. The BAE curriculum required an inordinate amount of time studying performance data. I supposed that British Aerospace had to protect themselves against litigation. A number of the attendees were company pilots with relatively little experience.

Type and instrument ratings were carried out by Gerry Ranscombe on Alan Bristow's private 125. Meanwhile I needed to build up hours on type to fulfil the Shell contract requirement. This was achieved by crewing on the weekly Lagos crew change during the summer of '79. These two successive overnight flights were physically demanding. An evening departure meant an arrival at Lagos in the small hours the following day and it was difficult to get any sleep before the return that evening. After landing back at Gatwick in the early morning and keen to get back to Devon, I found that I could drive safely for about 30 minutes. It was summer, and after a 40-minute power nap at the Dorking Gap I was sufficiently revived to manage the next three and a half hours down the A30/303.

The 125 required a refuelling stop in Algiers. After that came the long haul over the Sahara. Navigation beacons ran out over the desert, but the 125 had the precursor to satnav in the Omega Global Navigation System. Based on VLF radio transmissions, it was good enough for ocean or desert crossings.

With nothing to do but monitor the autopilot, keeping awake was a problem. Gerry always had forty winks after departing Algiers, and I took my turn when he woke up. Gerry often fell asleep when I was having my nap (he was getting on in years and approaching retirement). There being no air traffic control for a couple of hours, aircraft gave position reports to avoid conflictions. Falling asleep was a common problem, and during long periods of silence someone would call, on air, "Wake up, wake up!" Most airlines operated their long-haul African routes at night.

Arrival time in Lagos was around 3.30 am and by the time we got to the General Manager's house in Ikeja it was 4.30. The GM and his wife always received the 125 crews in person, as they were keen to unwrap the goodies they had ordered. The bar was open for a nightcap, and in order to sleep through the morning we took the opportunity to sink one or two more than usual.

On my first trip the GM was in mellow mood and his wife, a real flirt, took advantage. Ready to turn in, I took a shower and returned to my room. Wearing just a towel, I opened the door and bumped into her. She was wearing a short see-through nightie and was bending over, pretending to turn back the covers. I backed off, alarmed at her audacity. Her husband was still up and about!

The next morning we went for a wake-up dip in the pool, and she remarked that swimsuits were not necessary. I smiled but kept mine on. The lady apparently often made a pass at visiting pilots, the GM apparently not bothered by his wife's quest for extra-marital kicks.

Back at Gatwick I occasionally acted as co-pilot on Mr Bristow's private flights, and these were a welcome change. Bristow had a yacht in the Mediterranean and we either delivered or collected him from wherever it was berthed. These flights were provided with catering. The other 125 captain, Derek Jordan, was a foodie and always over-catered, keeping uneaten delicacies for himself. Nothing got past Mr Bristow of course, and he eventually cracked. After landing in Malaga he ordered his chauffeur to collect all the remaining food. Jordan, infuriated, chased after them across the airport apron swinging a tea bag bellowing "You forgot something!"

Jordan had high blood pressure, his moods were unpredictable and the slightest inconvenience could spark a mighty rage. His complexion gave warning of an impending outburst when a red flush rose up out of his collar. He could lose it in an instant. On one occasion, having been overtaken on a roundabout (traffic circle) by a police patrol car, he accelerated, overtook and after heading them off pulled them over to give a lecture about dangerous driving. The officers were not amused and charged Derek with the same offence. Derek challenged the charge and successfully defended himself in court! He was nobody's fool, pity about the temper.

When I found out Jordan was to be the Miri chief pilot I groaned, as this would definitely take the shine off the experience. His co-pilot for most Gatwick-operated flights, Mike Howard, coped well, having developed a thick skin for bolshie captains.

Shell selected the old Viper-engined 125/400B for the Miri contract. We collected it from Stuttgart, Bosch had replaced it with a new 700. It had been well maintained but had a vicious wing drop at the stall. Having studied the fuel planning in depth at Hatfield, I realised that it would not meet the correct fuel requirement for the Miri-Kuala Lumpur sector. My concerns were brushed aside; Shell called the shots and I was still a junior with Bristow.

Meanwhile Janet and I carried out intensive research for a suitable boarding school for Tia and Leon. Our parameters required the school to be within budget, co-ed, character building and most of all, fun .

This narrowed it down to three. Only one of these, Clayesmore in Dorset, was in driving range of Devon, which was important because Mum and Dad would be in loco parentis. Driving down to Clayesmore, Janet and I were holding our breath and hoping the school would come up to expectations. If it did not, we would be stuck.

On first sighting the school buildings, our hopes began to rise. Originally the Iwerne Minster Manor House, the school had retained the surrounding parklands. The buildings and grounds, set among quiet Dorset farmlands, invoked a feeling of peace and calm. We crunched to a halt on the gravel in front of the main building and were approached by a couple of pupils who asked with a smile if they could help. Janet looked at me with a big grin.

Mr Beeby, the headmaster, explained that Clayesmore had many years of experience caring for children whose parents were overseas, and he personally showed us the facilities. Tia and Leon were overawed and a little intimidated by the grand setting but they were eager to start. They would commence at the co-located preparatory school.

Dave Collinson was responsible for crewing. He decided I should also be Twin Otter qualified as a Miri back-up pilot. I self-studied from the Flight Manual to pass the technical exam. For the flight training and test I flew out to Nigeria on the 125 and we used the Lagos operation's Twin Otters.

I was reminded of Ikeja chaos by a pile up on the Agege Motor Road just outside the crew house. A van and its driver had skewered themselves on to steel reinforcing bars protruding from the back of a stalled low loader. They remained there for a couple of days. Gruesome.

I was to start flying in Brunei two months before the main Bristow deployment to Miri. Shell Aviation had been operating fixed and rotary-wing services for Brunei and Sarawak Shell from the Anduki airstrip. Dependence on the services of Brunei Shell had proved unacceptable to the Malaysian government and was the reason behind the establishment of the Miri operation. As a temporary measure, for two months, I was to be loaned to Shell Brunei to operate the Beech 99 and act as co-pilot on the Beech 90 until the Bristow aircraft arrived in Miri in the new year.

First I had to attend a Beech 99 technical course in the US. I arrived in Wichita just after midnight, with the temperature at 80°F although it was now mid October; I had to carry my jacket. The next morning it was 36° and snow was falling! At the Beech training school I had been booked on the King Air B90 course instead of the B99, great.

Kansas was a dry state, and in order to get a drink I had to formally join the hotel "club". Reading the local papers it appeared the alcohol laws did nothing to prevent carnage on the road. I was woken in the early hours by a mighty "crump" as some vehicle flipped over the central reservation.

On the way out I stopped over in San Francisco to see my youngest brother Roger. Married to an American girl and living in Mill Valley, Rog showed me the sights downtown and we finished the day at a genuine English pub. The 17th-century timbered building had been shipped complete with roses and red-brick garden path. Coincidentally the manager was an ex Shell Aviation pilot, and he became quite animated as we recounted our flying exploits, but he turned quiet when I asked how he was enjoying SF. He didn't seem too happy with his lot, probably due to visits by a 300lb police officer. This cop rolled in while we were there and was given a bottle of champagne. Roger raised his eyebrows and shrugged. We never found out what was going on.

My journey to Brunei took me via Honolulu, Hong Kong and Singapore and I finally landed, exhausted and jet-lagged, in Bandar Seri Begawan. The Shell fixed-wing Chief Pilot, Captain Currie, met me at the terminal and drove me down to Seria and the Shell camp.

For the two months flying Brunei-registered aircraft I operated on a local PPL while training on the B99 and B90 was carried out by Currie. The 99 looked the part, but Beech had failed to resolve the trim problems satisfactorily. The electric trim had to be motored immediately on flap selection to prevent elevator forces from exceeding the capability of the pilot. Several accidents had occurred in the States and the aircraft was not allowed on the British register. Currie stressed the various before-flight trim tests and checks. Failure of the "out of trim" warning system was a no-go item.

Anduki airstrip was a grass field close to the Shell residential area, and it proved a pleasant enough operations base. Unfortunately the passengers boarded from their air-conditioned lounge into the B99, whose aircon could only be operated with the engines running. Unlike the Twin Otter, the 99 had no external cockpit door, which prevented a free flow of air. A DIY trolley-borne aircon unit passed cool air via a hose through the document port prior to engine start. In the minute or so that cooled air was not available the cabin was transformed into a fearsome sauna. Knowledgeable passengers carried a spare shirt, but pilots remained soggy, getting progressively more grimy as the day progressed. The outside temperature could reach 36ºC, the humidity 90%.

Enough whingeing. The occasional KL flights in the B90 were an eye opener, as with a full fuel load we arrived (sometimes at night) with only VFR reserves. Shell aviation procedures were not up to the standard required of their contractors.

Anduki was only just long enough for a V1/Vr rejected take-off for the B90, so imagine my concern when as co-pilot with Currie we taxied out after heavy rain on to a runway flooded with about three inches of standing water. We had full fuel for the flight to KL. On application of full power with the brakes on, the propeller disc was so close to the surface that a funnel of water was being sucked into each engine. I pointed and Currie looked, but clenched his jaw and released the brakes. As we ploughed our way through the water I prepared myself for a rejected take-off ending in the brush. We just made it, clearing the foliage by inches.

After refuelling the 99 at Miri I spotted a vaguely familiar figure standing on the other side of the apron next to a Cessna 172, and saw that he was staring in my direction. We both started walking at the same time. Recognition dawned - it was my old Zambia protagonist, Graham Knock. A High Noon scenario was played out as the distance between us decreased. My imagination ran riot. Would Knock take a swing at me when we met in the middle?

Knock was unable to sustain the steely-eyed look and broke into a broad grin. "Flexman you bastard, what brings you here?" he said.

Knock was now employed as an instructor by the Miri flying club, and from what I gathered from scuttlebutt continued to engage in activities outside the conditions of his work permit, to put it lightly. He gave me a free check ride in the Cessna 172, but I never got around to hiring it as I didn't trust the maintenance. The engineer was a very likeable local, but his enjoyment of Miri night life was excessive to say the least. Knock eventually did a runner, flying the 172 across the border and abandoning it on the apron at Bandar Airport. Bristow subsequently received a flyer advertising his new "Bachelors Only" resort in the Philippines.

I was to move to Miri in the new year of 1980 when Bristow had set up their operation. On Christmas Day one of the Shell helicopter pilots (ex RN and friend of my brother Rob) invited me to his home for lunch and celebrations with his family. The highlight of the day was the visit by Father Christmas, who arrived totally pickled in the middle of a tropical downpour. Sopping wet and bedraggled, he had to present his gifts on the veranda as his crimson robe was leaving a trail of red dye.

Bristow arrived in Miri during the last few days of 1979 along with the 125, two Twin Otters and five Pumas. I transferred to Miri. Our aircrew took the Air Law exam and were issued with Malaysian licences. After a day or two setting up and familiarisation with the local area, Bristow commenced operations.

Janet arrived while the GM, Bill Pollard, was battling to get housing at reasonable rates, so we had to remain in the pokey (but clean) Gloria Hotel. One of Mark Salmon's kids had the incredibly inconvenient habit of planting or posting car keys in pots, down drains or wherever. This at one stage threatened to bring the whole operation to a standstill.

Derek Jordan, now the fixed-wing chief pilot, insisted we join him for dinner, be it in a fancy restaurant or at a roadside stall. This arrangement did not last long as Derek's temper got the better of him. With his sudden loss of temper and bad language, we no longer wished to be associated with him. In the Asian culture "face" is important, and Derek, with his brutal insults, was breeding resentment wherever he went. On being served a not-so-cold beer by a gay waiter, he loudly suggested that the bottle be rammed up the guy's arse. All present were dumbstruck.

The Borneo jungle looked mysterious and intriguing from the air. Determined to explore, I had bought a Suzuki Jeep from a departing Shell pilot. This vehicle could go where other four-wheel-drives feared to tread, as it had high ground clearance and was light on its feet. I was warned about its high centre of gravity and the need to corner with care. In the jungle it excelled, handling the muddy logging tracks with ease.

I had a roof rack for carrying my surfboard, but Miri waves only measured up a few days each year. The alternatives were sailing and diving, so a few of us fixed-wing chaps embarked on dinghy-building projects. I partnered with Steve Aitcheson.

Shell managed the Gymkhana Club of Miri (not a horse in sight) and had granted Bristow employees the right to membership. This establishment was a lifesaver for hotel occupants, as apart from having a pool, squash, tennis and badminton courts it boasted a sports field, a theatre and of course a bar and restaurant. The colonial tradition of Sunday evening movies was maintained with all the drama that operating 16mm projectors entailed. Bulbs blew and reels of celluloid fell off or broke, which provided an interval for glasses to be recharged. Things were never the same after VHS video arrived.

Next door to the Gloria was "The Pub", a wild and woolly disco where the music and bar girls were hot and loud. It was good fun and the transvestites were an amusing bunch.

The Bristow co-pilots were in heaven. They were allocated a large house in Luak Bay, staffed by a bevy of beautiful Iban girls; they could not believe their good fortune. Janet and I had tried to obtain one of these South China Sea beachfront houses, but the management, hardcore helicopter guys, had grabbed them first. Janet settled on a small but practical house on Medical Store Road. It was conveniently located midway between the club on the edge of town and the airport.

Many of the houses we had been offered had been designed by the owners, a common trait in Malaysia. This led to strange architectural quirks, as architects never informed their clients that the end product would be weird for fear they'd lose the contract. Massive staircases that descended into the centre of the living room were currently the in thing.

We spread the word that we needed a maid and a couple turned up seeking the position. Bibi was half Iban, half Chinese, and her husband Gerald was a Tamil Indian. A two-year-old adopted daughter of mixed origin and a cat completed the package. Despite misgivings about a small family sharing the house, we took them on. They were both cheerful and capable. Gerald would be out most of the day working as a telecoms engineer. The whole setup was made manageable by having a wet kitchen and veranda out back, complete with table and chairs.

Miri had not yet developed into a busy oil town and it was still possible to enjoy a quiet coffee and curry laksa at one of the kopitiam, Lim's Kedai being our favourite. Janet excitedly explored the market stalls, recognising produce she had not seen since her Trinidad days. Some of the Bristow families, especially those from Aberdeen, found it difficult to adapt to local fare. Western-style supermarkets had yet to arrive and Chinese restaurants offered too many unrecognisable dishes.

The locals predicted bad luck for Bristow, as no blood sacrifice had been made on the foundations of the new hangar. Normally a chicken paid the price, but management could not bring themselves to practise a pagan ritual.

Not long after Bristow had settled into the completed hangar, the crew transport was en route to the airport during an intense tropical storm. It was early in the morning and still pitch black, and floodwater had washed away the road. The driver saw the hazard too late and crashed into the culvert. No one was killed, but our Scottish stalwart, Jackie Gorman, lost an eye.

Shortly after that, one of the Twin Otters skidded into the ditch at Lutong. Although the damage was major, no one was hurt. The aircraft was disassembled and shipped out for repairs. No replacement Otters were available, so an Air Anglia EMB 110 Bandeirente was flown out to fill the gap.

Then we lost a Puma over Kuala Belait due to main rotor gearbox failure; it crashed into swamp and no one survived. Engine failures are manageable, but if the gearbox goes so does the rotor. The oil community was stunned and Bristow dejected.

One more disaster and we would lose the contract. Bristow was under a cloud. It was not easy.

Meanwhile Jordan had insulted a Singaporean air traffic controller over the air and was banned from Singapore air space. As the 125 route to KL was in the Singapore FIR, he was effectively neutered. Shell had already received complaints regarding his offensive behaviour and requested his removal. Les Ingham, up to now operating the Gatwick 125, was drafted out as replacement Chief Pilot - we meet again. The new TRE/IRE was Harry Hood, a real gentleman. The periodic flight tests, base checks and instrument ratings were now enjoyable as opposed to being a trial as they had been under Jordan or Collinson.

The 125 got fungus in the fuel tanks and Shell got even more annoyed. Refuelling away from base now had to include the manual addition of fungicide, which eventually became a standard additive in the tropics. Meanwhile 125 pilots had to personally add the chemical during refuelling. The 400 used over-wing refuelling, as it had no pressure connection.

The flights to KL enabled me to get my back sorted out. Although held in disdain by Western medical authorities, the traditional Chinese massage worked wonders. The problems initiated by lifting tons of lobster for Baylee gradually disappeared. Massage was available in Miri, but it tended to be sensual rather than therapeutic, and it could get you a reputation.

Our kids travelled out on their first school holiday as unaccompanied minors. For the first few trips they flew to Bandar Sri Begawan in Brunei, which required a journey by road to collect them. The Suzuki came into its own, as the road between Miri Baram River and Kuala Belait was unmade. In the rainy season it was impassable by anything other than four-wheel drive. As you had to take a ferry at both the Baram and Belait rivers, the whole journey could take anything up to five hours. The unmade section was only twenty miles, but it took two hours in four-wheel first gear. The road ran parallel to the sea, and some were tempted to drive on the beach when the tide was out. This was OK if each stream was crossed using the bridge back on the road - if not quicksand would trap the vehicle and the tide would cover it before any rescue attempt could be arranged. Recent wrecks could be seen submerged in the sand, and they would eventually be swallowed whole. The Suzuki usually dragged one or two vehicles out of the mud on each journey. The kids found the journey exciting, if a little time-consuming.

Tia and Leon, only vaguely remembering their time in Uganda, were entranced by Miri and its tropical surroundings. Asia has a different resonance to Africa, despite similar latitudes.

At the Gymkhana Club, Miri Amateur Dramatic Society (MADS) flourished with all the shenanigans associated with the thespian lifestyle. The annual pantomime provided light relief and in July classic stage plays challenged the limits of amateur ability. Janet and I started as stagehands, eventually reaching the giddy heights of Stage Manager and roles on stage. As Stage Manager Janet donned an all-black outfit with the initials SM embroidered on her back. For post-performance drinks she wore thigh boots and carried a whip. Amateur dramatics is like that.

Sunday barbecues on the beach were frequent - just bring food and a grille. A perfect fire could be built with the plentiful logs and driftwood. Mark and Ann Salmon with their two kids accompanied us on many of our beach trips; it was a very relaxed life.

Sometimes a bunch of us would spend the day at the Lambir Falls. A half-hour drive, followed by a twenty-minute walk through the rainforest, would bring you to a classic jungle waterfall and pool, ideal for cooling off. There weren't many mosquitoes, but if you ventured up to the top of the cascade you would get smothered in leeches. Dangling one's feet in the pool was safer, and it attracted shrimps that cleaned your toes and feet.

On one occasion, after a beer or two and entering into the spirit of things, I decided to do the Tarzan thing and swing across on one of the vines. Having selected a suitable location, I began climbing up the surrounding cliffs in my swimming gear. My enthusiasm for the project began to wane as the thorny brush took its toll. I reached the chosen launch pad and dragged the liana back toward me. The intention was to swing out over the water and drop into the pool.

Releasing my secure handhold and grabbing the ant-covered vine with both hands, I was committed. My Tarzan cry faded to a whimper as the vine took charge, swinging in a completely different direction from that intended. Out over the rocks, I could not let go, and horror of horrors, I was swinging backwards into unknown territory. This was not how I imagined it would play out. I was now concerned that I would not be able obtain a purchase to halt my unpredictable flight path. As I crashed back into the dry branches of a dead tree, an image of me suspended helpless over the rocks flashed through my mind.

Just into the forward swing, I managed to grab a rather jagged branch. The termite-riddled tree disintegrated and I dropped into the bushes. During the following few minutes I endured a painful climb back down to ground level. The rest of the gang were hysterical.

Back at the hangar, Murphy's Law struck with a vengeance. The company transport failed to pick up the engineers on the early shift and we had to cram them into the crew bus. Arriving at the hangar there was a rush to prepare the aircraft, which was still inside. Instead of carrying out their normal hangar duties some of the ancillary staff lent a hand. The 125 was towed out with an unqualified guy in the cockpit. As soon as the aircraft was parked, some of the Puma crew chipped in to help, as the 125 was the first to launch. The co-pilot, thinking too far ahead, removed the ground locks before entering the cockpit. The previous night's work on the hydraulics had left the system with no pressure and the landing gear lever was still selected

UP. A Puma engineer thought it would help if he manually primed the hydraulics, but as he pumped away inside the rear bay the nosewheel retracted and the 125's nose thumped on to the concrete.

The previous night the engineers had serviced components in the wheel well. In order to avoid the time-consuming business of putting the aircraft on jacks they had left the undercarriage locks in and selected the landing gear lever up. Using the hand pump the landing gear doors opened with the wheels locked down. This allowed access for maintenance.

The lever had been left in the up position because the unqualified brakeman had not done the proper checks. The co-pilot had commenced the pre-flight out of sequence. Hydraulic pressure had been restored without notice. The Shell MD would not make his appointment and the 125 would require extensive repairs in Singapore.

As a result of these interruptions of service in both fixed-wing and rotary operations, Shell ordered a major safety audit. They came down very hard, with a report that heavily criticised Bristow procedures. There was much exaggeration and a number of false accusations made by unqualified investigators trying to justify their jobs.

The head of Shell Aviation in London came out in person to present the report to our management. While addressing the GM and Chief Engineer in the hangar, he made an unguarded statement in earshot of Harry Hood, our 125 TRE/IRE. "Shell expects a degree of professionalism similar to our own" he said. "Your pre and after flight external inspections are not carried out with reference to the checklist."

Our normally mild-mannered Harry Hood fired straight back from across the hangar floor. "When I was operating out of Heathrow your Shell 125 crews didn't do any post-flight checks, I often saw them lock the door and walk away" he said. Our top team were stunned, work stopped and silence reigned. No one had ever spoken to the clients in that manner.

After a moment's hesitation the team retired to the GM's office. I reckoned Shell thought it best not to pursue the matter any further. Our GM told Harry that he should have been more diplomatic. Operations soon resumed, and our standard operating procedures remained unchanged. The audit did however focus the minds of those who had allowed their standards to slip.

Our first co-pilot, Lee Hong Seng, resigned. Although legally qualified for captaincy, Lee had been baulked by the high command hours required by the Shell contract. Harry Spriggs, a friend of Les Ingham from Nigeria days, was happy to fill the vacancy. Harry, a previous helicopter and BN2 captain on the Nigeria operation, wanted to build up jet time and was happy to act as co-pilot. The frequency of flights increased and Dave Hansom and Peter Kinsey from the Bristow 125 joined us on a temporary basis. Dave, an ex RN Phantom pilot, was so laid back he almost floated away. Local pilots soon replaced the UK "temps".

Our "milk run" was the two-hour flight across the South China Sea to Kuala Lumpur. That area is a great place for storms, and I never got bored observing the awesome cloud formations and electrical displays. Passengers always worried about lightning strikes and we were often questioned about them. Strikes happened frequently in the vicinity of recent thunderstorms. Pilots and passengers usually remain unaware of a strike; the cabin is actually quite a safe place to be. Burnt static discharge wicks have to be replaced and occasionally a tiny pinhole burn in the wing tip or tail will be found.

I watched a lightning strike in slow motion, this time in clear air. Coasting in over Kuantan between two giant storm clouds, I observed this freaky lightning leave the top of one cloud, zigzag its way across blue sky, enter one wing tip and exit the other. It continued on to the storm on the other side.

On the ground the gust fronts that accompany the downpour can be fearsome, blowing down trees and lifting roofs. Out on one of the platforms an unsecured Puma was taken by surprise and blown over. The pilot, GM Peter Grey, was having a tea break.

On the home front we suffered a robbery during a thunderstorm. I was away in KL and Janet heard nothing. We lost a TV and video recorder, but other than that no harm was done. From that moment on Janet kept my Toledo sword at her side whenever I was away.

Just a few months later as she was watching late night TV, the front door began rattling; a prowler was attempting to get in. Janet, sword in hand, leapt at the door, which opened outward, and slammed it open. The intruder was knocked to the ground and stared up in terror at Janet wielding the Spanish blade. The sword was raised head high and the would-be burglar fled, our warrior in hot pursuit. Attempting to leap the picket fence he clipped the top and fell headlong into the monsoon drain, before scrabbling out and haring off down the road and into the night.

Janet then realised that she was naked, as her sarong had fallen off. A classic Amazon spectacle greeted the neighbours as they peered over the fence, woken by the racket. They cheered. We suffered no more burglaries.

I was given a sharp reminder regarding correct procedures during an early-morning flight to KL. Routing via Kuching, I carried minimum trip fuel on the first sector as we would have to refuel there anyway before going to KL. The forecast was fair en route, with a 10 percent chance of thunderstorm in Kuching. Sibu, the diversion airfield, was "Loud and Clear" (fine weather), but on arrival Kuching was experiencing a tropical downpour.

Three aircraft were in the hold. It would be at least fifteen minutes before we could start an approach. The pilot of the number one aircraft, an MAS F27, told ATC that he would delay starting his approach because of the gusty conditions. The F27 should have been sent to hold away from the stack, but infuriatingly MAS always got priority, so we were all delayed. I chose to consume my Sibu reserve (45 minutes) by holding at Kuching, Sibu was clear with no traffic inbound.

Finally our turn came. Peter Kinsey, the co-pilot, was flying, and he carried out a precise ILS, but at decision height we saw the runway too late. Peter carried out a missed approach and we had no option but to divert to Sibu. Having only one passenger and little fuel the climb away was very very steep. For minimum fuel expenditure a maximum rate climb was followed by the final descent.

As I checked the fuel gauges my heart skipped a beat, for they indicated empty. We were both very frightened. The only option was to follow the profile. If the engines cut we would consider the options.

Then Sibu called to say that early morning fog was forming and that their ADF approach aid was off the air. Peter started to say something, but I said that we must continue as planned. At the top of the climb we poled over into the descent and throttled back to idle. The fuel gauges responded immediately, returning to the figure originally calculated. We could see Sibu through a thin layer of mist. I asked Peter to carry out a steep approach in order to retain visual contact with the runway.

After landing we had the correct fuel for one visual circuit to land. The flight manual performance data was proved accurate, but I wished they had told me about gauge error in the climb. My legs were so wobbly I only just managed to open the door for the passenger.

For a relaxed evening out of the public eye, the Bristow contingent patronised a bar in one of the bachelor houses. The bar also facilitated the mandatory in-house darts competitions. Initially this co-pilot's house was the place to be, but the hormone-driven relationship between these young lads and their girls produced an atmosphere so highly charged that non-residents felt they were intruding. We felt like voyeurs, and the venue was moved to the bachelor engineers' pad, where everybody could let loose… and did, frequently. Looking back I fail to understand how we coped with work, for most nights just about everybody stayed until 1.30 am.

Quiet evenings at the Brighton Beach food stalls were a delight. Set on the coast overlooking the South China Sea, this gourmet's paradise offered an amazing selection of seafood cooked Chinese style. Watching the sunsets with a cold beer and curried crab was an experience I still savour. Never mind the sauce that splattered your shirt and dripped off your elbows.

Bristow personnel were finally allowed to become social members of the Shell sailing club, much to the annoyance of Shell die-hards. A GCM diving section was initiated, the amateur dramatics section flourished and the Hash House Harriers carried on in style.

Our Bristow gang were determined to make the most of the opportunities available. Steve Aitcheson, Kevin Jones and myself were building dinghies, another bunch joined the newly established GCM scuba-diving section. This activity was sponsored by Shell, who gave us free use of a supply boat and provided a compressor to recharge the scuba tanks.

Shell registered the diving section with the British Sub Aqua Club, who stipulated very thorough training. One of the Shell professional diving contractors provided instruction, ending each session with the warning "If you don't do as I say you will die" We called him Dr Death. My first dive on to a coral reef brought me face to face with a shark. It looked huge, but was in fact only two metres long and asleep.

One of the Bristow technicians, an ex-French Legionnaire paratrooper, suggested forming a sky-diving club. This idea was received with enthusiasm and the company subsidised the enterprise. As soon as the brand-new equipment arrived, training got under way. Surprisingly, there were as many wives on the course as there were menfolk; it helped that the instructor was tall dark and handsome and spoke with a disarming French accent.

Returning from KL and turning on final approach one day, I was surprised to see three or four parachutes descending over the airfield. ATC had said nothing about this. I chose not to carry out a missed approach, as any vortex might collapse the canopies. I landed and braked hard, watching the last of the participants land in front of me. As I taxied back I saw Janet tending to Dennis Stoten, one of the Twin Otter pilots (ex British Airways), who had broken his ankle on landing.

An ambulance arrived, but it drove past Denis to collect a more serious casualty. The wife of one of our engineers was incapacitated, having broken her back landing in a monsoon drain. It was a disaster for those concerned and a chilling experience for the onlookers.

The drop had taken place in a stiff breeze and some of the jumpers had been unable to turn into wind. There was heated debate as to whether the instruction had been comprehensive enough, or if the students had understood. The skydiving club was shut down, never to be revived.

Gerald and Bibi took us to their friend Mr Mapan's longhouse for Gawai (The Iban Harvest Festival). It was deep in the jungle near the Niah Caves, and the drive took three and a half hours down the rutted laterite highway. At Niah we transferred to Mapan's longboat for another hour and a half upriver. As the size of the waterway shrank the waterway was obstructed by fallen trees. This occasionally required all hands to jump into the water to haul the boat over the branches.

If it had not been for the splendid dinner of wild boar sluiced down with *tuak* (rice wine), we would never have slept. We settled down for the night on the hardwood floor with only a straw mat for bedding. The odd grunt, cluck and other strange sounds from the animals underneath provided the night-time accompaniment. Waking the next morning was a painful experience, and ablutions in the cool river did nothing to ease the stiffness.

Mapans longhouse was of Christian persuasion. They did not observe *gawai* (harvest festival or Thanksgiving), considering it a Pagan festival - those pesky missionaries have a lot to answer for. To experience the festivities we had to make a 45-minute trek through the jungle to the neighbouring "thirty door" longhouse. For those not in the know, longhouses resemble apartment blocks lying on their side. Raised on stilts to about eight feet off the jungle floor, all apartments share a common veranda where most of the social interaction takes place. Before the main celebrations we were proudly shown a cockfight featuring their prize birds. It was not the sort of entertainment we would have chosen, but it would have been rude to refuse. Fortunately the experience was mercifully quick. The bouts were a fight to the death, but as the cocks were fitted with razor sharp spurs it was all over in about ten seconds.

For the celebrations each family laid out food and drink on a large mat in front of their door. Guests and neighbours were expected to sample food and drink at each door. Each visitor was expected to partake of at least two glasses of *tuak* before moving on. Needless to say, by the time we got to the last door we were incoherent. We were put to bed, although I do not remember how.

The following morning Mapan woke us with the instruction that we had to attend a service at his church. Staggering back through the jungle, we were finally seated in a small tin-roofed affair fitted out with an altar and pulpit. The sun rose higher, the service droned on and it became unbearably hot. My headache was accompanied by an attack of nausea. Hemmed in at the back, I had visions of throwing up as I clambered for the exit. It was a test of endurance, but we all made it to the end of the service without embarrassment.

A trip to the Niah Caves provided some excitement. The object of the trip was to see how the much-prized (by the Chinese) swiftlet nests were collected. The harvesting was achieved by nimble climbers ascending poles strapped together and guyed with wire. The whole setup allowed precarious access to the roof of the cave some 120 feet above.

This adventure was not a favourite with some of the girls, as the floor of the cave was wall-to-wall guano. The journey through the caves had to be made in single file because of the narrowness of the footpath. Guides at the front and rear held pathetic torches, but our gaze focused on the roof above, resulting in occasional knee deep missteps into the morass. The droppings from bats and swiflets were feet deep and heaving with cockroaches and centipedes. Stepping off the pathway into the mess raised the hair on the back of one's neck.

After those few days of back-to-basics living we were quite relieved to be returning home. Fatigued and feeling unwashed, we clambered into the boat loaded with gifts of local produce and bundles of smelly laundry. It started raining, and by the time we got to Niah everything was sodden. Jamming all our stuff into the Jeep, we set off down the road through torrential rain. Visibility was poor, and when we hit a flooded gully carved across the road the massive jolt sheared the engine mountings. Amazingly, the transmission and other connections remained intact. We strapped the engine down with jungle creeper and continued gingerly back home. The hot bath was heaven.

The repair revealed extensive corrosion caused by driving on the beach, so the Suzuki needed a rebuild. The Miri body shop fitted a complete new floor and back axle, and charged us US $300.

Mr Bristow flew out on his 125 to negotiate the sale of the operation to MHS (Malaysian Helicopter Services). Alan Bristow knew nationalisation was inevitable and the transfer of ownership was accomplished smoothly. His 125 flew in during the annual Bristow-organised Miri Raft race. It zoomed down the river over the competitors and the overloaded pedestrian walkway chose that moment to break away from the road bridge, decanting a dozen or so spectators into the river. Several others leapt in to save the kids; it was a miracle no one was drowned or injured.

Much to our dismay (we had become very spoilt by the easy life), runway lighting was to be installed in Miri. This upgrade, paid for by Shell, facilitated late returns from KL. Landing at night with only runway edge lights is not recommended. Having experience of unlit approaches, I suggested that night circuit training and night base checks should be carried out at Miri before commencing night operations, but they weren't. Being some distance from town there were no lights to assist with perspective. The "black hole effect" came into play; the absence of approach lighting can lead to a dangerously low approach (our helicopter guys were familiar with these conditions as most rotary operations are in remote areas).

When late returns from KL were possible, the pressure on Shell's management to complete business by early afternoon would disappear. Before the installation of lighting, the deadline set by Miri airport closure (open daylight hours only) ensured a prompt departure from KL. Under strict instructions from Shell, the 125 delayed its departure for no one.

One late passenger managed to persuade ATC to instruct us to return to the apron and wait for him, but we were already taxiing out and refused. This fellow, a ship's captain, caught the flight the following day. After I had finished the safety briefing in the cabin he asked if I had been the pilot the day before. When I said I had been, he launched a scathing verbal attack. The other passengers were embarrassed. I told him to put his complaint in writing, but he continued his tirade. I advised him that upsetting the pilot constituted a flight safety hazard, and the other passengers glared at him. He turned purple.

After the night returns began, Murphy's Law struck again. Returning home after a long day in KL, the co-pilot was flying the aircraft. On final approach I called "too low" twice, but he made no noticeable correction. We descended into the "clearway", the trees on either side becoming visible against the night sky. I called "I have control" but he did not let go, so I had to forcibly apply power and take control.

When the landing was complete I had to carry out all the after-landing checks by myself, because he was sulking. Such an incident requires a written report. The co-pilot, an expat, had much experience on other types and should have known better. He was furious, denying his approach was in any way dangerous.

Meanwhile back on the social scene, Steve "Aitch" handed over his share of the dinghy project and the hull was transferred to my car port. I soldiered on with it. Photocopied instructions and homemade templates had been mailed from UK, while basic materials were obtained locally. The only parts to be shipped from UK were the 4.75 metre mast and rigging.

The UK supplier informed me that British Airways, who flew direct to Brunei, could not fit the mast into the 747 hold and asked if they could cut it in half. One of our technicians, Bill Hayde, was a wizard with aluminium, so I said OK. When the mast arrived Bill fixed it, no problem.

In those days Miri could only offer expensive professional power tools; DIY was a primitive business. I made do with a plane made from an auto spring, a hand brace and a handsaw. I finished the dinghy, a fourteen foot Phantom. It was heavier than spec. but went OK and was fast and quite sophisticated. It featured mast bending (a bit stiff, with the sleeve join) and mast tilt.

The kids didn't use the dinghy, as it took time to rig. As for washing it down after use - forget it. Their friends had the use of quick and easy Lasers. But it taught me a thing or two and was fun. I had a trolley made but it was a disaster; with no shock absorbers and lively springs it almost bounced itself (and the Jeep) off the road. I had to park the Phantom at the Shell boat club, hoping no one would object.

As our kids grew it became apparent that we needed a house with a bit more space. We found the ideal pad, the old Residence on Tanjong Lobang. On top of the hill with a view through the trees of the South China Sea, it was constructed Somerset Maugham-style on stilts but with modern materials. It had beautiful wooden floors throughout and the front veranda joined the living room when the folding doors were opened. Bibi and Gerald had their own suite of wooden chalet-type rooms along a raised walkway out back.

Intrigued as to why the rent was so cheap, we made some enquiries. It turned out the locals thought the house was haunted by the ghost of the wartime British resident. He had been executed by the Japanese on the front steps.

As Tia and Leon developed into teenagers, their holidays in Miri began to resemble the "brat pack" movies. Most of the expats working in Miri were middle management with teenage kids. This community of party freaks, about forty strong, organised their own social life on a spontaneous basis, avoiding parental control. Shell management attempted to keep things in order by organising sailing and water skiing etc, but these kids knew exactly what they wanted - freedom. Tia and Leon were away for days at a time, but they did call to let us know they were OK. A pile of dirty clothes indicated that they had passed our way, and occasionally we came home to find the house in disarray, kids crashed out all over the house.

Then the manager of the Gymkhana Club had a heart attack and died. Janet stood in for a few months until a suitable replacement could be found. As the club had major renovations in progress this was no easy task, but the chairman of the management committee, Jan Buizen of Shell, gave Janet all the support she required.

More and more Malaysians qualified as fixed-wing and helicopter crew. MHS (Malaysian Helicopter Services) retained only senior administrators and training captains from Bristows. After five years in Miri my time was up. Gary West, the ex Chief Pilot from Lagos, deserved a break and was given the job in Miri. Lagos and Twin Otters was Bristow's only other fixed-wing operation. If Tia and Leon were to complete their education at Clayesmore I would need to continue receiving a tax-free income. Lagos it had to be. I was offered the Chief Pilot's job but turned it down, as it would be far too much hassle.

The two-year contract meant eight weeks on site followed by four weeks home leave, quite disruptive for the family. Janet would live in Portland House, and with the kids still at boarding school she planned to get involved in village life. We had never been apart before. It would not be easy.

Chapter Sixteen

NIGERIA AND THE TWIN OTTER

February-April 1977

The new international terminal at Lagos airport was now open, and company staff met inbound staff airside and escorted them through the formalities into waiting Bristow transport. This procedure helped avoid any harassment and extortion by customs and immigration.

Waiting in the immigration queue was painful. Standing for up to an hour observing surly staff interrogate those in front made newcomers feel distinctly ill at ease. This intimidation had occasionally pushed new employees to the point of resignation.

Customs had no green channel in those days, and bags were trashed by officials unless some "freebie" was passed across. Outside the terminal self-styled "porters" attempted to grab and carry bags in the hope of earning "dash". In Nigeria dash is the all-encompassing term referring to tokens of appreciation, and it ranged from small change to millions of Naira.

Settling into the company transport, I was surprised when five minutes later our man Simeon announced our arrival at the Bristow complex. Bristow and their Nigerian partners had been forced to build their own residential compound, the BRC. The cost of renting accommodation around Ikeja, coupled with the logistics required to get everyone to work, had made the project financially worthwhile. The only problem was the location; although conveniently close to the international terminal it was in the industrial suburb of Isolo. The surroundings were less than salubrious (for those who know Ikeja, it's near Aswani textile market and Oshodi). Approaching the complex along a potholed laterite road, the walled perimeter, topped by razor wire, had a foreboding appearance. Fortunately it was a totally different scene inside, where trees and flowering shrubs gave the modern accommodation a relaxed atmosphere.

The "resort" featured both squash and tennis courts and a swimming pool. The complex was completely self-contained, with its own borehole and generator. The borehole had to reach 200 feet to be sure of uncontaminated water. Most company reservations featured independent services, as the state utility companies were totally unreliable. Power and water could be off two or three times a day and sometimes were unavailable for days at a time.

Arriving at the car port all passengers disembarked straight into the company bar, the Spread Eagle, all of two yards. I recognised a few ex-Miri hands and over a beer I was advised to present myself to the Chief Pilot, Dave Cooper.

I was first given a word of caution about their dog. This mongrel, much adored by Dave's wife, was given the run of their small garden and when a visitor came through the gate it would appear, furiously wagging its tail. "Don't be fooled" I was told, "If you turn your back, it will bite your arse!"

Sure enough, as I rang their doorbell the dog trotted round the corner of the house, looking pleased to see me. I patted it on the head, then turned back to the door on hearing the locks and bolts being freed. Keeping an eye over my shoulder I saw the pesky creature launch itself at my rear. Whirling round I hoofed the mutt square in the chest, at the same time hearing a cry of anguish from Mrs Cooper, who was now standing in the doorway. I explained my presence and was ushered in with a furious gesture. Needless to say my welcome was brief, and terminated with the weary instruction "See you in my office tomorrow". Back in the bar, my report on the incident was greeted with cheers and laughter. Cooper entered during the accolade and cocked a raised eyebrow in my direction.

The traffic problem was as great as ever. The journey to the hangar for the early morning shift was OK as the transport departed at about 6.30 and took only twenty minutes. Later in the day, until about 10.00 at night, the same journey could take up to an hour and a half. The company transport was old and tired and the air conditioning never worked. Driving with the windows open led to an arrival at work sweaty and covered in grime.

As a beginner I made the mistake of buckling up, and arrived with a diagonal black mark across my uniform shirt front. It was the first time the belts had been used. Dust coated all, not only in the hangar; inside the offices all surfaces were covered with a fine film. The air-conditioning filters were cleaned at least once week. In those days computers had not yet been adopted, and the enormous stacks of files that lined the walls appeared to be the final resting place of much airborne pollution. Somehow everyone resigned themselves to this threat to their wellbeing and soldiered on regardless.

The meeting in Dave Cooper's office passed without further embarrassment. Dave had been in Lagos a long time, having worked for Aero Contractors (the competition) before switching to Bristow. By now he had developed the impervious stoical look acquired by those resigned to the purgatory of a Lagos existence. Dave did not mention the dog-kicking episode, but had marked me as a potential troublemaker.

The Twin Otters were still being operated single crew, which allowed our collection of sometimes eccentric pilots the freedom to develop their own operating techniques.

The second training captain, Rod Rea, carried out my base check and line training as Sam St Pierre was on leave. Rod, an ex-Rothmans aerobatic pilot, was a likeable fellow despite his addiction to all things macho. With a rugby player's build and sporting a beard, he had all the latest electronic kit, the hottest sports car and a glamorous wife (in the UK that is). He also flew the Shell executive aircraft, a Mitsubishi MU2 Solitaire. This demon machine suited his character, but they had to shoehorn him into the tiny cockpit. I would have to wait my turn, as Rod and the other MU2 pilot, Steve Kiley (ex Miri), jealously guarded their status as "VIP" pilots.

The Twin Otter was fun to fly, especially for arrivals into Warri, where the airstrip boasted a narrow and demanding short runway of only about 700 metres. The runway width was only twenty feet, not wide enough to meet UK standards. With maximum passenger loads, low fuel states and no fuel available at the diversion to Benin, the pressure to land rather than divert was intense. Landing during tropical storms could lead to an excursion off the runway, but that did not prevent some from trying. If crosswinds and poor visibility led to deviations from normal approach criteria, it was best to apply power and go around. The boundary fence was only another thirty feet from the runway edge, so kicking off drift and braking on touchdown could slew the aircraft into the fence. Aero Contractor's less experienced pilots occasionally managed to park their aircraft in the undergrowth - the wrong side of the chain link fence.

Initially the Twin Otter schedule was pretty basic. With two aircraft, one departed early to Port Harcourt, returning in the evening, while the other departed in the afternoon, stayed in PH over-night and returned to Lagos the next morning, all flights routed via Warri. The Shell" terminals" in Warri and PH were crappy prefabricated affairs with basic seating. "Sloppy coffee" was-served from behind bamboo fronted, Formica-topped counters.

I was taught an early lesson - hang on to your flight bag at all times. Leaving the bag in the cockpit, I had rushed into the terminal for a pee during refuelling, and when I returned to complete the tech. log, the bag was open and my passport gone.

At PH an ancient Bristow VW Beetle would take us in to the Shell Residential Area (RA), where a small bungalow had been allocated to provide a quiet place to rest. It didn't take long to become immune to the incessant rattle of poorly-maintained air conditioning, but the food provided in the Shell restaurant was dangerous. With the incessant power cuts the deep freezers failed to keep food frozen, and food poisoning was a frequent occurrence. It always attacked so fast that I never had time to make it to the airport, let alone the aeroplane. I wondered what passers by must have thought observing a pilot, in uniform, vomiting by the roadside.

I reverted to canned food when not cadging meals from the local Bristow families. It annoyed me that Bristow was frequently reprimanded by Shell regarding safety issues when they so often failed in their own back yard. When I called the Shell doctor he said "I'm not surprised". The problem was never tackled seriously because Shell expat staff ate at home. The locals either had cast-iron stomachs or accepted it as a fact of life.

The real health issue in Nigeria was malaria, and few escaped this scourge. Weaving my way between thunderstorms on my way back from Port Harcourt, I suddenly felt cold. Thinking that the combination of night and altitude (we were at 10,000 feet) was responsible, I turned the heating on. Minutes later one of the passengers tapped me on the shoulder, saying it was too warm in the cabin. I was surprised to see beads of sweat on his brow and turned to Amaechi the co-pilot who, with sweat pouring down his own face, nodded in confirmation. Amaechi's bald statement "You have succumbed to malaria" surprised me, as I had never previously suffered from the pesky disease. I was allowed two or three days off the flying programme to suffer the side effects of chloroquine. Artemisinin had not yet arrived on the scene.

The cure was often more painful than the disease. Nausea, dizziness, blurred vision and headaches were common, and those were not the only side effects. Bristow personnel were asked to take daily paludrin tablets which were available on the breakfast table, but these also produced side effects - not good for pilots. The other problem with prophylactics was their tendency to mask the symptoms. One could have the disease for some time before finally realising that the tired and achy feeling was more than just old age or hangover.

After work the company bar was first stop. Everyone would be desperate for a drink, having been stuck in the "go-slow" for an hour or two. Those with greater than average willpower took a break for a shower and a meal before returning for a game of snooker or darts. The serious drinkers remained in the bar. Getting these guys washed and fed could be a problem, as dinner finished at nine and they were loath to give up drinking time. These hardened boozers often missed their evening meal. I just hope they showered before retiring for the night.

At weekends the infamous Crocodile Bar came into play. Tucked away in a shady hollow by the Oshodi interchange, it was operated by the redoubtable Karl Souter. Karl was a raucous German-speaking Swiss national whose core business was supplying and maintaining industrial looms to the textile industry, but his obsession was running this wild but hugely stimulating bar and restaurant. Carl was married to Nancy, a Ghanaian, and had a small family. His staff lived in a series of cabins adjacent to the saloon. A live crocodile lurked in a low-walled pond alongside the pathway to the bar. The Ikeja Hash House Harriers were based at the Crocodile.

On Friday and Saturday nights the Croc was packed. With seating for about thirty and with a small dance floor, it regularly catered for up to 150 customers. The rule stating "dance floor for dancers only" was strictly enforced and offenders would receive a barrage of obscenities from Carl if they encroached. Evidence of Karl's previous failed aviation enterprise was a bent propeller pinned to the wall behind the bar.

Good-time girls came from miles around in the hope of picking up an expat lunch ticket. These girls revelled in each others' company and had a wild time regardless of whether or not they were successful in landing a catch. When first entering or squeezing through the crush to get a drink, one became a target. The girls would press against you with their ample bums or boobs, grabbing your hand to try and stuff it inside their underwear. If you failed to resist, the next ten minutes could be spent trying to disentangle yourself from the assailant.

Not all girls were in attack mode however. Those who were young and cute knew it would be only a matter of time before they had company. As the night developed, going to the loo could prove a tad risky, as the more extreme of the "night fighters", high on drugs, would ambush the unsuspecting while they were relieving themselves. One such crazy confronted me in the loo. My need to have a pee was overwhelming and I could not abort the mission. I pushed her into an open booth where the pan caught the back of her knees and she sat down with a thump, temporarily stunned. I had almost completed my task when the "zombie" launched herself in my direction screaming invective and threats of bodily harm. I dodged clear and rushed for the exit. I finished my mission in the bushes outside.

Both male and female customers came from a wide cross-section of Lagos society. Occasionally partnerships were set up and some arrangements lasted several years, one or two even resulted in matrimony. These liaisons only survived in Nigeria, because the girls missed their friends and became bored if relocated to civilised surroundings.

At weekends Bristow provided a minibus and driver for trips to the

Croc. On the return journey some of our guys would be accompanied by one of the girls. The trouble was that nobody checked who was accompanying whom, and very often a few "extras" used the transport to bypass our security and enter the bachelor quarters. These freelance operators would knock on doors, hoping for a room for the night. Sometimes chaps who had mellowed out in the Spread Eagle bar would oblige. Rejects would crash out in the TV room.

Incidents were frequent. Once while I was in the shower, one of these roaming types managed to enter my room (BRC rooms were not en suite). I returned to find the girl undressing for bed and grabbed her clothes and struggled to shove her out the door. Hearing the ruckus, Steve Aitcheson, my neighbour, threw a red smoke signal into my room. His stunt produced the desired effect, sending the intruder off down the corridor. The flare rolled under my chest of drawers, and all my shirts and underwear turned bright orange.

Senior managers were normally married-accompanied and they got hell from their wives for tolerating this nocturnal activity, but all international companies in Nigeria experienced the same issues. The majority of expat employees were unaccompanied, wives being reluctant to accompany their men to such an intimidating environment. Another possibly more pragmatic reason was the incredible cost of providing accommodation for families.

On the aviation front, Twin Otter line training was basic. Weight and balance compliance was mandatory but not monitored or even enforced. Deviations from standard fuel states and payloads were frowned upon. Advice was given regarding weather, use of diversions and navigation, and pilots had little choice from the few available options. The standard diversion for Lagos was Cotonou in the neighbouring state of Benin. Being only twenty minutes away, it allowed reasonable payloads to be carried from Warri and Port Harcourt, but diverting into Cotonou was a nightmare. We had one new pilot (a nice chap but hopelessly naive) who flew by the book, diverted to Cotonou and discovered the realities of life in Africa. Fuel and airport charges had to be paid for in US dollars in cash and passengers were not allowed to leave the aircraft, never mind that the Twin Otter had no toilet or air-conditioning.

Pilots would be targeted if they were known to hold a cash float, so a special flight was required to pay airport charges. Arranging this took all day (or night) to organise. Cotonou Airport did not allow credit, and opening an account required a very large deposit, which was not advisable. Thus the stranded crew and passengers were placed in an unpleasant situation. With this in mind it was not surprising that when the weather was below limits most pilots landed at Lagos anyway. There were two main causes of bad weather - tropical storms, and the harmattan dust haze. The dust often reduced the visibility to as little as several hundred metres and encouraged early morning fog. It often kept airports closed until mid morning.

At the other end of the route, afternoon pilots departing Warri for Port Harcourt had to bear in mind that they only had enough fuel to return to Warri should they be unable to land at PH. Warri closed at dusk, so flights had to depart on time. In the early days, if flights got airborne late, they would know there was nowhere to go if Port Harcourt developed bad weather or suffered a power failure (which was frequent). Management were aware of this problem, but left it to the captain's discretion. This meant that some pilots took the risk to avoid any hassle, while others, annoyed with the commercial pressure, played it by the book and stayed overnight at Warri. This presented Shell with the problem of what to do with their passengers, as safe accommodation was in short supply. Shell were quite naughty, making it known that contractors like Bristow were expected to be "very co-operative" in regard to their operations. In the early days our management passed the buck without giving pilots direct instructions to ignore the regulations. Eventually Shell gave in and officially sanctioned Warri night stops when afternoon flights were delayed.

The Bristow/Shell fixed-wing operation was originally initiated with light aircraft operating into small strips. The nature of this flying had attracted individual and adventurous pilots. Although undoubtedly capable, some were decidedly odd. Operating procedures and standards were becoming more professional with time, but those long-serving pilots retained the old "can do" attitude. This suited Shell so long as there were no incidents.

Having been given carte blanche to make their own decisions, most of the Twin Otter pilots became victims of personal pride. Being the first to land at Warri strip as the morning fog lifted accorded the pilot some degree of kudos. Aero Contractors (part of the Schreiner Group, and our main competitor) operated the Warri strip, and landing before they did gave us a certain smug satisfaction.

Even though it was only certified for visual conditions, a privately-installed radio beacon and visual approach cues gave pilots enough information to pull off landings in relatively poor weather. Homemade approach charts (Jungle Jepps) were produced by the various operators, and although technically illegal they made a significant contribution to accident prevention in the Niger Delta.

The competitive spirit and desire to press on led to exciting moments. Approaching Warri once, I decided to go under a developing storm rather than divert or turn back. The storm broke before I could land, and penetrating the gust front at 200 feet was a chastening experience. I felt sorry for the passengers as we hammered our way through, bucking like some demented bronco. The landing was a bit rough and I expected complaints, but surprisingly the passengers gave a round of applause on shutdown. They were always pleased to get to their destination unharmed. Be aware that travelling anywhere in Nigeria is an extremely risky business, especially by road.

This business of having no alternative to Port Harcourt gave Murphy's Law a free hand. Sure enough I was presented with an approaching gust front. The crosswind exceeded the Otter limits, but it was getting dark. The aircraft would surely tip over if a landing on the main runway was attempted, so I configured for a STOL landing, reducing the speed down to about fifty knots. Crabbing down the right side of the runway with about 45º of drift I gradually turned into wind as I approached the left hand exit to the GAT (General Aviation Terminal). The landing was into wind on the taxiway at 90 degrees to the runway. It was a smooth landing with a ground speed of around 5 to 10 knots; very little braking was required.

Silence from ATC and the passengers. Raising the flaps, I had to remain pointing into wind until it reduced enough to allow parking.

Shell laid on R&R weekends for their staff, giving them respite from the heat and stress of life in Warri and PH. They had established a guest house in the plateau city of Jos and Bristow of course flew them there. It was a three-hour grind in the Otter and with headwinds during the harmattan season took an extra fifteen minutes. Those extra minutes deleted the alternative airfield from the equation, meaning you were committed to land at Jos, but by then actual weather info would be available.

The new airport runway was very long indeed (altitude 4000 feet), but as yet had no functioning let-down aids. Jos local radio did however have a very powerful transmitter, so we used that, tracking in on a radial that would take us across the airfield. The runway could be spotted by looking straight down through the haze and fog patches and would be followed by a tight descending turn into the circuit. The Otter was ideal for this type of approach. The point of no alternative when you were committed to land at Jos occurred about twenty minutes before arrival. During the harmattan season the dust remained, but clearance of early morning fog was guaranteed.

Departing Lagos was a matter of well-judged timing but it couldn't be left too late, as the aeroplane was required back in Lagos for the afternoon shuttle.

Harry Hood, Dennis Stoten and engineers Mark Salmon and Martin Duck arrived from Miri as the nationalisation of that operation progressed. Keith Gaston-Parry, the MD and an ex marine, did his best to entertain his troops (us lot), occasionally taking us out to dinner. These treats usually meant feasting at one of Ikeja's two excellent Chinese restaurants, and although it was intended to keep the wild ones on the straight and narrow it only served to prime them for the Crocodile Bar.

Operations in Nigeria were fascinating, but the cycle of eight weeks on, four weeks off was extremely disruptive. Back home, with the kids in boarding school, Janet got involved in village activities, becoming an enthusiastic member of the Chagford scene. After one or two jobs in the village she joined our old Baylee friend Glen Ponsford and his new partner Larry in their new air charter enterprise. They had previously operated Glenline, an Exeter to London low-cost coach service. They had cleaned up but unfortunately their success was noted by those with deeper pockets. A new company, Stagecoach, deliberately undercut Glenline, bankrupting their fledgling company. Glen and Larry, undeterred, then set up their air taxi service. (When later on this also went bust, Glen and Larry did a runner to the Turks and Caicos Islands.)

Returning to Lagos on August the 27th 1985, I was given a last-minute reprieve when in the departure lounge all passengers on the Nigeria Airways flight were advised to reclaim their bags. There had been a coup in Nigeria and all airports there were closed, so I got an extra week at home.

Back in Lagos, the airport had terminated the temporary privilege allowing airline vehicles to cross the airfield via the perimeter track.

This short cut had been a boon for Bristow vehicles as it had cut the journey time down to twenty minutes. Now the ever-resourceful drivers had found a time-saving short cut through the shanty town of Mafoluku. This district had to be seen to be believed. With no established roads, vehicles clambered their way between the shacks and buildings, and the ground was so uneven that great care had to be taken in order to avoid rolling the wagon on to its side or into improvised drains. Ground impact with the underside of our vehicle meant we could only proceed at snail's pace.

This slow progress made possible a detailed study of the extraordinary surroundings and its amazing array of advertisements for small businesses. The local quacks erected explicit hoardings in English with crude graphics. These promoted not only the skill of local artisans but cures for bodily malfunctions and sexual problems. The latter were the clear favourites, producing much amusement for the otherwise tedious journey.

Finally I got my type rating on the MU2 or "pocket rocket". It justified its scary reputation but I loved it, tons of power and highly manoeuvrable. It was not a machine for the inexperienced, being unstable around all three axes. In the US, because of its small size and high speed, it had become a favourite for wealthy owners.

The MU2 was designed for single-crew operations, so a lot of the flying was carried out by the businessmen themselves. With only a private pilot's licence and little experience they frequently ended up as accident statistics. 831 MU2s were built, including the Marquise, its slightly larger sister; they clocked up 142 accidents and 339 fatalities. The machine was never approved by the UK CAA due to its engine-out characteristics.

To ensure Bristow MU2 pilots were capable, pilots new to the type first flew about 25 sectors with experienced captains. As an ex-combat pilot I found that the instability of the machine brought back memories, and I thoroughly enjoyed flying the little devil.

Shell had chosen the MU2 for its ability to operate out of the old Warri airstrip. The powerful Garret engines drove huge four-bladed props which not only gave a short take-off but an amazingly short landing run. Full span flaps allowed low approach speeds and on touchdown the application of reverse pitch produced fearsome deceleration. Acceleration on the take-off roll was equally exhilarating, reminding me of my Navy days. Sam St Pierre, the QFI/IRE (senior examiner) with Bristow Lagos, refused to fly the machine, saying quite correctly that the flight manual performance figures were wrong and that an engine failure after lift-off or on short finals would be uncontrollable. Initially Sam's protests were pushed aside, as he was known to be a testy character prone to criticism of the management. But when Shell aviation became more professional they quietly sold the MU2 and switched VIP flights to the King Air.

The MU2 was not allowed to fly single crew without a functioning autopilot. I found out why when flying the Shell MD down to Port Harcourt; the autopilot tripped off and could not be reinstated. The return trip was empty, so I figured I could return to base as a non-public-transport positioning flight. The departure and climb out went well, and after levelling off and thinking the aircraft nicely trimmed I started filling in the navigation log. Being in cloud, there was no visual reference. But half way through filling in the blanks I became aware of increasing wind noise and checked the instruments. The pesky machine had sneakily rolled into a spiral dive, and I had lost 1500 feet. There was absolutely no sensation to indicate that this uncommanded manoeuvre was in progress. Being out of radar coverage, my altitude excursion went unnoticed, but in Europe or the US it would have caused considerable alarm. Rod Ray had warned me, but I thought he was exaggerating.

The Shell GM booked the MU2 for a trip to Gabon. Nobody had any information on the facilities and setup in Libreville, so I requested

Shell to arrange a handling agent to sort out the formalities on arrival. The customs and immigration formalities leaving Lagos were carried out in the aeroplane - the Shell MD is a big deal in Nigeria.

At the other end in Libreville, the agent, a sturdy British girl, breezily announced that no formalities were required. She saw the MD into his waiting car, then took me straight to a French restaurant for lunch. The dessert was airflown strawberries... the French were firmly in control. As we passed the barracks it was French soldiers we saw on the parade ground and even the hamburger stalls were manned by expats.

I spent the three days in Libreville indulging in fine food, which was a great change from Lagos. I checked out the craft shops and bought some scary-looking masks. On the last day I was given "the tour", courtesy of the agent. As the young lady was a member of the yacht club, she treated me to a seafood lunch at the beachside restaurant. The lunch of garlic prawns and salad was delicious.

That evening I started to feel queasy during our ten-pin bowling and asked to be taken back to the hotel. I had no appetite for dinner and retired to my room. Lying on the bed, I was suddenly gripped by violent stomach cramps and nausea and fled to the bathroom. After two hours of violent retching and diarrhoea, I was exhausted and unable to reach the phone in the bedroom, I collapsed on the tiles.

I eventually recovered enough to shower and call for a doctor. They pretended not to understand my French and put the phone down on me - not good PR for the Sofitel. I gave up trying to sleep, resting on the bed for an hour or so before getting dressed for the return flight to Lagos. I could not trust myself to eat breakfast, but managed some water.

At the airport I made one final visit to the loo before the GM arrived, packing my underpants with toilet paper. He asked me how I had enjoyed my stay and I replied that it had been excellent (it doesn't do to alarm the passengers). On the two-hour flight back I had to clench my sphincter a few times, a difficult manoeuvre when busy on the radio. The flight took two hours and twenty minutes, but I managed it with only minor leakage.

Another of the MD's jaunts took us to the Yankari game park in Bauchi State. The game spotting was hopeless, just one or two mangy lions, but I had the chance to swim in the hot springs. Naturally carbonated, it was like bathing in champagne! The 20-foot-wide stream flowed straight out of a cave at the bottom of a cliff.

Residents of BRC were allocated a secondary duty, which not only saved the company money but occupied the spare time of those who might otherwise have slipped into less wholesome activities. The engineers plumped for bar services which were separated into accounts, stock, cleanliness and games. Darts were the all-time favourite and the MD, Keith Gaston-Parry, had been persuaded to fork out for a second hand, full sized snooker table. The chess and checkers sets had gone missing, but Uckers was still played with enthusiasm.

My responsibilities included the video room and swimming pool. I chose rented tapes from a travelling library, and much to the chagrin of our sex addicts I limited the porn to one tape per week. I managed to get a second VHS recorder, hoping to build a library of copies, but the project failed due to constant theft of tapes.

I took on the task of "Chop Master", which entailed devising the menu, purchasing the supplies and balancing the account. This job could be rewarding if the groceries available downtown matched the planned menu. It was fun going shopping with truck, driver, and Gabriel the local BRC foreman. Due to time restraints Gabriel and I shared the tasks of searching for the required supplies. I had to strike a fine balance between allowing Gabriel to collect his "cut" from suppliers and confronting him about the expense. Gabriel could obviously obtain goods cheaper than I, but he presented me with inflated invoices. The next week I went shopping with his assistant, and this tactic proved more economical.

BRC volunteers were required to take a food basket to Kiri Kiri Prison for two of our engineers, Ken Clarke (whom I knew from Miri) and Angus Patterson. They had been charged with conspiracy to steal an aircraft. They were acquitted, but re-arrested outside the prison.

Mike Howard, previously a co-pilot on the Bristow 125 and now a freelance captain, had accepted the task from the British owners of repossessing their impounded 125. Leased to a Nigerian, it had been caught smuggling currency and was now parked on the General Aviation apron. Howard, ostensibly on holiday with his fiancée, asked our two guys for assistance. Howard informed Ken and Angus that the export formalities were being processed, so they charged the aircraft battery and carried out a few systems checks (for free, or maybe a bottle of whisky).

At night, Howard and his girl boarded the 125, started it up and taxied out without notifying anybody. The take-off was carried out without radio contact with ATC. Having been unable to refuel in Lagos, Howard staged through Abidjan on the Ivory Coast. The aircraft was impounded on landing. Howard and friend were arrested, but luckily they were handed over to the British authorities before the Nigerians were notified. They were promptly whisked back to the UK. The 125 was returned to Lagos by the Nigerian Air Force and Ken and Angus were arrested.

Despite Kiri Kiri's appalling reputation, the British High Commission had managed to obtain improved conditions (beds, for example) for Ken and Angus. The general consensus was that they were held as bargaining chips for the extradition of Umarre Dikko, who had fled to the UK after a failed coup. Dikko had previously been the subject of a dramatic but foiled kidnap attempt arranged by Nigeria and carried out by ex-Mossad agents.

On my visits to Kiri Kiri Ken seemed able to maintain high spirits, but Angus was in a bad way and took no part in the conversation Ken and I struggled to prolong.

Collinson arrived from Redhill for a flying standards audit. He carried out a few line checks and finding the Lagos Operation proceeding well enough, spent the remainder of his allotted time getting a sun tan by the pool and challenging the rest of us to tennis and squash. My squash was OK, but when we got to the stage where he might lose the match, he whacked me across the backs of my legs so hard he broke his racket. I gritted my teeth and offered to lend him my spare. When he declined, I claimed victory. He said the leg strike was an accident - he would, wouldn't he?

Back at Redhill, Mr Bristow finally got fed up with Derek Jordan's temper and he was "retired". Collinson took over the 125/700 operation at Gatwick and needing another experienced 125 pilot, he offered me the job. My two-year Lagos contract was soon to be completed and Janet and I needed to lead a normal life. We would try a UK-based existence again.

To celebrate my departure from Nigeria, Keith Gaston-Parry arranged for us all to visit musician Fela Kuti's "Shrine" in darkest Ikeja. The music, a unique style of African jazz, ran non-stop. Fela himself did not perform before 1 am and by that time we were all stoned, a result of our passive inhalation of marijuana smoke. The establishment was thick with the aromatic haze. Roving waitresses served joints from a tray, just as in the old-time movie theatres.

Chapter Seventeen

GATWICK - BRISTOW AIR CHARTER

June 1987 - April 1991

The Bristow 125 was now operating an executive charter service to defray costs. At Gatwick the General Aviation Terminal acted as an agent. At Heathrow, MAMI, the operator of Robert Maxwell's Gulfstream, arranged high-end clients.

It was a relief to see an end to the schizophrenic eight on/four off existence and the dreaded return to Lagos. The transfer to the UK meant another domestic upheaval as working from Gatwick meant relocating to the Surrey area. I felt pretty mean telling Mum and Dad that we would have to sell Portland House, but with Dad having had a stroke Mum was keen to move to a smaller, single-storey property. Chagfordian old timers reckoned we would have to sell the house at a loss, but they were wrong. We actually had two competing buyers and sold it at a respectable price to the Irish artist Kenneth Webb.

Initially I had to commute weekly from Devon to Gatwick, staying in the company guest-house in Horley. When not flying I rushed around looking for a suitable property not far from the airport.

When Portland House was sold, Janet joined me in East Grinstead (Cult City) for the final decision on which property to choose from my short list. The house we finally agreed on was a little over budget, but being a split-level semi overlooking the Ashdown forest we could not resist it. The vendor was the sole member of the East Grinstead communist party.

Tom Frost OBE carried out my refresher training on the Bristow 125 and showed me the ropes regarding executive charter flying. Tom, originally from South Africa, had served in the RAF, qualifying as a test pilot. After leaving the RAF he became Chief Test Pilot for Armstrong Siddeley and Rolls Royce, testing the Concorde engine.

When not flying I was required to be in the office at Bristow HQ, Redhill Aerodrome, planning pre-booked flights. The operations department had a computer but this was used only for accounts and correspondence as the internet was not yet up to speed. We laboriously compiled flight logs by hand from charts and manuals. For regional airports where handling agents were not available, catering, customs immigration attendance, transport and accommodation all had to be booked by phone.

Every flight required a cabin attendant, and we had a number of part-timers who we called when required. These ex-first class attendants, no longer on any payroll, enjoyed the challenge and excitement as well as the extra income. Often carrying VIPs and stopping over in exotic destinations, the 125 provided a welcome break from their now less demanding lifestyles.

Val, our original 125 cabin attendant, had extensive experience in British Airways first class. Being an attractive blond and a 36B to boot meant that Tom could not refrain from teasing her with sexual innuendo. Val remained unfazed, having been trained to cope with this all-too-common occupational hazard. It didn't help that Val sunbathed topless during our Mediterranean day stops; this surprised me, but I wasn't complaining.

There were several notable charters. Tom Frost and I flew Norman Tebbit MP to Milan, Italy. En route Tebbit, who was an ex-BOAC captain, came up to the cockpit. He and Tom Frost, a South African, got engaged in a conversation which made my ears burn. They both assumed I would hold similar views on immigration and carried on a twenty-minute tirade while I managed the flight. I am unable to quote any details as I can not remember it word for word but the tone of their conversation veered to the right of, shall we say, Genghis Khan.

Again with Tom, we got logged by the CAA for landing in Kirkwall when the airport was closed. Kirkwall in the Orkney Islands is one of the most remote airfields in the UK. Tom was in command, so I did the flight preparation. I failed to notice that Kirkwall was closed on Sundays.

Before our descent the Scottish FIR controller handed us over to Kirkwall tower, assuming we had arranged for the airport to be open. We got no reply, and a quick check in the Jepps confirmed our suspicions that it was closed on Sundays. It was a bright sunny day with staggering visibility, absolutely unlimited. Tom looked at me and raised his eyebrows and I said "go for it", though we knew retribution would follow.

Fire cover should attend all public transport aircraft movements. The next morning, when we went in to pay landing fees and file the flight plan for our departure, the senior controller called me over. He looked daggers at me, saying "You landed yesterday". I nodded and he lost his cool, threatening to prevent our departure. When I told him we were taking Armand Hammer of Occidental Petroleum to Tel Aviv he relented, but informed us, still shouting, that he was reporting us to the CAA. Tom Frost was not fazed but as usual, I worried.

At the subsequent enquiry Collinson came out strongly in our defence, arguing that it was a private positioning flight to collect passengers. That is technically no excuse, but it was a mitigating factor. No penalty was imposed but we were cautioned.

In Israel we did the tourist thing. We read newspapers in the Dead

Sea and visited the Church of the Nativity in Bethlehem. In the little crypt downstairs it was very crowded and I was pushed off balance by a large group of French nuns, when I staggered on to the brass star that marks the supposed birthplace, they shrieked at me. J.C. would have smiled.

On October 16th 1987 Peter Grey, the former Bristow GM from Miri, invited us out to dinner. Saying our goodbyes at around 11 pm I remarked how very warm it felt, almost tropical. On the drive home the wind picked up rapidly. By the time we got back to East Grinstead the car had become very difficult to control and I had to reduce speed to a crawl. Later, in bed in the early hours, we were woken by crashing and banging noises. Getting out of bed to investigate, we realised that the hurricane pooh-poohed by BBC forecaster Michael Fish had struck. The garden fence had been torn from its mountings and was bashing the back of the house. If I didn't secure the thing it might smash the kitchen window. I struggled outside and pulled it clear. Looking up I saw a sky full of debris. Apart from the many leaves, branches and much household garbage, I could see, several hundred feet up in the air, sheets of corrugated iron, dustbins and other potentially lethal items. I rushed back inside just as the greenhouse exploded.

Not being able to sleep (the roof tiles were rattling alarmingly) we drank coffee until the wind subsided. I was surprised how soon it was all over. The next morning we realised how lucky we had been. Our house, being in a relatively sheltered position, had suffered only minor damage. Many trees were down and all roads were impassable. There would be no work for a day or so.

During the next few days we walked around East Grinstead surveying the damage. Sadly most of the centuries-old oak trees in Estcots Park had been brought down. What struck me most was that some of their trunks had sheared, even though they were four to five feet in diameter.

Collinson gave me the task of recruiting and briefing more cabin attendants. We all had contacts in the industry, and from word of mouth the applications trickled in. After the interviews the short list remained surprisingly small. We needed to have a reasonable number on the list, as most of these girls had other commitments and were sometimes unavailable. Experience of first-class service was essential as our clients usually travelled this way when using the airlines.

Normally the execs we carried were preoccupied with paperwork and weren't a problem. There were notable exceptions however - some bullied the girls in an attempt to humiliate them, and some got fresh. James Goldsmith littered the cabin with newspapers and other rubbish and refused to allow the mess to be cleaned up while he was on board (his daughter Jemima was embarrassed). One Arab passenger flashed one of our girls (this happens more often than you might think), but they were trained for these eventualities and handled them unfazed. The putdown was usually on the lines of "What would your children say?".

At the Redhill head office we were preparing a trip for Trafalgar House which included several resort destinations along the Turkish coast. Dave Collinson threw a file on my desk and said "I will crew on this one, call this girl". I opened the file and saw the photo of an applicant I had rejected. Her picture, taken at a party, showed an effervescent young thing sporting a come-hither smile, shoulder strap awry. The picture must have been taken when she was about twenty years old. Her CV quoted her age as thirty five and her experience as having been obtained in the Middle East (regular airline attendants referred to these girls as "flatbackers"). Collinson had made up his mind and would not be deterred. I was worried, as the client was one of MAMI's best customers.

To my dismay Collinson nominated me as Co-Captain. The 125 had been parked outside the BA hangar at Heathrow, where MAMI had office space. We drove up from Gatwick, meeting the girl at a Heathrow security gate. Sure enough she was barely recognisable from the photo, she had put on a fair amount of weight and had lost her spark. Collinson was shocked, but quickly recovered his demeanour. I showed her the 125 galley area and it became apparent she was hopelessly out of her depth. I had to prepare the galley myself and was instructed to greet and brief the passengers.

Once level in the cruise, Collinson told me to go back to the galley and help prepare the dishes. The passengers twigged what was going on and were not amused; they knew our reputation for good service. The atmosphere in the cabin became strained. The next few days would be painful.

At the Hilton in Istanbul, the three of us ate dinner in silence. We had two more days in Turkey and the return flight to manage. We struggled through. In Dalaman, the girl and I got a taxi to the market stalls and selected lunch for the trip home, but she played no part in the endeavour, remaining mute. We landed back at Heathrow late at night and delivered the passengers to the agents at terminal one.

Taxiing back to the MAMI ramp beside the BA hangar, Collinson instructed me to pay off the hostess and open the door near the airside car park. He did not want MAMI or the next crew, who were waiting to take over the aircraft, to see the girl. We dropped her off, engines running, and she disappeared into the night. After we parked on the apron Collinson explained to our replacements that our girl was in a hurry to get home. Val and Tom Frost raised their eyebrows. Val was furious when she discovered she had to clear up the mess before setting up.

Collinson could be a pain. Although not a harsh boss, he enjoyed manipulating our emotions. As the training captain he carried out our check rides, taking the opportunity to belittle our attempts. It is easy to make things difficult for a candidate. His favourite trick was to sigh heavily and look away while we were handling a practice emergency. It was effective. We lost our focus.

Collinson enjoyed fine dining and on stopovers we followed his example. He allowed us to claim for one bottle of wine with dinner. As a crew of three this meant a sensible two glasses each. Inevitably we ordered more, especially if we had a late start the next day. We all put on weight. For exercise I checked out the East Grinstead Hash House Harriers. By coincidence the Grand Master and founder, Tim Waller, lived on the other side of the road, Estcots Drive. The EG Hash were heavy-duty runners, the trails were across open country or established footpaths and the going was fast. Runs normally lasted about an hour and a half with the On-On (weird Hash ritual and beer) at a country pub.

The EG Hashers consisted mainly of the rugby club and the local constabulary, thus ensuring the chosen location would not be monitored by patrol cars. I found the running too strenuous, so I gave up hashing and joined the squash club. Frequent unexpected call-outs resulted in many cancelled squash appointments. I gained a reputation as an unreliable partner, which put an end to the venture. It was now back to brisk walks in the forest.

Apart from the 125, Bristow operated a Learjet 35 for Loftur Johannesson, an arms dealer. He was known in the trade as "The Icelander". Although not in current practice he was an experienced pilot, having flown for the Red Cross. His Panama-registered company, Techaid, operated from his office and apartment in Victoria, Central London.

Collinson and Simon Risley had flown the Learjet to the US, where Techaid had secured new business with the US government (see *Charlie Wilson's War*). Wanting to tie up loose ends, Loftur had decided to stay on a further ten days. Collinson, not wishing to remain away that long (Christmas was coming), informed me that I should get to Washington Dulles the next day; tickets had been arranged. I was told that the Lear was operated on a private basis and that my not having any knowledge of the aircraft was not important; I would only be required to do the navigation and radio.

Collinson and Simon Risley met me on arrival at Dulles. Collinson checked in for the flight to the UK and Simon drove me to Loftur's house on the eastern shore of Chesapeake Bay. Some house - it was a replica of a French mansion. We were allocated the beachside villa, which was luxurious by any standards, and given a Jeep to get around (Loftur's personal vehicle was a heavily-modified Lincoln Town Car). When we were stopped for speeding, the cop told us "You guys must obey the laws while you are here, your boss will be informed". Loftur cautioned us when we got back.

Simon made the most of the situation. During the day we did the tourist thing and in the evenings we dined at the best restaurants. I exercised before breakfast by running around the estate; Simon slept in.

No customs or immigration were present for our departure from the small airfield at Easton. Loftur appeared to be exempt. Not having the required navaids to operate a direct trans-Atlantic flight, the Lear had to route via Newfoundland and Iceland. This suited Loftur, as he could visit friends and family. The take-off with fuel load for Goose Bay was unnerving. As the Lear was operated as a private jet there was no requirement for rejected take-off capability. Getting airborne just before the end of the runway was good enough. To allow jets to operate the runway at Easton had been lengthened, and the extension had a steep downhill gradient. On take-off this down slope meant a large rotation was required after lift off; at low speed this was not a comfortable manoeuvre.

At Goose Bay Simon asked me to do the paperwork at the AIS office in the terminal while he monitored the refuelling. Leaving the aircraft, I realised why! I had not anticipated the severity of the

Canadian winter. It was blowing snow and -18°C. I was not dressed for the short walk across the apron and needed a hot chocolate to unfreeze.

Reykjavik was a surprise, +11°C; we landed at the very convenient general aviation airport in town (the international airport at Keflavik was to far away for Loftur).

We had dinner at a restaurant in the heart of the small capital, where our window seat allowed us to observe the intensity of the local night life. At 9 pm the streets and clubs were jumping. Many people were seriously drunk and one chap was lying in the street waving his arms in the air. A normal night in town apparently.

Back at Redhill I was asked if I was interested in becoming a Lear 35 captain - I was. It was great fun to fly. Loftur's Lear was registered in the Cayman Islands and operated as a private aircraft. I was issued with a Cayman Islands Private Pilot's Licence. I flew as co-pilot with Simon Risley for a couple of flights to Périgueux and a trip to Zürich. Just before I was let loose as captain, the CAA told Bristow that the rules had changed. The type was fast and sophisticated and pilots now had to be UK-type rated. A wise move - the Lear, like the MU2, demanded depth of experience.

As usual, I was not given a manufacturer's course. Swotting for the exam got me immersed in the flight manual (no bad thing). The type rating was carried out by a non-Bristow examiner from Biggin Hill, Captain Faulkner.

The problem was the contract. The little jet was for personal as well as business use. Loftur liked to spend weekends with his wife at their château in the Dordogne, which meant most weekends away. Collinson said that with more pilots rated on the type, weekends away would be shared out. What he didn't say was that he had blotted his copybook and had been banned from staying at the château. After a drink or two he had taken a horse from the stables and galloped it around the estate in the middle of the night. As Collinson was not prepared to stay in the nominated hotel in Périgueux, the rest of us were lumbered with the Périgueux weekends. I found out too late that the other pilots, an Aussie captain and Simon, fed up with weekends away, had both tendered their resignations. I was lumbered.

Favourite destinations apart from Périgueux were the financial centres of Zürich, Geneva and Luxembourg. The runway at Périgueux was a trifle short for the Lear, having been built for propeller-driven types. Simon told me that Collinson had gone off the end of the runway on to the grass, and although no damage was done Loftur was not amused. Cleaning the brake units had proved time consuming. Collinson was a capable pilot and very knowledgeable, but his reactions were a tad slow. When flying with him to Périgueux I carried out the landings. With reverse thrust and normal braking you could turned off at the intersection, 4000" from the threshold and before the downhill section. All it needed was a positive touchdown and snappy deployment of reverse.

Collinson gave me the next Lear flight to the US. I had never flown transatlantic except the previous return with Simon, so I expected at least a route familiarisation flight with another captain, but he crewed me with Jock Young, desk wallah and occasional co-pilot. Jock, an old and not-so-bold ex helicopter chap, had seen better days. He was unfit and tired, with too much desk time and no exercise. He normally manned the office but had acted as co-pilot on the Lear and the 125.

The day before our flight he called in sick, but Collinson persuaded him to fly anyway, so he sat in the cockpit, read the checklist and retrieved the appropriate maps and charts. Jock did look pretty rough - I wasn't sure if this was a cold or a hangover; he was famous for packing a bottle or two of Black Label on stopovers. I worried our way across the Atlantic via Reykjavik and Goose Bay, and on reaching US airspace was totally flummoxed when given an unrecognisable arrival clearance for New York Teterboro. We scrabbled about, filling the cockpit with opened charts while we searched for the way to go. Fortunately the controller heard my accent, noted the foreign registration and figured out what was going on. He slowly spelled out the VOR beacons to follow and we managed. I was staggered by the amount of traffic in the New York Terminal Area, but we were threaded through, finally landing at the General Aviation hub.

Take off for Easton was scheduled for the following afternoon. Due to unfamiliarity with US procedures we decided to get everything ready early, which was just as well. In the aviation sector the Americans do not follow international standard procedures - they have their own way of doing things. My self-briefing in the UK afforded us little help, and the Teterboro operations office was unmanned. Computer terminals linked to air traffic control were there to assist. Flight planning and payment of fees were automated, which was fine if you knew how to proceed. The simplicity of the system gave the impression we were missing something, but when we checked with other crews they looked at us blankly, confused by our accents. In the end a call to the control tower sorted it out. We refuelled using my credit card, adding a whole bunch of air miles to my account.

When the time came to depart for Easton late in the afternoon, tiredness and jet lag had set in. We were carrying a light fuel load, as the flight was only 35 minutes and the runway at Easton was quite short. After take-off the Lear launched itself into the sky like a rocket, briefly exceeding both the speed limit and our assigned level, but there were no comments from ATC. We left controlled airspace and headed for our destination, where luckily we saw the field. In the Lear an old fashioned NDB letdown on to a short runway makes for an "interesting" arrival.

Loftur was driven off in his limo while we carried out the refuelling and cleaned up. With no handling agents this also meant removing the toilet. We emptied the contents in the airport lavatories and took the contraption back to the villa for cleaning (essential). When I had flown back on the previous occasion, each time the lid was raised a nauseating waft of ammonia had filled the cabin.

It was the month of May, and during our two weeks the weather switched from winter to summer. Spring lasted two days. It was a nice break for us, two weeks with only one flight to New York Teterboro. Jock and I did a quick tour downtown with a visit to the top of the World Trade Centre and lunch in Battery Park.

Back at the villa Loftur okayed our use of the speedboat. Great fun, we thought. After fuelling up and greasing the reluctant telex cables, Jock drove, and I got back into form water skiing. The water in Chesapeake Bay had retained its winter chill and this, combined with the exercise, made us ravenous. Sandwiches would not suffice, so we set course for St Michaels, where there were many seafood restaurants.

We sped round the headland into the quaint little fishing port and tied up at a likely looking place (Foxy's) with its own jetty. We were a trifle early for lunch and the place was empty, but a waiter told us that they were fully booked. We ordered beer and checked the menu, to be stunned by the prices.

Things began to add up when a large and opulent private yacht approached the main jetty. When this gin palace tied up, uniformed crew fussed about deploying the gangway. The male passengers were dressed in blazers, white slacks and spotless deck shoes; the ladies wore designer creations. I realised what a shabby picture we presented, dressed in baggy shorts and oil-stained T-shirts. Jock's considerable beer belly protruded from the gap between shorts and shirt, displaying a navel like the eye of the Cyclops. We were both covered in grease from preparing the engine and our windblown hair was encrusted with salt.

Jock was about to cause a fuss regarding non-delivery of our second beer. "Jock, I think we should try a different place, I don't have enough cash for another" I muttered. This struck a chord with Jock's Scottish instincts and he agreed. I paid for the drinks and we descended the steps on to the floating jetty. The manager, standing back in the shadows, looked mightily relieved.

Once aboard, I managed to get the outboard started on the fifth pull. In best nautical fashion I ordered Jock to "let go aft", but he looked blank (ex Air Force, you see). I explained quietly and he untied the stern line. While I was untying forward Jock realised that the stern was swinging out from the jetty and leapt aboard. His foot caught the gunwale and he rolled arse over tit in the ski paraphernalia, legs in the air.

By now we had an audience. I tried to look cool, but this became difficult when each time I engaged reverse from idle, the engine died. The rusty control cables were still playing up. I could get idle or full power, but nothing in between. With my repeated attempts I could tell the ageing battery would not last much longer, so there was nothing for it but to select reverse at full power.

We leapt back, water flooded over the transom and I selected full forward. We shot ahead, straight for the gin palace. I slammed it into reverse again but we hit with a thump, leaving a long black rubber streak on the gleaming white hull. Reversing again with more water coming over the stern, I managed to turn the wheel and engage forward at the same time, slewing the craft in a dramatic U-turn followed by a high-speed exit from the scene of the crime. I fully expected to be chased by the harbourmaster, but at forty knots we were soon out of sight.

That evening Loftur invited me over for cocktails (Jock was in bed). I thought he knew about our St Michaels escapade, but no, he and his friend were interested in my time in Africa. They assumed I had been either a mercenary or a spy, but didn't pursue the matter.

He told me how he had got into the arms business during the Biafran war. He and a few other entrepreneurs had flown arms and ammo into Uli airstrip near the city of Enugu. After delivering their goods the DC7s and Lockheed Constellations were parked in the bush or bulldozed off the runway if they broke on landing - interesting stuff. Later he showed me his gun collection in the cellar. It was just like the movies, with racks of assorted small arms filling the cabinets. Would I like to try some? I chose the Magnum .44. I asked where the range was, and he laughed and said "outside in the garden". They stuck a piece of A4 card on one of the shrubs and I loosed off about ten rounds from twenty feet, eight on the card, they were surprised.

With Jock now fighting fit, the flight back to UK via Goose and Reykjavik was less stressful. After landing at Gatwick Loftur said he now wished to go on to Perigueux. I called the office to request a change of crew and the Europe set of Jeppeson charts. The flight bag contained only the UK, Atlantic and US Eastern Seaboard charts. Collinson said that a crew change was not possible and that there was no time to deliver the "Jepps". I was not to worry. as the flight management computer could get me to Perigueux and he was sure I could remember the instrument approach!

Foolishly I went along with this and we departed feeling quite vulnerable. If the weather turned bad we would come back to Gatwick.

Instead of staying in the cheap and cheerful Perigueux Ibis I had arranged to stay with my old Bradninch friends Sue and Alex, near Lalande. We hired a car and joined them for a few glasses of wine and dinner. In the middle of the meal Loftur rang and told us that on Monday morning (it was now Saturday evening) we would be going to Budapest, not back to the UK. After putting Janet in the picture (now really fed up) I called the office and asked Collinson to put the European navigation manuals on a BA flight to Bordeaux, and I would collect. He refused and told me he would fax the charts. Rural

France was a bit behind the times, and the only fax machine in Perigueux was in the Post Office.

When I arrived at the PO the next morning I found the staff in a panic. The fax machine had been busy overnight and was still churning out charts. They were mightily relieved when they realised I was the recipient and would actually pay the bill. It took the rest of the day to cut and tape the whole puzzle into some semblance of order. The fax had been set on "normal", which rendered some of the fine print unreadable, but it would have to do.

The morning of departure found Jock and Loftur in the Lear with myself up in the control tower. We were waiting for air traffic control permission to get airborne and join the airway. The booked slot time was not for another hour and a half, but we were prepared to go hot off the blocks when an opportunity arose. Périgueux did not have a ground power unit, nor the Lear an auxiliary one. If we listened for our radio clearance in the aircraft the battery might go flat. I waited for our call up in the control tower. After twenty minutes we got our break and I raced down the three flights of stairs, fired up and got airborne. Passing 4000 feet the tower informed us that I had left my briefcase behind - did I want to return? I was now without my passport and licence and our destination lay behind the Iron Curtain. I took a deep breath and said no, we would continue. It was a day stop. I would stay on the aircraft and Jock could complete the formalities. Loftur had powerful connections and could sort out any problems if it came to the crunch.

We managed to decipher the smudgy small print and find our way to Budapest. After a boring six hours and too much coffee (lucky the weather was mild) Loftur returned. Fortunately for me he wanted us to drop him off at Périgueux, so I could collect my briefcase.

I added the King Air B200 to my licence when our Bristow machine arrived from Nigeria. Jim Lawn, an affable, easy-going, long-time Bristow employee, came with the aircraft. With his smartly-groomed beard, Jim resembled the Players Navy Cut sailor.

Charter business was increasing and the small Bristow hangar by the Gatwick control tower was now full; more pilots were needed. Two more joined the team. The first, John Kennett, I had known from the Fleet Air Arm, and though now retired from British Airways he was good for a few more years. A gentleman like his brother, he kept us amused with his dry-as-dust humour and wry comments. John was followed by the upwardly-mobile Paul Weddick. Paul had considerable helicopter experience on various Bristow operations. He had acquired enough fixed-wing time to start working his way up the fixed-wing ladder. He was very ambitious and did this in record time.

Ambulance conversion kits were acquired for both the 125 and the King Air, adding a lucrative new dimension to our expanding portfolio. The ambulance business kept us busy returning damaged holidaymakers and decaying retirees. The 125 door could manage the vacuumed bean bag stretcher. The King Air's entrance door was narrow and the steps steep, so we used a Neil Robinson scoop. Overenthusiastic helpers often had to be restrained in order not to disengage any drips attached, or worse, drop the stretcher. It had to be tilted steeply to enter the cabin.

During the summer months the King Air air-conditioning could barely cope with the door closed, and open it was useless. Medical evacuation flights from the Mediterranean were torture. The protracted business of loading the stretcher turned the cabin into a sauna, and it was worse if there were delays in receiving our start and take-off clearance. Normally ambulance flights had priority, but in the busy summer months in places like Majorca, delays were inevitable. In situations where the patient was in critical condition the insurance companies authorised medical teams to use the more expensive 125.

Tourist casualties included obvious survivors of motor accidents and drunks who had looked the wrong way crossing the road. A surprising number were broken necks - the result of diving into shallow water, either at the wrong ends of hotel pools or off jetties when the tide was out.

Most paramedics who assisted with stretcher loading were calm and professional, but there were exceptions. During one evacuation at a small airport in rural France the situation turned farcical when the ambulance crew were too hasty. They dropped the stretcher, throwing the patient on to the tarmac. With equipment scattered and drips disconnected the patient lay there, robe in disarray, exposed to the world. The pilots, the medics, the crowd on the viewing terrace, all were stunned - it was the stuff of nightmares. Our UK doctor and nurse carefully reinstalled the patient, and it then took a few more minutes to load the stretcher as we struggled to get the Robinson through the B200 doorway. I hope the onlookers appreciated our little drama.

If a patient died en route, or even in the ambulance on the way to the airport, the paperwork always stated location and time of death as the destination airport. This avoided any complications. Imagine trying to sort out the legal implications if the death was over a country other than that of departure or arrival.

Due to the variable nature of the task, charter flying is a challenging business. Air ambulance flights were trickier than most, as the flights were mostly set up at short notice. One of our longest charters was an ambulance flight to Nairobi to collect a heart patient. This flight required several diplomatic clearances, and not all were obtained. There being no response from Ethiopia, we flew across passing only traffic information, ignoring their requests for details. Addis Ababa were obviously familiar with this behaviour and soon gave up. We were very tired for the midnight arrival into Nairobi and only just managed to follow the descent profile required to avoid high ground. We finally got to bed (after a nightcap in The Hilton bar) at four in the morning.

The alarm woke us at seven. We rushed off without breakfast to prep the aircraft, pay the fees, and get the paperwork ready. We managed to get everything done for the scheduled 9 am departure. The ambulance failed to arrive and there was no response from contact numbers provided, so I phoned our Bristow ops back in the UK. About thirty minutes later they called back saying the patient was just leaving the hospital. I was worried, at 5000 feet altitude even the long runway would not be enough when the temperature increased. We ate breakfast while waiting for the ambulance. The catering was magnificent.

We were about to postpone the flight until late that night when the medical team arrived. The medics fussed about, taking longer than expected to settle the patient. By the time we were ready to depart public transport safety margins had disappeared. We would get airborne with only a few hundred metres remaining; yet another judgement call. The patient was slowly deteriorating so I chose to go, nagged by worries that our take-off ground speed would exceed our tyre limiting speed.

Rolling down the runway I had never experienced such poor acceleration. As we passed the point where any attempt to stop would result in an overrun, we held our breath. We tentatively eased the 125 off the ground and the end of the runway flashed underneath.

With full fuel for Cairo the initial climb out was tediously slow, but the rate of climb returned to normal as we climbed out of ground heating. The Cairo agents provided a remarkably quick turnaround and we finally landed at Southampton. After unloading the patient and medics to a waiting ambulance the engine failed to start for the short return home. Some days we got lucky.

Ambulance call-outs sometimes occurred in the middle of the night, but if a life was at stake crew duty limits were waived. This led to the return leg being flown when we were very tired, so we took turns to nap. During the summer most of these emergencies were alcohol-related accidents. Many hooligans were repatriated from Spain (not too far) but a surprising number were collected from Yugoslavia, a long haul, especially if the King Air was used. Callouts to Zadar, Split and Dubrovnik are listed in my logbook.

Collinson was becoming a bit of a pain. If we didn't join in pub stops on the way back from the airport or join him at the dog track etc, he got annoyed. I was also getting fed up with consistently being called in on my days off and having to spend an increasing number of Learjet weekends in Perigueux. Family life was suffering. I looked around for alternative employment.

My colleague from Lagos, Rod Rae, had joined TNT express freight services. Air Foyle operated the HS 146s for TNT and were expanding fast. Rod was their senior training captain and put in a good word for me. The interview went well and I was offered a position starting as co-pilot. The only problem was the schedule. The 146 was so quiet it could take off and land at night without infringing noise regulations. "Whisper" jet status meant most flights were at night. Routing from city to city, crews stayed in hotels for a week at a time. I was in two minds about it, but the chance of getting a 146 type rating made me persist.

I submitted my letter of resignation, mentioning my unwillingness to continue working with Collinson. The Bristow Operations Director, Alastair Gordon, called me up to his office and requested I hold on to my letter pending the outcome of an unfolding scenario with Collinson. Collinson had manoeuvred himself into the position where he had sole control of Bristow fixed-wing operations. Now he was demanding much improved pay and conditions and had threatened to resign if his demands were not met.

Alastair told me I was not alone in finding Collinson difficult and Bristow had refused his demands. I should await the outcome. I agreed.

Collinson was informed that there was to be no change in his terms of employment. He refused to back down, thinking himself indispensible. He tendered his resignation, it was accepted, and I stayed.

After a short simulator course and a check ride with the CAA, I became a 125 type rating examiner. I then trained Paul Weddick on the type. The operation could now manage without Collinson, who was still working out his notice in the vain hope that Bristow would cave in and ask him back. Paul, a senior Bristow employee and instrument examiner, took over the reins when Collinson departed. With the operation now back on an even keel, work once again became fun.

The King Air had a regular run to Waterford in Ireland to collect flowers and plants from the Mount Congreve botanical gardens. The cabin retained the fragrance of the blooms, which was very pleasant. Ambrose Congreve himself accompanied the flora, even though he was verging on eighty years old (he is still with us at the time of writing). We collected him from Fairoaks and returned him there. This airfield in the Heathrow control zone was very basic and limited to visual approaches in sight of ground. It was surrounded by obstacles and had limited runway length, which posed a challenge in marginal weather conditions. Speedy use of checklists and radio procedures were required, as several ATC handovers were required during the approach. Normally only "puddle jumpers" and the Twin Otters of Antarctic Survey used the field.

The airfield operators needed the income from landing fees and we needed the contract, so rules were bent, Heathrow ATC were very understanding. Waterford airfield was not much better, as at that time it had no approved landing aids. We always felt a sense of achievement after successful completion of a Congreve trip. John

Kennett found the challenge especially stimulating after the hidebound British Airways.

The longer flights were always a challenge. On one oil company charter we were required to visit Tripoli, Libreville, Port Gentil and Cairo. The passengers, American oil execs, were alarmed when they found out we were refuelling in Kano, Nigeria, outbound, and Khartoum on the return. These airfields have a reputation for impounding aircraft for improper documentation. Having previously operated in and out of Kano I had old contacts and Bristow furnished original stamped diplomatic clearances. These documents, along with receipts for landing fees and fuel, had to be presented with the outbound flight plan before start-up clearance would be approved. The passengers remained sceptical and showed extreme apprehension after landing.

I descended the aircraft steps and commenced the trek round the airport offices. The only approved handling agent was Nigeria Airways, but I knew them too well to trust them. Twenty minutes later, when I entered the cabin, the passengers stared in disbelief when I told them we could start up for Libreville. They only relaxed after lift-off.

In Libreville the agent turned out to be the same girl responsible for my previous food-poisoning débâcle, so gracefully refusing her offer of dinner, we ate in the hotel. The schedule the following day was a day return to Port Gentil, which we did with no special formalities. I always felt uncomfortable when normal procedures such as temporary import documents were dispensed with. In Africa these omissions can be used to hold the crew, passengers and aircraft to ransom. On the leg to Cairo via Khartoum the passengers were in better spirits and the turnaround was achieved quickly with the help of the agent arranged by Jeppeson Aviation Services. Jeppeson always came up with the goods, but Collinson had previously avoided them because of their relatively high charges. We spent the two days in Cairo being tourists, visiting the main mosque, the museum and the pyramids in between beer stops for Jock and mint tea for me.

The trouble with executive jet charter in UK was that all prices were artificially low. 90 per cent of the business was carried out by under-utilised company aircraft. Chartering was used to defray costs, not to make a profit. Consequently all competing outfits reduced their charges in an attempt to gain market share. This ensured no money was ever made. Attempts to organise ourselves into some form of cartel failed miserably due to the intense rivalry.

On another of our trips we were chartered to fly a group of secretive wheeler-dealers on a round-Europe tour. They requested that no cabin service be provided. On the longish leg from Stockholm to Berne I opened the cabin door to enquire if they needed refreshments, and the passengers looked as horrified as if I had suggested group sex. I hastily shut the door.

This bunch had amazing luck with the weather. We warned them that a blanket fog had been forecast to cover Europe during their trip and we could not guarantee successful landings at any destinations, especially Berne (limited landing aids). In fact it turned out that the only airfields open to traffic were those on their itinerary and only at time of arrival - unbelievable! Finally, for the last departure out of Stuttgart, they arrived half an hour late. We had missed our airways entry time and had applied for an opportunity slot. We told the passengers that the only way to ensure not missing our chance was to wait on board. No sooner had they boarded than the call came and off we went. We never found out who they were.

Jan joined our team as a regular cabin attendant. She was a winner, ex-Caledonian first class, a slim, tall blond and fit enough to handle the sometimes demanding tasks imposed by a full load and cramped galley. Jan had a wicked sense of humour, so extreme that it occasionally took our breath away.

Jim Lawn, Jan and I flew the TNT top honchos to Stockholm, where they had ordered sumptuous catering. After landing around lunchtime, at least half the dishes and several bottles of wine remained. When Jim and I had finished refuelling and done the paperwork Jan took us into the cabin, where she had prepared a slap-up meal including the wine, the best china, and the silver cutlery. We were to fly back the next day - no problem, we enjoyed an extended lunch. Hours later we weaved or way across the apron and into the terminal. We wore our raincoats to cover the gold braid - mustn't bring the profession into disrepute. Checking in at the hotel, Jan told reception that one room would do as long as the bed was big enough. I collapsed in a fit of giggles while Jim sorted it out.

Generally our little outfit had a good reputation. British Aerospace used us as their long distance option, and funnily enough it was with them that we had two of our most serious aircraft system failures (the 125 is their product). They were very understanding and continued as a regular customer.

Just before the top of descent into Geneva we suffered an hydraulic failure. We put it to them that landing in Geneva would mean they would have to return with the airlines and we would be stuck with a logistics problem, or we could return to Hatfield (their HQ) and try again that afternoon. We went back to Hatfield, the problem was fixed and we delivered them as promised. The other incident occurred returning from Toulouse, when the main cabin pressurisation duct disconnected and we had to switch to the alternative supply. The air now entered directly from the engines into the cockpit, and was unconditioned. The cockpit temperature rose to about 50 degrees C, but although the very dry air caused us discomfort it did no damage. The trouble was that we had an hour's flying before the landing at Hatfield.

BAE gave us free tickets to the VIP enclosure at the Paris Air show, which was brilliant, pity we had to abstain from drinking the free wine. Tom Frost met his old mates from Aeromacchi and there followed an animated discussion of his time as a test pilot on the MB 339. Not speaking Italian, I felt a trifle excluded.

Paul McCartney used our services to ferry him from his home airfield (Lydd in Kent) to Heathrow, where he connected with the US-bound Concorde flight. We had to be positioned early, as he liked the reassurance of knowing the aeroplane was waiting ready to go. This involved waiting on the apron with the APU (Auxiliary Power Unit) running for up to two hours. Although refreshments were available on board I liked my tea out of china (not Styrofoam), and with the occasional Danish, so we dived into the small terminal. Sure enough, as soon as the goodies were on the table a runner came rushing in to say the Rolls Royce was waiting by the aircraft. Before we could board the aircraft a stern call of "Captain!" halted us in our tracks. Tom winked, said "I'll start her up" and disappeared into the cockpit. Getting out of the Rolls, McCartney gave me a dressing down right there on the apron. He liked to hear the engines spooling up as he opened the car door.

The flight to Heathrow took fifteen minutes. There was never any delay getting clearance for Heathrow if they had been advised your passengers had a Concorde connection. Linda always checked that the catering matched her order. She rarely smiled, but her face lit up when she did.

Other showbiz characters we flew included Rod Stewart and Genesis. We took Rod and his friends up to Glasgow to see the big match, Celtic v. Rangers. They were quiet and polite on the flight up, but raucous on the return leg. We waited ready at the General Aviation Terminal for several hours past the scheduled departure time. Rod and friends finally arrived in the early hours of the morning in very high spirits.

When Jan brought us our coffee she was smiling and reported being mooned. When I asked her how she had handled it she said she had asked them in best schoolmarm style, "Now boys, what would your mothers say?" they sheepishly composed themselves, apologised and ordered more scotch.

We flew Genesis to Rotterdam for a performance one day, returning them in the small hours. Phil Collins came up front for the landing and sat on the jump seat. I think he might have had flying lessons or even a private licence, as he asked a lot of questions. He requested a smooth landing and Collinson gave me control. I was flattered, but "greasers" as we called them are normally things to be avoided, as they wear out the tyres in quick time. A positive (not heavy) touchdown is best, especially in rainy weather. (skimming the wheels in the wet may generate superheated steam, the steam eats the tyre, making an expensive tyre change mandatory).

Light relief was available. The Hong Kong Civil Aviation Authority used our 125 to keep their admin pilots in current flying practice. Their nominated pilots required ten hours per annum, including the proficiency test and instrument rating. The chosen method of achieving those flying hours was to select a desirable long-range location to carry out the training, eg Venice or Casablanca. Paul Weddick did the necessary training at the destination. Family members, including Janet and me, enjoyed the sightseeing.

Harry Goodman, founder and CEO of Air Europe, gave us a week's free holiday in Faro, Portugal when he required the 125 to remain there on standby. Janet flew out separately to join us for fun and the food.

We carried out a charter for Rupert Murdoch during the period when French air traffic controllers were working to rule. This industrial action caused a delay to our departure from Madrid; Murdoch came up to the cockpit to enquire about the progress of our clearance. He asked a few pertinent questions, revealing that he new intricate details of the reasons behind the problem. Murdoch seemed to know an awful lot more about my business, aviation, than I did. Now he is asking everyone to believe he was unaware of nefarious dealings by his own staff at News International.

When the Learjet contract came to an end, I was to collect it from Fort Lauderdale and deliver it to UK for the new owner. Gary Booze a locally based Lear captain would be the other pilot. I flew over as a passenger via New York and was met at Fort Lauderdale by Gary and his girl Tammy. Despite my protestations I was immediately whisked off to a hangar party. I was very tired and jet lagged, but tried to enter into the spirit of things by throwing a few drinks down. I then confused everyone with verbal dyslexia in an English accent.

After a disturbed night I got a call At 7 am inviting me down to breakfast. I had no idea who it was, but they said they were friends of Gary. Two guys introduced themselves to me as I entered the buffet area. They looked like the heavy mob, but said they were FBI. I was intrigued but perplexed when they tried to explain. Handing me their cards, they asked if I would use my good offices to pass on to Gary their apologies for their previous behaviour and hoped that their relationship with him could get off to a fresh start. No further explanation was forthcoming.

When Gary picked me up shortly after, I passed on the message. He nodded, and without revealing any details said his air charter company had carried out a number of flights for the FBI, the DEA and other government departments. There followed some interesting stories, some relating to the ferrying of arms to Central America and around the Caribbean.

Gary considered the bags under my eyes, laughed and said he would fly the first few sectors, so I could relax. Loftur joined us and we took off for Easton, Maryland. That evening Gary chose the location for dinner as he loved the local delicacy, soft shell crab. I was still a bit woozy, so he drove the Jeep, dropping me off by the door while he found a parking spot.

I walked straight into the plate glass window, thinking it was an open door, and split my nose. Blood poured down my chin. Holding my nose and feeling a fool, I walked in through the adjacent door. At the counter, when I asked for a napkin and a table for two, the staff stared apprehensively, expecting a tirade and possible litigation. I got the impression that I was not the first person to have hit the glass. They said nothing but escorted us to the best table in the house. I had to hold the swab in place for most of the meal, but the bleeding stopped in time for coffee.

Just before we departed the next day, Loftur offered me one of the geese he had shot just a few hours before. If I could freeze the bird quickly it would be just the thing for Christmas dinner. I put the bird in a maintenance bay on the underside of the Lear and we departed (appropriately) for Goose Bay in Newfoundland. On arrival at Gatwick the bird was rock solid, as the temperature at altitude had been -55°C.

Janet cooked the goose for Christmas. It was OK, but during the preparation the bowl of goose grease (at least a litre) slipped out of her grasp. You have no idea how long it took to clean up.

The operation was booming, so our office was relocated to larger but less stylish premises in one of the Redhill hangars. Dedicated operations staff were employed, but our pay remained stagnant. The cost of living in the Home Counties was high and we had virtually no disposable income. I had landed at hundreds of different airfields, including some of the most challenging. It was time to move on, and earn some real money.

Bristow needed another DHC 6 training captain back in Nigeria and were offering an attractive package including married accompanied status. Although charter flying had been fascinating, our quality of life in East Grinstead left much to be desired. Irregular hours and the high cost of living meant no social life. Janet agreed that we should accept the posting. We got tenants for the house in East Grinstead; the rent covered the mortgage.

Chapter Eighteen

RETURN TO NIGERIA

October 1990 - September 2002

It was comforting returning to Nigeria with Janet; it would prove to be a very different experience from the time before.

On our arrival we were greeted by the Chief Pilot, Phil Hewitt. Phil, a dapper American of slight build with a walrus moustache, showed us around and carried out the introductions. Having previously lived at the Bristow Residential Complex (BRC) I felt more at home than he did. Phil was a well-meaning and caring character and a Born Again Christian, surely a round peg in a square hole at BRC. At the office he questioned me extensively. I recognised the symptoms immediately. My flying experience and company record intimidated him, so I told him not to worry, I did not want his job.

Toby Taplin, the Twin Otter training captain, carried out my check rides. If Toby's name brings to mind a jolly rotund fellow who enjoys his cups, you get the picture.

Our operation had acquired a number of Nigerian pilots, including Johnny Uku, a CFS qualified instructor and ex-NAF squadron CO. Johnny was building up his hours on the DHC 6 and along with Enid Otun, our only lady pilot, was impatient to get his command. I didn't blame him - he was more professional than most of our expat captains.

Our expat pilots were a mixed bunch. Finding personnel who could survive the conditions in Nigeria was difficult. Alistair Gamley, an ex-Navy colleague, joined the operation. Alistair was a capable and resourceful chap but he was disdainful of his colleagues, especially the management. Evenings in the Spread Eagle were often enlivened by his loud voice and forceful arguments.

Chris Puddy had returned to fly with us, having found that working as a fortune teller on Blackpool Pier was financially non-viable. Another of our characters, he was into the power of crystals and claimed to have healing hands. Bob Burstall, a large and affable Australian, was also on the team. Aussie Bob was a Hash-running stalwart who was notorious for bedding young Nigerian girls.

At the other end of the spectrum came Alan Goodenough, an ex-career naval officer and real gentleman (I had known him at RNAS Lossiemouth). He managed to maintain his poise along with his good nature and gentle sense of humour. Alan had previously flown the Bristow HS 125. Why he came to Lagos we never knew.

Gabriel, the local estate manager, had retained his position and he found us a very jolly and capable maid. Abigail was from Akwa Ibom, formerly Cross River State, in the oil-rich Niger Delta. Abigail had followed the local custom of preparing for marriage by building up her constitution. Some turned to fat, but Abigail, although small in stature, had just become tough and chunky. Having worked for a very wealthy blind Nigerian, she was also a trained masseuse.

Our first-floor apartment was quite spacious with a very large living/dining area. Unfortunately it had been unoccupied for some time and had been raided by other residents. The custom of exchanging new for old left us with a complete range of crap furniture. On top of this the company had not redecorated, so the overall effect was pretty damn depressing. Every refurbishment had to be fought for, but we managed to make our residence presentable. Phil Hewitt had not been given control over anything but the flying programme. Any other requests, especially those incurring expenditure had to pass

John Black, the General Manager. John was a proud Scot and as tight-fisted as the stereotype (more about that later).

Shopping for curtain material and bed linen took place in Yaba market, a maze of densely-packed stalls set up in the concrete structure of an abandoned mall project. If I was working Janet took streetwise Abigail for personal protection. Bag snatchers roamed the markets, and although mostly successful some were caught. These unfortunates suffered summary justice, Nigerian style. They were "necklaced" - hogtied with an old motor tyre placed over their heads. This was filled with petrol and set alight. Certain death followed. Janet saw one such robber caught in the act, but Abigail rushed her away.

Life was cheap and scenes of tragedy common. While stopping at a roadside stall to buy potted plants, an excited little girl ran out of nearby school gates and was struck down by a speeding car. We witnessed traffic accidents on several occasions. Driving back to Lagos after golf, we were overtaken by an 18-wheeler when its nearside rear bogie detached from the axle. The two wheels, travelling at speed, peeled off on to the hard shoulder and slammed into the rear of a VW minibus. The vehicle, which had stopped to pick up passengers, disintegrated. We felt helpless, as stopping to help was pointless. The many times we saw accidents unfolding in front of us made us realise how frequent these events must be. We saw the remains of fresh accidents four or five times a week.

It wasn't long before I caught malaria and for the same reason as before, failure to spray the interior of the company transport. I became familiar with the symptoms and usually caught it early enough to continue flying. Dr Okupa still ran the Bristow-approved clinic at the other end of the road (Lateef Salami Street), and was delighted to see me back. Insecticide was issued to the drivers, with strict instructions that they should spray their vehicles first thing in the morning, but the cans promptly disappeared.

Bristow had promised that a car and driver would be available on request for shopping and the occasional night out. These arrangements never worked out and we were forced to purchase our own vehicle. Initially we used off-duty Bristow drivers, but there were so many no-shows that we had to employ our own. The driver was charged with ensuring the vehicle was kept roadworthy. The most common vehicle on Nigerian roads at this time was still the VW Kombi, so thinking that spares and maintenance would be rendered simple, we bought one. Not trusting a local, previously-owned vehicle, we purchased an ex-Swiss army example imported by Jimmy, a Nigerianised Irish guy who ran a motor repair workshop.

Expats were advised not to drive themselves around Lagos, as extortionists would jump at the chance to stage a collision. With the collusion of the police large sums could be extorted from the unfortunate victim for damage or "injury". Our first driver was a splendid fellow named Levinious.

Janet and I joined the local Hash House Harriers, and our vehicle became the transport of choice for the wild girls of the Ikeja HHH. Most expat hashers were single or unaccompanied and were paired with one of the good-time girls. Girls that had landed an expat travelled with them, while we trucked the "spares", who were a very raucous crowd and great fun. The Ikeja Hash was still based at the Croc, and Peter Palm, the MD of Hoechst Nigeria, was the Hash Master. In the world of the Hash those in charge were normally referred to as the Grand Master, but our bunch refused to dignify anyone with this title. Karl Sauter was the RA, or Religious Advisor. The Ikeja Hash only laid trails in the jungle/bush and was famous for its "shiggy" runs. Shiggy, for those unfamiliar, is a term used to define anything from puddles to quagmire. Some runs were almost entirely "run" through swamp. We saw real village life and the jungle in the raw and it was priceless. Shiggy, although intimidating, is clean as long as there are no villages nearby.

With all the beer consumed at the "On-On", pee stops were frequent on the return home. The girls joined the men at the roadside and peed standing up. They had to accomplish this with legs a little wider apart, a revelation.

Returning from a midnight Hash (with torches) at three in the morning, our train of vehicles was stopped at a road block. I could see the police were delighted by our arrival, anticipating rich pickings. They couldn't have been more wrong. The hashers decanted themselves out of the vehicles, utilising the occasion to relieve themselves. Mission accomplished, all burst into song and danced around in the road, and the half dozen or so police could not make their demands heard and became totally confused. Making a snap decision, they zoomed in on the lead vehicle. The driver, a French guy, was so drunk he had to remain in his seat. On being asked to step down he fell into the road, unable to talk. We all assumed he would be arrested and his vehicle impounded, but for the officers of the law this was way outside their experience. They were flummoxed and stuffed him back into his car with shouts of "go, go!" We all jumped back into our respective vehicles and sped off.

Getting to work in the morning was a stressful event in itself. The pesky mosquito bites you got while sitting in the "go-slow" were not a good start to the day. Minor collisions and a new corpse by the roadside did not help. One such cadaver lay in the road just outside our general aviation entrance; each day it suffered more damage. We all privately vowed not to look, but the urge to see if the remains were still evident proved irresistible. Night-time scavengers took their share. Finally some brave person pushed the backbone and a few ribs to the verge. Garbage and vegetation finally obscured the remains.

It was this gruesome scene that probably lay behind our rescue of a hit-and-run victim. We had become familiar with the lady in question, having noticed her looking lost and confused on the roadside verge. Although a vagrant dressed in rags, she had none of the verve and ingenuity of the common beggar. She had the look of a lost soul who had long given up hope.

When I first spotted her, I found the depth of despair in her dark eyes deeply distressing. I arranged with Janet and our driver to give her a bottle of water and some bread each time they passed. Then one Saturday we set off to join the Hash, and as we were checking traffic prior to pulling out on to the main road we saw her lying in the middle of the swerving traffic, trying to sit up, both her legs badly broken. I turned to Janet and we knew without a word that we would have to act.

The advice given to expats is not to get involved, because even if it is not set up as a scam, the opportunity to gouge some quick cash is not missed by passers by. We were aware of these warnings, but we both knew we would not be able to live with ourselves if we drove on.

I turned into the road and stopped our VW in position to divert oncoming traffic, which then screamed past with horns blaring. There was no time for assessment of injury, we had to get out of there fast. Lifting the poor woman into the Kombi, we drove straight round to Doc Kupa's. All the staff assumed we were responsible for her condition but Kupa knew us better. He quickly put her on a drip and sent us off to the WHO orthopaedic hospital on the Ikorodu Road. A&E accepted the casualty after payment of admittance charges. Janet briefed the doctor as best she could as the lady remained mute and the staff thought she was just another "mad" person. They recorded our details and commitment to pay. It was now up to us to try and track down her family.

Janet went back to the hospital every day and by keeping her company with gentle conversation eventually extracted enough information to contact her relatives. Originally a school teacher in Benin, the woman had been ostracised and turned out of her home for having an affair. Unable to find work in Lagos, she had run out of money and ended up on the streets.

We had to find a way of notifying the family. We now had the house address but Nigerian mail was delivered only to PO boxes. Janet asked some of the Hash girls if any of them came from Benin, and fortunately Lizzie, a Hash girlfriend of one our engineers, knew somebody who often travelled there. They were prepared to deliver a message. It worked, and six members of the family showed up at our front door. They were extremely grateful and had come to thank us. They were obviously not wealthy people and when we made it clear we did not require payment they burst into tears, dropped down on their knees and prayed on our behalf. Embarrassed, we choked back tears. Our teacher recovered and was welcomed back into her family.

Every Sunday we went to the beach at Tarkwa Bay. It was just west of the entrance to Lagos harbour and a delightful escape from the hassle in Ikeja. The local villagers kept the beach spotless and ensured touts and petty thieves were kept away. The setting was idyllic, and because it was shielded by two enormous breakwaters it was free from the heavy surf prevalent along most of the coast. Canvas sun shelters could be hired at minimal cost, and we became friends with the family who maintained our basha and arranged for tea to be served mid afternoon - wonderful. We still communicate by Facebook

Food and drink to suit any taste was available, the specialities being fresh fruit, suya and fresh baguettes from Cotonou. The suya was among the best kebab style snacks available anywhere. It consisted of tender beef morsels, thinly sliced, covered in chilli and garlic powder and served with diced fresh onions and tomatoes.

Tarkwa was the Lagos Riviera and resembled a mini Copacabana. Traders walked up and down selling an incredible range of goods. The usual handicrafts, audio tapes, CDs, fireworks, radios, cameras and kitchenware were available. One of the Bristow engineers bought a two thousand-dollar NATO laser rangefinder for peanuts, only to have it confiscated by UK Customs and Excise. Windsurfers could be hired and the local Lebanese put on an average display of waterskiing and water-scooting. Girls paraded up and down in bikinis and sometimes wet T-shirts; people watchers had a bonanza, while nationals of many countries and cultures shared in the fun.

Fishermen could try their luck from the breakwaters and surfers could round the point to Lighthouse Beach. Lighthouse was less frequented, as it was not protected. Possessions were occasionally pilfered and prostitutes plied their trade. Woe betide any who took up an offer from one of them, as mentioned before, it sometimes resulted in loss of more than just the wallet. When the innocent customer was naked in the bushes, accomplices would appear from behind the trees and depart with all possessions, including apparel.

Because of its reputation Lighthouse attracted the guys who enjoyed the wild side of life, including some of our hashers. Beer was consumed in formidable quantities. Knowing the dangers of undertow or riptides, they were careful not to swim or go for a pee out of their depth. Despite this precaution, disaster struck. We were alerted when two distraught hashers came up to us asking for assistance, as one of the group a Brit, had suffered an accident.

It took ten minutes to walk across to Lighthouse (it is impossible to run on soft sand). We found the victim flat on his back next to a group of American students. One of their girls had bravely applied mouth-to-mouth resuscitation for ten minutes, but she said he was a goner. Apparently he had only gone into the surf for a pee, but the next his friends knew his body was rolling in the shallows.

Janet went back to the landing stage at Tarkwa and negotiated for one of the boats to shift the body to Victoria Island and the British High Commission. Making a stretcher from the canvas and supports of one of the shelters, we managed to carry the surprisingly heavy remains the mile or so back to Tarkwa. We had to walk the length of the beach, and it must have spoilt the afternoon for some. Fortunately the High Commission was only yards from the landing stage and leaving Janet with the body and the increasingly impatient boat driver (he wanted to offload the corpse and depart), I went in search of the duty officer. At the High Commission I phoned the DO, who referred me to the duty doctor, who told me to get their ambulance and driver to deliver the victim to the hospital. The key could not be found.

In the end the DO abandoned his Sunday afternoon with friends and came over. Our VW was parked nearby. We loaded the body with great difficulty, as rigor mortis had set in. The corpse was large and heavy and the Kombi only about five feet wide. We had to travel to the hospital with the door open and the poor man's legs and feet protruding into the traffic, but at least it was a Sunday and not busy.

At the hospital the duty doctor made it clear that he would not provide a death certificate until he received dash. The DO looked at me and said he had a directive not to bribe. I could not find enough cash and he got annoyed, saying he was using his own cash, and I should not be under the impression HM government was involved. How green did he think I was? He would recover the expenses somehow.

Further inducement was required to persuade the mortuary attendant to accept the by now expanding remains. The doctor told me I should report the fatality to the police, as they would be informed by the hospital as a matter of course. A feeling of dread crept over me as I realised the implications. Hiding my worries from Janet, I drove to the nearest police post on Bar Beach.

The sergeant behind the desk met all my expectations by screaming that I had killed my friend in a drunken brawl. I resigned myself to the looming negotiations. Luckily for me, a superintendent was in the back room checking the log, and he suddenly appeared and politely asked for an explanation. After I gave him the facts he turned on the sergeant and delivered a series of hard slaps about the head. He then invited me in impeccable English to write a brief statement.

While I was in the process of doing this I had a sneaking feeling this was too good to be true - but no, the superintendent accepted my statement and apologised for the "impossible behaviour" exhibited by the guy behind the desk. We were waved on our way with a smile. I was reminded of one of our expat sayings, that one should never exclaim "Now I have seen it all". You would be proved wrong on a daily basis.

The drowned hasher was accommodated at the Crocodile bar as an employee of the Japanese company supplying new looms for Karl Sauter's business. We reported the matter to Karl. The Japanese made all the arrangements to ship the body back to the UK and on top of this they paid off his mortgage, allowing his widow to keep the house.

Deciding to expand our social horizon beyond that of the Hash, we took up golf. Besides being a darn sight healthier, Janet could play at the local Ikeja course and meet a selection of lady friends at the smarter end of the social spectrum. At weekends we could venture out of Lagos, to the Portland Cement courses. Being in the open countryside provided relief from the stresses of the downtown rat race. The return journey was an instant reintroduction to reality. If the roads were free and the police checkpoints were not in evidence, it could take as little as forty minutes.

If the main highway was used en route to Shagamo, one could take in the auto accident scene. Normally it was the big trucks that lost control and rolled in to the monsoon drains.

Meanwhile back at the ranch, I was amazed by the variety of operating procedures employed by our captains and the absence of paperwork. The technical log was the only record that was properly completed. As a new training captain I found any advice and instruction was met with resistance.

Most of our pilots had come from single-pilot operations and had their own way of doing things. Flight logs were not filed, as chinagraph pencils were used to jot down ETAs on a plasticised clipboard. The checklist was impractical, never referred to, and when co-pilots were crewed they were rarely allowed to have control of the aeroplane. The contrast between our fixed-wing and helicopter operations was stark. Bristow management and Shell had allowed our little operation to slip between the cracks.

Concerned that this might become an issue resulting in loss of contract, I got the go-ahead from Paul Weddick in Redhill to reform our operating procedures. As a start I produced a simple user-friendly navigation log. The existing form under the film had been copied from an airline and was unnecessarily complex; the boxes were so tiny that they were ignored.

The crux of the problem was the fixed-wing operations manual. It failed to provide proper guidance and it was a hotchpotch of random instructions and last-minute additions. The whole tome, although supposedly following company format, was full of paragraphs literally pasted in to fulfil legal requirements. These were inserted without any attempt at editing. No wonder the pilots were doing their own thing. If I were to make any improvements the manual would have to be completely rewritten from the ground up.

I had no office and no computer. A request to use one of the secretaries was met with scorn. After creating a fuss I was reluctantly given a desk in the tiny dust-filled operations room, but it was hopeless, a computer was the only answer. The MD, John Black refused any expenditure on the IT front, but I was told Bristow would be prepared to ship out a machine of my own – whoopee!

When my computer arrived I kept it in our flat, and much to Black's chagrin spent much of my time working from home. He thought I was shirking.

When the manual and checklist were ready I issued each pilot with a copy of the revised Normal Procedures section, along with questionnaires to be completed for their next line check. I had a hard time getting any response, so I threatened candidates with failure if the procedures were not followed or the questionnaires not returned. Phil Hewitt was alarmed at my new broom approach, worried that he would not have enough pilots left to fill the flying program. "Give them time" he said. I followed up with a compromise solution that involved placing pilots under review. This process required Phil Hewitt to respond with appropriate action.

As Shell expanded their operations so their demands increased and new pilots were hired. Our workload grew from the provision of morning and evening shuttles into a never-ending shuttle service between Lagos, Warri and Port Harcourt. The training task increased dramatically, and in order to lighten Toby Taplin's workload Bristow arranged for me to complete the IRE (Instrument Rating Examiner) course at Gatwick. It was fun and I passed, despite temporarily losing the plot on the check ride.

Chief Pilot Phil Hewitt was more or less pushed out by John Black (or his wife Helen) and Martin Lampitt arrived as a replacement. Martin, a very decent ex RAF fellow, tried hard, but he didn't last too long either. It was rumoured that Helen Black demanded subservice from "junior" wives and would pressure John to remove any Chief Pilot whose wife refused to buckle under.

New pilots arrived. Chuck Pillette, an American, joined us after resigning from Pan African. Chuck was very bright, a career cynic, and kept us amused with sardonic comments regarding Bristow and Nigerian aviation. Fortunately he appeared to be an anglophile. He was added to our growing list of eccentric recalcitrants.

Tony Dhont from Belgium had done a last-minute runner from a self-destructing Congo. He had worked his way up there from bush flying and crop dusting to corporate flying in a Canadair Challenger. Tony was qualified to maintain the PT6 engine as well as fly the Otter, he was accompanied by his wife Denise, whom he had met while flying for missionaries in the jungle, and he became the residential handyman. Tony was a wizard with the estate generator, so the establishment was now kept in good running order.

These were the sort of guys we had on our team, capable and self reliant but not used to the team player thing. They struggled with two crew co-ordination; some were openly defiant while others pretended to go along. Feedback from the co-pilots made me realise it would be a long hard battle. I understood their problem, as embedded habits are hard to fight. During check rides it was patently obvious which guys were not complying, they did not appreciate my comments in the flight report. It took two years to get all pilots to toe the line, just in time to comply with the compulsory two-crew requirement demanded by Shell, now backed up by the arrival of their new aviation guy, Ray Reynolds.

Johnny Uku and Enid Otun finally made it to captain. Johnny had enough command hours to fly as captain on the Shell contract, but Enid could only use her command on the King Air private charters. Johnny was big and likeable but sometimes morose; he reminded me of Bluto from Popeye. Enid was small and thin, very likeable but very private, she reminded me of Olive Oyl. The co-pilots did not find it easy taking instructions from a lady captain.

Ray Reynolds, the Shell Aviation Manager, persuaded the oil company aviation contractors to form a flight safety association. The oil-producing areas in the Niger Delta stretched from Escravos in the west to Calabar in the east. Mixed helicopter and fixed-wing traffic had up to now used rudimentary separation rules and visual procedures to avoid conflictions. These were now inadequate and had resulted in a number of close calls. If nothing was done it would be just a matter of time before there was a mid-air collision.

The Delta Operators' Association was formed, but remained unregistered due to the participants' concern over liability. Being our nominated flight safety officer, I represented Bristow Fixed Wing at the monthly meetings. Initially the position of Chairman/Secretary rotated between the various operators, but it eventually ended up in my lap as they preferred my minutes and my ability to sooth tempers. Bristow and Aero Contractors, the main players, agreed on any changes at preparatory meetings, and the others would follow on. On the whole these meetings went well, and resulted in a much-improved operating environment. Ray Reynolds had to be reminded that he was attending only as an observer. Ray, an ex-Bristow helicopter pilot, was pushy but had the good manners of a professional smoothie.

The workload was high, with many trainee pilots to process. To ensure standards were maintained initial proficiency checks (when new on type) were supervised by a Nigerian DCA examiner. The current nominee, Jerry Agbeyegbe, was head of the Flight Calibration Unit and a splendid fellow. He was straight as an arrow, had a quiet sense of humour and could be relied upon to be totally fair. Jerry created the Nigerian Air Safety Initiative, challenging many players who were influential in Nigerian aviation. He carried out his self-appointed tasks, refusing to be intimidated by those in power.

Jerry was later murdered outside his Lagos home. His body had received 29 bullet wounds.

Earlier I had been under pressure to approve one of our recently-acquired Nigerians for command. I told Phil Hewitt that this guy was OK during normal circumstances but found it difficult to cope during simulated emergencies. Phil had been instructed by Bristow management, themselves threatened by the Nigerian authorities, to accelerate the nationalisation of our flight crew, and despite my reservations I allowed his promotion.

Meanwhile our current Chief Pilot, Martin Lampitt, had had

enough and was replaced by Pat Roofe, a more forceful character - some would say belligerent. Pat exposed John Black's policy of limiting the Chief Pilot's authority, and made a considerable number of improvements both at BRC and at the hangar. Roofe made Redhill aware of John Black's stranglehold on the Lagos operation.

In order for BRC to be secure it was surrounded by an eight-foot-high wall. Pat removed the shards of glass on top and replaced them with razor wire, and new guards were employed. These precautions were necessary as our area (Isolo/Oshodi) could get pretty hairy. The guy across the road in the "big house" was assassinated. A hit team followed him home and shot up his car when it stopped for the gate to be opened. The gunfire reverberated around BRC.

There were more eventful stories about everyday life in Nigeria than there were in aviation. My VW bus seemed to return from maintenance in worse condition than before. Janet had to use her hairpins to repair a broken clutch cable! Suspecting that my wagon was being used as a reliable spare parts source, I bought a new Hyundai bus (dealer serviced). This was great for a while, but the fuel injection was vulnerable to contaminated fuel.

Nigeria was notorious for receiving toxic waste, and it was reported that the wife of the then president (Abacha) was into this in a big way. Having received large payments from some Middle East country to dispose of tar-contaminated gasoline, the problem was solved by forcing distributors to sell the stuff at roadside filling stations. The engines of thousands of vehicles were destroyed when the valves jammed. Fortunately I had only had a small top up.

Frequent topping up with fuel tanks was required, as one never knew when a fuel shortage would occur. Even a rumour would result in long queues at the pumps. The problem was that tanker drivers smuggled their fuel across the border. Vast profits could be made, thanks to the government subsidies on domestic petrol. Fuel queues were so bad that we had to send the driver to queue overnight. If you were desperate you could buy a can from a tout at ten times the pump price.

Having a new vehicle made me nervous, so I bought a big old truck for rough roads and late nights. The Swedish Chief Engineer of Pan-African, Mat Todesson, was selling his old Bronco. It had been fitted with sturdy crash bars all round and much extra lighting (see picture). I was hooked, it had real style.

Unfortunately Mat saw the gleam in my eye and I paid well over the going rate. The Bronco had been modified and had received a new paint job, but this couldn't disguise the fact that it had enjoyed a very exciting existence. It did the job, and with its imposing presence and the muted roar of its 5.8 litre V8 we were quickly waved through police road blocks. In the traffic snarl-ups we were given a wide berth. On two occasions overloaded mini buses ran into the back of the Bronco. Not bothering to step down we drove on, disengaging with much graunching, clattering, and tinkling. Later inspection of the rear fender showed maybe a small dent or two and paint from the offending vehicle.

Our driver had up to now been an amiable and reliable chap, but he had now changed, becoming shifty-eyed and unreliable. We discovered he had been using the Hyundai to carry passengers during the time he claimed he had been waiting in all-night fuel queues. Further investigation revealed other problems relating to maintenance, so we released him.

Personal drivers are classed as casual labour, but the convention was to pay a gratuity of one month's pay for every year of service. It seemed this was not enough for him, and we received a letter from some dodgy solicitor claiming ill treatment and unpaid wages. We managed to sort this out with advice from Doc Kupa, but shortly afterwards the police arrived at BRC and ordered me to accompany them. I refused to go and called witnesses. This stunned them, as ordinary Nigerians obeyed immediately, fearing a beating.

When I received a letter requesting my presence at the police station, I decided to attend. I knew the police were collaborating with my ex-driver to extort money. It was ridiculous, about 1M Naira. The visit to the station was typical and they used all the tricks in the book to intimidate me. This included a long wait with an adjacent interrogation in progress. Sound effects included harsh beating and screaming - it sounded very genuine and may well have been the real thing. When John Black at Bristows realised the police were not going to give up hassling me, he finally stepped in with a letter from the solicitor general. I enjoyed the final meeting, when a chief superintendent informed the inspector concerned, my driver and his brothers (the instigators of this plot), that they had no case and should desist. These collaborative schemes normally succeeded, with everyone involved receiving substantial payouts. The plotters were dumbstruck. I would like to have known their fate. One of the favourite scams down in Warri involved a variation of the "honey trap". A drunken expat would be charmed into taking home one of the many bar girls. Later when the inebriate was sleeping heavily, the girl would open the door, allowing an under-age girl to take her place. Shortly after, the police would arrive. The "settlement" could reach millions of Naira.

Isolo was an unattractive but lively neighbourhood. Down the end of the road a row of small shop-houses caught fire in the middle of the night. Several BRC residents watched from the roof of our accommodation block and were rewarded by an amazing display of pyrotechnics when a store containing gas cylinders blew up. They hastily took cover when chunks of metal casing crashed down around their ears. The shrapnel took chunks out of our concrete roof.

The main highway to reach BRC from the airport had never been adjusted to take into account the switchover from left-hand driving to right. This failure necessitated awkward U-turns back up the entry lanes, an ideal setup for police extortionists. One day Janet got caught on her way to play golf. When the vehicle slowed to negotiate the turn, an officer of the law opened the front passenger door and jumped in. Our driver was instructed to drive to the nearby police post, where the vehicle would be impounded for an "illegal U-turn". This was normally an expensive business.

On arrival at the compound the police corporal told our driver, Francis, to step down and hand over the keys, but he refused and received a slap across the face. He was about to receive more abuse but Janet intervened. Incensed, she leapt out of the wagon and grabbed a seven iron from her bag, shouting "If you don't stop I will hit you!". This little drama attracted the attention of the cleaning ladies and food stall mamas, who circled round to give Janet moral support. Janet demanded to see the officer in charge, and the now nervous corporal said he wasn't there. The cleaners shouted "Oh yes he is!" and sure enough he was now approaching to investigate the ruckus.

When he arrived he told Janet she should pay 500 Naira (a moderate "fine") and go. "Where am I going to get 500 Naira at this time in the morning? And you're making me late for golf!" she said. Her response made him pause. The officer, aware that most of the local bigwigs and well-connected played golf at Ikeja, hesitated. He thought Janet might be playing with some of them. Now surrounded by women, he said "OK, go" and walked away.

Janet very rarely backed down. After many confrontations she became well known at the roadblocks and was waved through with a smile.

The BRC residents occasionally provided unplanned entertainment. I was awoken early one morning by shouting and angry female screams. I managed to stop the "Walhalla" by paying off a hooker on behalf of a beleaguered and embarrassed customer. It doesn't pay to get on the wrong side of these girls, for they were tough. Down on Victoria Island there were gangs of them at every stop light and street corner. Scantily dressed in the extreme, they would try and enter the vehicle even if the other occupants were wives or girlfriends.

We often got invitations from other expats in downtown Lagos, and occasionally John Black would freak out and arrange a night on the town. These occasions did raise morale, but the late-night journey home overshadowed the event. Carjackings were a frequent enough occurrence to cause concern, but more often than not the police road blocks and the shakedown that came with it were the norm.

Road blocks were present night and day and occasionally caught thieves. They were arranged in a spontaneous and non-predictable manner, often causing tiresome delays, and sometimes they could be the cause of serious accidents. In order to catch highway drivers by surprise they were often situated over the crest of a hill. This was not a good idea, as heavy goods vehicles were overloaded and had poor braking ability. On three occasions that I know of, petrol tankers had ploughed into tailbacks caused by roadblocks. Fuel pouring from ruptured tanks flowed downhill under the line of stationary vehicles and ignited. These queues included busloads of passengers who were incinerated, over 300 of them on one occasion.

Returning to the subject of carjackings, one enraged expat wife finally made it to the nearest police station only to find that the officer delegated to take the report was the man who had taken her vehicle. Another time a bunch of our hashers had their wagon taken and were told to lie face down in the road and not move. As they were being immobilised with tie-wrap, one of the men, the Second Secretary at the Australian High Commission, turned his head and they shot him six times in the legs.

Back at the hangar, the company had been told by the DCA licensing department to take on a pilot who was a relative of one of their senior staff. Non co-operation would result in problems regarding issue and renewal of Bristow pilots' licences. This "pilot" was not too bright. He was a slow thinker with appalling judgement, and could not even fly straight and level; I had to intercede on every approach to land. The guy must have known he was an accident waiting to happen, but he was determined to continue. As the Type Training Captain, I had no option but to fail him.

He claimed his rejection was Bristow's unwillingness to employ nationals (a heinous crime). Pat, under pressure from John Black, asked me to reconsider, but I refused to alter the assessment and added that I considered the chap very dangerous. The guy was grounded and the DCA carried out their threat - some of Bristow's replacement helicopter pilots (turnover was high) were rejected.

I was targeted for a hard time, and along with one of our new pilots had to endure a two-hour tirade from a DCA observer, Mobil Aviation's own examiner. The night time check ride was delayed so much it had to be abandoned for another day. I deliberately kept my cool, and as he was about to leave, sarcastically thanked him very much for his services and went to shake his hand; he quickly stepped back raising his arm, a look of horror on his face. He assumed I was going to strike him! I felt sorry for the guy, as we normally enjoyed a cordial relationship. I don't suppose he had any option but to follow DCA instructions if he wished to keep his position. The fate of the DCA's other examiner, Jerry Agbeyegbe, must have also weighed heavily on his mind.

Phil Waterer and Alistair Kennedy joined the team as experienced King Air captains. Phil, with recent experience in South Africa, had acquired a blatant disdain for Africans, fortunately he refrained from any outright demonstration of racism. Bear in mind that Nigerians handled racist treatment extremely well as they had learned to live with the much more serious tribalism. Apart from his aviation career, Alistair had been a gentleman farmer. Intelligent and capable, he nevertheless remained a little distant, appearing disenchanted and cynical.

The King Air charters were a welcome break from the tedium of the Shell shuttle, especially if they incurred a stopover of enough duration to check out the locality. I can't remember the name of the company in question, but a charter to Pointe Noire in Congo Brazzaville came up for grabs. I jumped at the chance. I requested Bristow use Jeppeson to obtain the diplomatic clearance, but John Black hated spending the pennies.

When our ops department failed in their attempts to obtain the clearance, Pat Roofe told me that he expected me to make the trip anyway, because "this is Africa". I said no, that Bristow risked having the aircraft impounded and that I might be incarcerated. Pat passed me on to John Black, who assured me that the clients, an American oil company, would take care of everything, no handling agents required.

Remembering my PA23 saga to Sfax, I assumed this would be the case and departed in reasonably confident mood. After landing, a limousine whisked the passengers away, leaving me to sort out the formalities. The refueller refused to deliver without a copy of my departure flight plan (he needed proof that my flight was international and therefore duty-free). I was required to pay in US dollars but only had enough to pay for my fuel at the duty-free rate. I trekked over to the tower, paid the landing fees, including a bribe for the clerk's attendance, and tried to file the flight plan.

"Where is your diplomatic clearance?" I was asked. I explained, but the guy behind the counter insisted the oil company had not delivered. I must pay a fine of $4000. I was dumbstruck. After some tricky negotiations I wrote a letter stating that the fine would be paid by the oil company concerned. I was amazed that this deal was accepted, and had the uncomfortable feeling that after refuelling, permission to start engines would once again be denied. Fortunately it wasn't. I taxied out and took off with that little tickle at the base of the spine, just like walking away from a levelled gun.

On return I went straight up to John Black and gave him the news. He had difficulty containing himself, knowing that Bristow would have to repay the $4000.

Meanwhile because of the increased workload I was flying with the effects of malaria. Those bloody mosquitoes injected their damn parasites into my bloodstream on more than twenty occasions during my time in Nigeria. I stopped taking prophylactics as I found they did not stop the disease, only masked the symptoms. Doc Kupa informed me I had suffered from all the types of malaria prevalent in Nigeria. It often took up to three attempts to cure resistant strains.

First-time cures returned with the advent of Artemisinin-based medicines. Kupa used Cotexin and there were virtually no side effects, a great relief from the chloroquine days when the cure felt worse than the disease.

Medical problems were easily acquired. Apart from salmonella and hepatitis the hazards of eating out included dysentery, which can reveal itself in many ways. When I had an intense pain in my stomach I thought it was some other problem, as there were no hurried trips to the toilet. Doc Kupa said it was appendicitis, and John Black shipped me back to UK that same evening. Hospitals in Nigeria were not recommended for surgery.

At the airport the immigration officer pointed out that my visa was expiring in three days' time and it would have to be renewed in Nigeria. Not concerned with such trivia and needing to get my health sorted, I boarded the flight. Bristow provided BUPA medical cover and I checked in at the convenient Gatwick Park Hospital.

Their tests proved no appendicitis but positive for dysentery. Medication solved the problem. I went to company HQ in Redhill and asked them to courier my passport back to Lagos for visa renewal. I was told John Black was livid and suspected me of pulling a fast one. Yippee, two weeks' holiday in UK. I had been watching the housing market closely and used the opportunity to purchase a London apartment. This was one of my better investments. When John Black eventually heard of my acquisition he felt it confirmed his suspicions.

Most of the many aviation accidents in Nigeria consisted of runway overruns caused by late landing decisions in bad weather. Some were fatal. At Lagos a Nigerian Airbus 320 ended up very close to the boundary fence and perimeter road, striking a spectacular pose nose down in the mud. With its tail in the air and both engines half buried in the ground it resembled a giant bull ready to charge. A Harka Air Tupolev 154 fared worse when it burst into flames. The survivors reported panic among passengers and cabin crew.

If the captain was well connected, the aircraft would be blamed for the accident. Nigerian Airways deleted the Fokker F28 from its inventory after one such overrun, another of their many expensive mistakes.

Given the lack of standard arrival and departure routes at Lagos, what we all feared most were mid-air collisions. It was unfairly left up to ATC controllers to work out the necessary separation of inbound and departing traffic. I got the feeling that the authorities found this system suited their mindset of being able to pass the blame. The controllers were convenient scapegoats.

It was the evening rush hour on the 7th November 96 and we were returning to Lagos in the B200 when we heard a somewhat confused ATC clearing an ADC 727 to descend. When we asked for our own descent we were informed our approach time would be delayed by thirty minutes as they had lost contact with the ADC flight. It turned out that they had been cleared through a flight level occupied by another flight. Suffering an apparent near miss, the 727 pilot overcooked the avoiding action by applying too much bank. He lost control and the aircraft plummeted almost vertically and near supersonic down into the Lekki Lagoon. Days later, debris was found floating in the water about eighty miles out from Lagos.

Then came our Twin Otter crash. Being on holiday in Tobago, I mercifully escaped the trauma caused by the loss of the captain. I felt vaguely guilty having fun in the sun while Pat Roofe was dealing with the fallout. Paul Weddick rang me at our hotel to mentally prepare me for the return to Lagos. I suppose it was the right thing to do, but it sure took the edge off my holiday.

A microburst had caught the Otter crew unawares. They had a fifty-knot tailwind for landing. The co-pilot was flying the aircraft and was about to start a missed approach when the captain took control, dumped full flap (not approved by Bristow for public transport operations), and landed. It was impossible to control the aircraft with such a tailwind and the captain, realising his mistake, tried to take off again. Unfortunately he had lost runway alignment. The Twin Otter jumped the monsoon drain and headed into the NAF apron, where it crashed into a derelict Nigerian Air Force F27. He was killed and the co-pilot was seriously injured. Luckily no passengers were hurt.

The accident kick-started a raft of flight safety initiatives. The "stable door" syndrome kicked in - better late than never. Shell instructed crew members to watch all available training videos on the subject of windshear. We received micro-burst training at Le Bourget – it was only on a Citation simulator, but it got the message across.

Shell cracked, and paid for crews to use the Twin Otter simulator in Toronto. De Havilland of Canada provided a Cockpit Resource Management training course. The instructor, Michael Moore, was very professional. We were taught industry standard CRM, learning how to manage any emergency with coordinated two-crew procedures. We also ran through differing wind shear exercises. The results were impressive. The recalcitrant loners were won over and co-pilots now felt an essential part of the team. However Chris Puddy couldn't handle it and retreated to an ashram in India.

Aero Contractors, our main competitor, were wise enough not to comment on the accident, and not long afterwards they themselves lost a Twin Otter and all on board. The aircraft was on the approach to Abuja when it struck high ground. The captain, Michael Arad (an old friend), was one of Nigeria's most experienced pilots.

Aero claimed the published approach plate had been drawn up without reference to appropriate surveys. The ILS glideslope did not provide enough clearance from a hill on the approach. With the arrival of GPS I drew up offset approaches for Bristow use. This was unapproved, but it was safer than the state published version. It seemed to me that the runway had been misaligned by four degrees, the prevailing magnetic variation. Surely such a basic error could not be responsible? A four-degree shift provided a dramatic increase in obstacle clearance on approaches to both ends of the runway.

Back at the ranch Aussie Bob got the boot, as he had fallen asleep in the cockpit one too many times. Shell insisted the cockpit door remained open, as passengers wanted to monitor the goings-on up front. Shell employees received brownie points for every safety memo submitted, so our actions were often the target of the upwardly mobile. Mostly they had no idea, but just occasionally they had a point.

Bob regularly burned the candle at both ends, his libido being his downfall. He was entitled to a BRC apartment as he had married one of the Hash girls, but he continued his adventurous lifestyle. Pat Roofe was quite relieved to see him go. Some of the girls Bob was seen with appeared no more than schoolgirls.

With our much-improved procedures we were well prepared when Shell announced their intention to upgrade their aircraft and construct a proper airport in Warri. We were all on tenterhooks, as Aero Contractors made a great show of their intention to gain control of fixed-wing contract operations.

Great speculation ensued as to which aeroplane would be chosen.

Finally it turned out to be the Dornier 328, a rank outsider. I had my suspicions, knowing how Dornier had obtained many of their other overseas sales. Operating costs were very high but there was no doubt that it was quite a performer. Being a corporate aircraft there was no requirement to make a profit, so why not? It had the latest technology and would be a great addition to the CV.

The D328 demonstrator arrived, and Captain Havenstein, their Chief Test Pilot, was to prove the rejected take-off ability from V1 (take-off speed). With a full load of Bristow, Aero, and senior Shell staff, the 328 accelerated down the runway. At take-off speed power was cut and full braking applied. It was very impressive. The 328 came to a stop with less than half the runway used. The brakes were now red hot, so if we taxied back in, by the time we got back to the apron the heat would transfer to the rims and burst the tyres. With enough runway remaining we rolled for take-off. The brakes released with a bang and a clatter. After take-off Havenstein left the wheels down for a good ten minutes and they cooled off OK.

There followed the usual fancy flying demo, after which he called me up to the cockpit and offered me the approach and landing. I couldn't resist the chance but this was a sneaky move on the part of Havenstein; he could blame me if there was a braking problem. I landed very gently and slowed to walking pace using reverse pitch. The nosewheel steering was on his side, so he had no option but to take control for the taxi back in. Lots of grinding noises from the wheels accompanied our return to the hangar. The aircraft was grounded, awaiting brake and wheel spares.

Shell had carried out safety audits on all the other potential operators, but there was no doubt it was down to ACN or Bristow. We were on a golfing holiday in Thailand when Paul Weddick called to tell me we had won the contract. I got very excited.

Mobilisation commenced immediately. The new contract required major extensions to our hangar and offices, the building of a new passenger terminal and provision of more apartments at the BRC. Extra accommodation was available in Ikeja. Colyn James had replaced Pat Roofe as Chief Pilot and took over the task of 328 mobilisation.

The chosen few from the Lagos operation joined newly-hired pilots Graham Hackett, Chris Calvert and John Maxton on the conversion course in Oberpfaffenhofen near München. Also to join us in Germany was something entirely new to Bristow Nigeria - cabin attendants. Those selected were the best, and a great bunch. The girls were street smart and ably deflected all advances made by our new pilots from the UK. It was February and bloody cold.

The course was by computer self study and quite effective, the only snag being finding an instructor for the clarification of confusing info. The initial 328s were five-bladed turboprops with state-of-the-art cockpits (Honeywell Primus 2000 avionics suite). This computerised glass cockpit made for a steep learning curve, as most of us were only familiar with clocks and dials.

During the course, instructors emphasised the actions for proper selection of ground idle and reverse thrust. Dornier did not mention the many problems the 328 had experienced with the power lever. If the lever cannot be retarded below flight idle after touchdown the residual thrust exceeds the ability of the wheel brakes to slow the aircraft, a go-around is the only option (more later).

For a weekend visit Dornier recommended a nearby monastery for its excellent food and beer, but our girls wanted to visit Dachau, so we went there. When our instructors cheerily asked how we enjoyed our weekend our reply left them devastated. Sorry, but we could not really deny these girls the opportunity to further their education. The following weekends we visited Neuschwanstein and beer halls in München, the Dornier guys were vaguely re-assured.

When the three new aircraft arrived in Lagos, Bristow was once again king of the hill. ACN and its Dash 8s were firmly relegated to second place.

Back at Lagos Bristow was in turmoil, with extensive hangar, office and accommodation expansion well under way. Janet had refused to accept the apartment we had been allocated and blew her stack when Colyn James applied pressure (he should have known better). Although the Shonibare Estate was one of the best locations in Ikeja, the apartment in question was on the ground floor and had so many burglar bars on the windows that they cut out the light. The approach was down an unlit corridor, and it felt like prison. It had been vacant and available for some time.

John Black ordered me to accept and I refused, so he suspended me from the 328 programme. I was to continue on the Twin Otter while the others gleefully commenced flying the new aircraft. Our newly-qualified crews flew under the supervision of pilots borrowed from Horizon Air, Portland Oregon, and others from a defunct Norwegian airline.

Horizon presented their operations manual as an example. This massive tome must have been formulated with litigation in mind, for it was four inches thick and covered every possible situation in great detail. Pilots would have no excuse if they strayed from the straight and narrow. Our guys would never read it – they risked personal injury just by trying to pick it up. Much of it duplicated information available in the flight manual. We said our thanks and published our slim easy-to-read version.

Two months later John Black relented, and said that if I signed a new two-year contract I could switch back to the 328. He had heard rumours that I was seeking alternative employment, and Shell were asking questions. I signed, happy to be back. Shortly after that Black was replaced by Fred Leyton, an American - he was OK, pragmatic and straightforward.

Shell, excited with their new toy, changed their R&R destination from Jos to a resort on the picturesque isle of Principe. The island's giant volcanic monoliths reminded me of "Bali Hai". With its considerable range the 328 could make it there and back without refuelling. The airport was tiny, but with its narrow track undercarriage the 328 could turn around inside the apron.

Cases of difficulty in selecting the 328 ground idle and reverse became quite common; most problems were overcome thanks to the length of runway normally available. Dornier insisted that it was the use of improper technique, but it seemed too frequent to be so easily dismissed. I suffered the problem landing at the old Port Harcourt airstrip, which was only 4000 feet long. After three deliberate attempts to close the throttles I was half way down the runway and still at touchdown speed. The co-captain Alasdair Kennedy suddenly chipped in, "Shall I shut down the engines?" "Yes" I yelled, and applied full braking. We stopped just inches before the end of the runway. The cockpit door was open and there was silence down the back. We started up again and had to put one main gear on the grass to complete the U-turn.

It was dusk and there was no airfield lighting. In retrospect I should have immediately reapplied power, got airborne again and diverted. Easy to say, I had successfully helped out co-pilots when they had the same problem.

Questions were asked and fingers pointed. Ray Reynolds required a full enquiry, and Dornier sent Havenstein back out to Lagos. Havenstein disputed my assertion that I had used correct throttle handling procedure. Initially he said my description of the lever's movements was not possible; some believed his interpretation and some mine.

There followed a deadly 328 runway overrun in Genoa and non-lethal excursions in Aberdeen and Mannheim. Shell later exchanged the prop version for the jet, sacrificing range for safety.

Osubi, Shell's spanking new airport at Warri, opened, and the wild oil town suddenly became closer to the rest of Nigeria. I advised Ray Reynolds to install gratings on the drains along the edge of the taxiway and apron, otherwise Murphy's Law would ensure that someone would put a wheel in the ditch. Nothing was done, and sure enough someone did.

When the NAF were taking delivery of their big new Russian-built Mil 25 Hind helicopter gunships, they took the opportunity to stage through Osubi. Taxiing in heavy rain, one tipped into the drain, with spectacular results. The blades hit the ground and rotor blade shrapnel shot through the air. Half of one blade soared over the terminal building into the public car park and other pieces peppered the surrounding area. Amazingly, no one was hurt. One of our 328s parked nearby escaped damage, but inspection found shards on top of the tailplane.

Back in town, Nigeria proved once again its capacity to beggar belief. A minister's wife, stopped at a road block, was discovered to be carrying four or five severed heads. These were to be used in a juju ceremony arranged to ensure her son's success in forthcoming exams. Instances of this practice were not that unusual, even taking place among the Nigerian diaspora in London.

In similar vein a body parts vendor set up his business under the Isolo flyover. He would trap and kill late-night vagrants before butchering them. After selling the much-sought-after organs the remainder would go into the pot (a 44-gallon oil drum) to be served to daytime passers by. He was discovered when one of his prey managed to escape, and the whole setup became a tourist spectacle. The police eventually had the place sealed off after coachloads of sightseers blocked the highway. Local entrepreneurs soon published wall calendars with grisly photos. I could not bring myself to buy one, but they were constantly on offer at the kerbside.

Road accidents became ever more disastrous, with articulated behemoths crossing the median to cause spectacular head-on collisions. On our way to Shagamu Golf Club one Sunday we were forewarned by two ominous plumes of smoke. Rounding the curve in the highway we slowed to a crawl as traffic ahead tentatively bypassed two fiercely burning juggernauts. One of the blazing vehicles was a 24-wheel diesel tanker, its cargo blazing furiously. Not being able to turn back against the traffic we were committed to pass the inferno; if we stopped we could be there for hours, holding up hundreds of impatient road users. Waiting for the fire to burn itself out was not an option. Some had vainly tried to U-turn down the hard shoulder, only to meet oncoming traffic.

Tempers frayed. Traffic approaching the burning tanker finally increased speed to avoid a possible explosion, or charred paintwork and shattered windows. As we passed the furiously burning wreck we saw what must have been the driver staggering between the lanes of traffic pleading for help. Nobody stopped. He was a dead man walking. His skin had been baked crisp and had split to a crazy patchwork of pink cracks. He was naked, his clothing burnt and fused. That image remains imprinted on my memory.

Accident wrecks often remained in place for days; one burnt-out minibus stayed on the median for weeks, complete with seated skeletons.

In the office one Saturday a call came in that one of our pilots had been involved in an accident on his way to the Hash run. The Bristow truck taking the guy, his girlfriend and Karl Sauter had turned off the highway and was about to pass under the carriageway. A crashed petrol tanker lay alongside the track and a small stream carried away spilt gasoline. Villagers were salvaging as much fuel as they could carry. The smell of petrol was overwhelming, but urged on by Karl, our driver continued.

The gasoline ignited, and a giant fireball enveloped the entire area. The scavengers were incinerated and the Bristow truck was enveloped in fire. All of them were burned. The driver died minutes later and our Aussie pilot died later in hospital. Karl suffered serious burns and was eventually flown back to Switzerland. I have since been told he recovered.

We returned to Oberpfaffenhofen and carried out transition courses for the 328 jet, which had been transformed. The jet engines gave it incredible acceleration and record rates of climb - only the cruising speed was on the low side, because of the straight wing.

Then came 9/11. I was called into the crewroom, to see that on the TV the first tower was ablaze. I was shocked, but knew it was no accident. I watched the second aircraft hit, and felt deeply saddened. I remember saying in the silence that followed, "This will change the world".

It was a bad time for us. The day before, our crew bus had been shot up when it unintentionally blocked a getaway vehicle. No one was seriously hurt, but Alasdair Kennedy got shrapnel in his bum and Leong a bullet wound to his ankle - two pilots out of action. Also on the bus were two engineers newly arrived from UK. Suffering from shock, they point blank refused to stay and caught the next flight home.

The day after, my bank called to ask me to confirm a transfer of all funds from my bank in favour of a Nigerian account in Switzerland. When I told the guy on the phone that it was fraudulent, he was stunned. I thought they would have been used to it by now.

Meanwhile we were having fun on the jets. Phil Waterer had an engine failure on take-off at Osubi, but thanks to much simulator training he handled it well, no problem. I had loss of oil pressure after take-off from Abuja and eventually shut down one engine in the climb. Instead of returning to land I continued to Lagos, home base, naughty, but appreciated by all concerned. Logistical problems can become seriously complicated in Nigeria. Apart from these two incidents the jets proved reliable and were very popular.

With the outbreak of religious tribal fighting in Jos, our 328s shipped out many of the vulnerable, often carrying twice as many passengers as we had seats. The fear was palpable - nearly 2000 people died in the tit-for-tat slaughter.

Our vacations, still referred to as "leave", occurred every six months. Having read an article describing the Malaysian retirement programme, we used some of the time to check it out. We had investigated Spain, Portugal, Florida, and Trinidad and were not too impressed by any of them, but Malaysia looked ideal. After several visits we bought a plot on Tiara Golf Resort in Melaka, found a builder and committed ourselves to building a resort-style house. Not having proper use of telephones, I used email and courier services.

Finally mobile phones arrived in Nigeria and suddenly communications became a whole different ballgame. Nigerian Telecoms made a last ditch effort to compete and we got a landline in the apartment - amazing.

On the 27th January 2002 on a stopover at the Bristow complex at Elelenwo in Port Harcourt, Janet called me on my new and clunky mobile phone. "The ammunition dump is going up" she calmly told me. Then, "I have to go". I heard the heavy boom of explosions in the background before the phone went "click".

I was left staring at the phone. There was nothing I could do. At breakfast the next day, there was nothing on the local news. I had to wait until we got back to Lagos to get the lowdown.

The dump was about 800 metres away across the road from our estate. As the intensity of the explosions increased, alarm set in. The noise could not be put down to the frequent highway crashes or yet another transformer going up.

The explosions were heard in downtown Lagos, and the British High Commission had tried to contact me - I was the current CLO (Community Liaison Officer) for our area, Maryland. Using the HF link provided for just such emergencies, they got no answer. They called on the landline to ask what was going on and why they couldn't get an answer on the radio. The HF set installed in the spare room should have been on air.

Janet went to check just as an almighty crump shook the building. She dived under the table to shelter from breaking glass and discovered that the plug for the HF set had been removed - presumably the maid had used the socket for the vacuum cleaner. She explained the situation, and there was relief at the other end. Instead of worrying about the airport being attacked by insurgents they now considered the coup scenario. The mundane truth turned out to be that the neglected site had become overgrown and a random bush fire had triggered the old munitions stockpile.

After briefing the HiComm of her intentions Janet took charge and evacuated the apartment blocks. The refreshments area in the lee of the squash court provided protection from falling shrapnel, and a headcount was carried out. One of the maids was running around in circles in total panic, and an expat manager could not be coaxed out of his bungalow. Cowering on the floor, his bearded macho facade was lost, never to be regained.

Meanwhile more windows in our apartment block shattered and aircon units were blown out of the wall. Across the road, shrapnel and live ammunition rained down on the Government Residential Area (GRA). Asbestos roofing was perforated by falling debris and a considerable amount of live ammo. Residents returned to their homes to find debris embedded in furniture and bedding..

Tony Dhont was on the roof of BRC taking pictures, The explosions continued for about three hours.

The villagers of Isolo and Oshodi near the Bristow Estate about four kilometres away evacuated their homes in panic. Fearing a coup they fled, seeking refuge in a large banana plantation. In the dark they stampeded into a canal, where upwards of 800 drowned or were suffocated as they piled in, one on top of the other.

With only a few months to retirement, I sold my UK properties and gave Vincent (the builder in Malaysia) the go-ahead to start the paperwork and confirm with the architect. During our next leave in Malaysia we found a plot, had a meeting with the owner, agreed the price, paid the deposit and signed the sales and purchase agreement, all in the same day. Vincent told me this was the way to go to avoid any last-minute price increases. We arranged to rent a house nearby to monitor the construction.

It was a strange feeling packing up our few possessions. Starting a new life as a retiree was weird. But the house is fantastic.

Flying hours - 17,800.
Aircraft types - 21 aeroplane, 6 helicopter.
Accidents – nil.
Incidents – many.

Life is still fun.....there is a monster go-kart track in Melaka.

Our children have done well. Tia is a painter of contemporary art and her work has been displayed in some of the best galleries in London. Her paintings have been shown in the Royal Academy Summer Exhibition on several occasions. Leon is now Director of Communications for Horizon, the company set up to build the UK's next two nuclear power stations.

I have not written much about my siblings, as they have their own amazing stories. Elizabeth has spent most of her life in the US, her husband Mike working for an oil-related company. In Little Rock Liz was sometimes referred to as Saint Liz, for fostering close to a hundred children from dysfunctional families.

Rob, as an RN helicopter pilot, instructed Prince Charles and fought in the Falklands campaign. After flying for the Omani Police and Omega Helicopters he finally joined Bristow and flew the coastguard helicopter at Lee-on-Solent.

As a schoolboy, Roger damaged his knee. When he overheard the doctors say he would never walk again he discharged himself, discarded his calliper and used a crutch. It wasn't long before he was playing rugby, skydiving and skiing. He ended up as a top Mercedes salesman in Beverly Hills. Now retired, he lives in Thailand.

They should all write their memoirs. I can't wait to read them.

ND - #0030 - 270225 - C67 - 234/156/21 - PB - 9781909020351 - Matt Lamination